And the Money Kept Rolling In (and Out)

ALSO BY PAUL BLUSTEIN

The Chastening

And the Money
Kept Rolling In (and Out)

WALL STREET, THE IMF,
AND THE BANKRUPTING
OF ARGENTINA

Paul Blustein

PublicAffairs
New York

Book design by Mark McGarry
Set in Meridien

Library of Congress Cataloging-in-Publication data
Blustein, Paul.
And the money kept rolling in (and out) : Wall Street, the IMF, and the
bankrupting of Argentina / Paul Blustein.
p. cm.
Includes index.
ISBN 1-58648-245-9
1. Financial crises—Argentina. 2. Argentina—Economic conditions—1983-
3. International Monetary Fund—Argentina. 4. Investments, Foreign—
Argentina. I. Title.
HC175.B665 2005
330.982'07—dc22
2004058743

FIRST EDITION
10 9 8 7 6 5 4 3 2 1

To my children:

Nina, Nathan, Dan, and Jack,

whom I will always love unconditionally,
even if they go to work on Wall Street

Contents

Author's Note and Acknowledgments

ONE OF the things I like best about my job at *The Washington Post* is that from time to time, I'll get requests like the one I got in early February 2002 when David Hoffman, the *Post*'s foreign editor, called me at home on a Sunday afternoon. "Can you go to Argentina as soon as possible?" he asked me. The *Post*'s regular correspondent in Buenos Aires had to rush home to the United States for a family emergency, David explained, and the paper needed to send a reporter who knew something about financial crises of the sort that had just knocked Argentina flat. Such crises were becoming a specialty of mine, in much the same way that other reporters specialize in airplane crashes or nuclear plant malfunctions; I had covered the crises of the late 1990s in Asia, Russia, and Brazil and had authored a book on that topic (*The Chastening: Inside the Crisis That Rocked the Global Financial System and Humbled the IMF,* PublicAffairs, 2001). As sorry as I was for the Argentine people, I was thrilled with the opportunity to better understand their nation's travails, and the next day I was on a flight to Buenos Aires.

That was the genesis of this book. During that trip, I tracked

down a few of the people who had held high-ranking economic policy posts in the Argentine government in the period leading up to
the crash, to ask for their recollections of the crucial turning points,
and I soon concluded that the saga of Argentina's rise and fall was
even more drama-packed than the tales I had just recounted from
the other countries. Upon returning to the States, I continued gathering string about the Argentine crisis when I could find time away
from my daily reporting duties. Initially, I thought I would write a
chapter about Argentina as an addendum to *The Chastening,* but as I
delved deeper into the events in question, I realized that this chron-
icle merited its own book. My conviction grew when scandals
erupted on Wall Street over the conduct of securities firms during
the stock market bubble, because I began to connect dots between
those scandals and the hype surrounding Argentina's huge borrowing on the international bond markets in the late 1990s. A couple of
phone calls with Peter Osnos, the publisher of PublicAffairs, got me
launched; Peter had inspired me to tackle my first book, and he
played a similarly formative role this time around.

The result is a book with a substantially higher indignation quo-
tient than *The Chastening.* The more people I interviewed, and the
more documents I obtained, the more appalled I became about the
part the international community had played in pumping up
Argentina's economy to a dangerous degree and then letting the
country down so badly when the bubble burst. So whereas my previous book has a more-in-dread-than-in-anger tone, this one reflects
my ire concerning a system that has caused misery to millions of
people and threatens to afflict millions more. This book also dwells a
great deal more on the buildup to the crisis, and on the role that
financial markets played in rendering the country vulnerable.

The book is based on interviews with more than 125 people—top
officials of the International Monetary Fund, U.S. government,
other G-7 governments, and the Argentine government, together
with many from the financial markets and a smattering of other crisis participants and observers. To a much greater extent than in *The*

Chastening, I have relied on contemporaneous material, especially internal IMF documents including memos, confidential reports, and notes of meetings. Quite a few sources, I am pleased to report, kindly furnished me with such material, and I would like to give them my heartfelt thanks for helping me write as accurate and comprehensive an account as possible. Not everyone was so forthcoming; many IMF officials recoiled at my request for memos from their files, and voiced consternation upon learning that I had obtained such documents elsewhere. But even these people were extremely generous with their time, in some cases enduring many bouts of questioning; by the end I was resorting to joking weakly that I would stop describing my query as the final round because that promise had proved false so often in the past. I am enormously grateful to all the people who took the trouble to answer my questions, and particularly those who good-naturedly accepted repeated phone calls and requests for meetings. In this regard, I am also obliged to Tom Dawson, director of the IMF's External Relations Department, for once again allowing me free rein to contact Fund staffers directly and meet with them privately; and to Tony Fratto, deputy assistant secretary for public affairs at the U.S. Treasury, for facilitating my interview requests.

Most of my interviews were conducted on a deep-background basis, so I could use the information provided but could not quote the interviewees or cite them as sources unless granted permission later to do so. Many sources were naturally reluctant to be quoted on sensitive matters, particularly because a number of the key players were still in their jobs. To the greatest extent possible, I have attributed quotes by name, but I trust readers will understand that in certain cases this proved infeasible, and I hope they can accept my assurances that unattributed material has been carefully researched and checked. For example, when people recalled conversations at meetings, I made every effort to confirm the accounts with other participants.

A list of interviewees appears in the Notes section, including those who spoke on the record, plus those who were interviewed on deep background and later granted permission to be quoted or named as sources for the book. Some people declined to be listed, and a couple of key players refused to be interviewed at all. In the case of people whose actions I have criticized or questioned, I made sure to seek their viewpoint, even if they did not want to be quoted in their own defense. These include several financial market participants. A personal aside is in order here: Despite my harsh judgments about Wall Street—and my swipe at the Street in the book's dedication—I genuinely like market folks, who are mostly engaging, personable, and blessed with wicked senses of humor. In depicting some of their conduct as socially undesirable, I hope I have made it clear that the problem should be attributed to the pressures under which they are forced to operate, rather than deficiencies of character.

Completing the research and writing required six months of leave from my job at the *Post,* starting in August 2003, as well as additional snatches of time away from my newspaper duties during 2004. I deeply appreciate the approval of my leave by Executive Editor Len Downie and Managing Editor Steve Coll, and I owe a special debt of gratitude to Jill Dutt, Assistant Managing Editor for Business News, who supported me in this endeavor and whose idea it was to use some of my research in a story that was published in the paper in August 2003. Jill and other editors bore the burden of arranging for my colleagues to fill in for me on various stories during my leave, the most heroic example being the coverage of the World Trade Organization meeting in Cancun by Kevin Sullivan of the *Post's* Mexico City bureau. Kevin was not exactly steeped in the minutiae of global trade negotiations, but by the tumultuous end of the Cancun meeting he was tossing around terms like "Singapore issues" and "amber-box subsidies" as if he had been covering the WTO for years. Kevin, I'm putting this in writing: I owe you. Big time.

The Smith Richardson Foundation, which had provided a considerable amount of financial support for *The Chastening,* came through for me again with a generous grant. I cannot thank Smith Richardson enough. There is simply no way I could have managed to do this book without that money. Allan Song, the program officer at Smith Richardson who handled my grant submission, has shown great enthusiasm for the work that I do; his kind words and guidance have also meant a great deal to me. By gently prodding me to sharpen my grant proposal, Al also played a significant role in helping me figure out what the book ought to say.

Important support for the project also came from the Brookings Institution, which named me a Guest Scholar and provided a comfortable office. Robert Litan, who headed the Economic Studies Department, graciously responded to my request for a perch from which to conduct my work, and I ended up in the Governance Studies Department, where department head Carol Graham and her colleagues provided stimulating company and good fellowship. Rob Wooley, Bethany Hase, and Sara Hommel cheerfully took care of administrative issues and made my stay at Brookings all the more pleasant.

Thanks to my Smith Richardson grant, I was able to hire several people in Buenos Aires who ably assisted me in gleaning various sorts of information. Two were American—David Shafer, who diligently searched the Argentine press for material that might be useful; and Brian Byrnes, an accomplished young journalist who did great work on the story I did for the *Post*, and who later helped me with other research. Another was Argentine—Mariano Melamed, a journalist of wondrous energy, curiosity, and talent who tracked down a number of people from a wide variety of social classes for the purpose of illustrating some of the book's economic concepts with anecdotal material. In Italy, Sarah Delaney did a nice job on interviews that were used in my *Post* story as well as the book. The well-designed Chronology was the product of Farhana Hossain, a *Post* colleague. I also appreciate the work of Maggie Kozek, a research assistant at Brookings, and Maria Ramos, a student at Bell Intercultural High School in Washington, who translated some material for me.

A number of people supported me in other ways without being

financially compensated for doing so. Santiago O'Donnell, a former *Post* reporter from Argentina who is boldly leading Latin American journalism into a new era of independence and creativity, provided me with all sorts of wise counsel and did one particularly great favor by referring me to the aforementioned Mariano Melamed. I am proud to say that Santiago became a good friend during the course of this project. Judith Evans, whom I first met in Buenos Aires nearly twenty years ago, was as always a source of insight, a fount of contacts, and a dear pal. Finally, several people helped me unearth and understand financial data and economic statistics that I desperately needed; three deserve particular mention—Freddy Thomsen, an astute Argentine economist; Jens Nystedt, a former IMF staffer; and Peter Marber, president of The Atlantic Funds.

Once a manuscript draft was ready, I asked three people with extensive knowledge of the events in question to read it. One was Nancy Birdsall, president of the Center for Global Development; another was Shinji Takagi of the IMF's Independent Evaluation Office; the third asked to remain nameless because of the sensitivity of her job. I am greatly indebted to all of them for preventing embarrassing mistakes from getting into print, and for offering numerous thoughtful suggestions. Having said that, I of course am responsible for any errors and omissions that remain.

The book would be far less satisfactory were it not for the superb editing of Clive Priddle at PublicAffairs. Over the phone, Clive exhorted me to confront big questions and explain broad implications; with a sharp pencil, he improved the manuscript immeasurably. Thoughtful and meticulous copyediting by Ida May B. Norton turned many sloppily worded phrases into gems. And as with *The Chastening*, I again appreciated the work of others at PublicAffairs, including Managing Editor Robert Kimzey, Production Editor Melanie Peirson Johnstone, Editor David Patterson, and Publicist Jaime Leifer.

Book authors typically become obsessed with their work to the point of antisociability, and I'm afraid I was no exception. So I want to thank my children, whose accomplishments and merriment helped me maintain my emotional balance by reminding me that being the father of such beautiful kids is more important than anything else I might undertake. My greatest debt, of course, is to my wife Yoshie. Many were the times when, as I sat silent and vacant-eyed at the lunch table, she indulgently bade me to return to my basement office because she could tell that my mind was overloaded with the problem of how to write some transition or chapter ending. Many were the times, too, when she coped with the antics of our two young boys on weekends or while she was preparing delicious dinners, enabling me to squeeze in some extra work. Her support for me, and my feelings for her, far transcend these matters of comfort and convenience; suffice to say that she once again proved herself the perfect marriage partner for a struggling author—this one, anyway.

Prologue: Up, Up, and Away

THE CONCEPT of a "mission" to a foreign country may conjure up images of swashbuckling idealists—the sort who might be played in the movies by Jeremy Irons or Harrison Ford—tramping through tropical forests, accompanied by pan pipes, trying to convert the natives to the way of true salvation. In the case of the International Monetary Fund, however, missions typically involve teams of brief-case-toting civil servants with advanced degrees in economics, flying first class or business class to a national capital, shuttling between a deluxe hotel and the country's economics ministries and agencies, scrutinizing budgetary and monetary data, and sending reports by e-mail back to IMF headquarters in Washington, D.C.

The IMF mission that traveled to Argentina in November 2001 closely resembled the norm—at least in superficial respects. After an overnight flight to Buenos Aires, the six members of the IMF team were chauffeured to their usual hotel, the Sheraton, a towering modern edifice in a city gilded with broad boulevards, European architecture, and elegant statuary. As on previous trips, the team set up an office in the central bank and spent many hours in meetings at the Ministry of Economy, on the Plaza de Mayo, the fabled square that has been the scene of countless political protests, rabble-rousing speeches, and torchlight rallies during Argentina's turbulent past.

Heading the mission was Tomás Reichmann, an economist from Chile who held chief responsibility for Argentina on the IMF staff. Sixty-one years old, Reichmann had a gentlemanly demeanor; a former colleague described him as having "not a single confrontational bone in his body." He had accepted a job offer from the Fund in 1973, after receiving his Ph.D. from Harvard, because he and his wife did not wish to return to Chile, which had come under a military dictatorship. He had spent the bulk of his career in the Fund's Western Hemisphere Department and had been working on Argentina in various capacities since 1996. Missions to the country were old hat to him. At the half dozen or so Buenos Aires restaurants where he liked to dine while on mission, the waiters recognized him as a steady customer.

Technically, the mission had a narrow purpose—to conduct a review of Argentina's progress in meeting the terms of its $22 billion loan package from the IMF. Such reviews are conducted every few months on most IMF loans, and if this review were "completed" successfully, meaning Argentina's progress was deemed satisfactory, the Fund would disburse a $1.24 billion installment that was scheduled to be lent to the Argentine government in December.

This seemingly modest issue, however, was enormously consequential, because a long-running crisis in the Argentine economy was reaching an acute stage. Global financial markets were panicking over the prospect that the country was heading into an economic cataclysm. Withholding approval of the IMF review not only would deprive the government of badly needed cash; it also would send a signal worldwide that Argentina was being cut off from international support at a moment of grave peril.

Most directly endangered was the cornerstone of the Argentine economy, its currency system, known as "convertibility," which kept the value of one peso fixed exactly equal to one U.S. dollar and allowed Argentines to use both currencies interchangeably. In the decade after its 1991 inception, the legal guarantee of the $1-per-peso link had proved remarkably successful in quelling Argentina's corrosive inflation and imparting a sense of stability among consumers, savers, and businesses. The peso-dollar equivalency was deeply ingrained in the nation's economic fabric: Millions of borrowers had taken out loans in dollars, even though their income was in pesos. Breaking the peso-dollar link would thus wreak havoc in the Argentine economy by generating bankruptcy en masse. Many borrowers were middle-class Argentines who had taken out mortgages on their homes; for a homeowner paying $1,000 a month on a mortgage, for example, a 50 percent decline in the peso would double, to 2,000, the amount of pesos required to make the monthly payments. That scenario loomed ever more menacingly as jittery investors and lenders pulled their money out of the country, depleting the reserve supplies of dollars that Argentina needed to keep the system alive and functioning.

In a bid to shore up the system, the IMF had twice granted emergency loans in 2001 to the Argentine government. In return, Economy Minister Domingo Cavallo, a man of intimidating personal force, had strained mightily to fix the country's underlying problems, demonstrating his commitment to fiscal frugality by cutting government salaries and pensions even though the economy was mired in a long recession. Despite these moves, the slump had deepened as every month of 2001 went by, and the markets were continuing to plunge, reflecting fears among investors and traders that the government lacked the wherewithal to maintain interest and principal payments on its $140 billion debt.

Without the lifeline that Reichmann's mission could extend, Argentina looked doomed—and for that reason, many in the markets were predicting that the IMF was certain to approve the loan disbursal as it had done on prior occasions. But within the IMF's highest councils, a powerful sentiment had taken hold that further assistance to Argentina would be an exercise in futility. "When we left Washington, the odds that the mission would complete the review were minimal," recalled Alberto Ramos, a member of Reichmann's team. The Argentine government had already acknowledged that its budget deficit for 2001 would exceed by a hefty margin the target agreed with the IMF, because the recession had caused a steep decline in tax revenues. And in examining the government's projections for the coming year, the mission's economists concluded that the amount of budget-cutting pain the government would have to inflict to balance its books would go beyond almost any conceivable bounds of political reality.

As Reichmann and his colleagues grimly sent word back to their superiors in Washington, a new financial shock rendered Argentina's situation even more irremediable.

Amid growing fears about the safety of bank deposits, a steadily increasing outflow of money from banks surged to full-scale flood stage during the final three days of November, when thousands of depositors queued up to pull $3.6 billion out of their accounts—about 6 percent of total deposits. On Saturday, December 1, the Economy Ministry announced restrictions on withdrawals aimed at halting the run. Under this decree, which would be dubbed the *corralito*, or "little corral," Argentines could take no more than $250 a week in cash from their accounts, although they could make payments by check or debit and credit cards. Furthermore, a comprehensive ban was imposed on transfers of money abroad except for those related to trade. People reacted with outrage to their inability to obtain cash from automatic teller machines. National television showed a woman screaming at presidential spokesman Juan Pablo Baylac: "How can I get my money? It's my savings. I'm furious." Radio talk shows were besieged with distraught callers asking how they were to pay their rent or electricity bills (checks and credit cards were much less commonly used in Argentina than in the United States). The government's assurances that the measures would be lifted after ninety days were dismissed as lacking credibility.

All these goings-on were being monitored closely at IMF headquarters, where a meeting of top officials and staffers convened on Monday morning, December 3. "A great feeling of defeat" pervaded the group, one participant recalled, because of the realization that the Fund's rescue effort had flopped for certain and was reaching the stage where the plug was going to be pulled. The last straw, as far as the IMF was concerned, was the country's imposition of the *corralito*, because it shredded the principles that lay at the heart of the convertibility system—the interchangeability of dollars and pesos, and the guarantee that the nation's monetary authorities would furnish dollars freely to anyone with a legitimate claim on them. IMF officials felt they had put their institution's money and credibility on the line based on Argentine insistence that the convertibility system was inviolate, only for the Argentines to abrogate its basic tenets without even consulting the Fund in advance.

"What does convertibility mean now?" demanded Anne Krueger, the IMF's first deputy managing director, at the meeting.

Back in Buenos Aires that day, Reichmann was in the midst of lunch with a prominent Argentine economist when his cell phone rang with a call from a superior at IMF headquarters informing him that the Fund's top management was calling an end to the mission. Reichmann was ordered to return home that evening, ostensibly to brief the Fund's executive board about the new and disturbing circumstances in Argentina. The IMF would officially announce two days later that it was "unable at this stage" to complete the review necessary to disburse the $1.24 billion. In simple terms, Argentina was being abandoned.

Now Reichmann faced the unpleasant task of informing Argentine officials about the IMF's decision. He quickly arranged after lunch to fly back to Washington on a United Airlines flight departing at 8:30 P.M. and tried to reach Cavallo to convey the bad news. The two men met around 4 P.M. in Cavallo's office in the Economy Ministry, where Cavallo made it plain that he was not going to let Reichmann off easily. "You can't tell this to me," he said to the IMF official. "You will have to explain it to the president."

That meant Reichmann would have to meet President Fernando de la Rúa at his residence in Olivos, about an hour's drive from downtown Buenos Aires. Reichmann protested that he didn't have time. "I've got an 8:30 plane to catch," Reichmann told Cavallo, but the economy minister retorted that he would arrange for a government helicopter to ferry Reichmann to the presidential residence and then to the airport. Reichmann rushed to the Sheraton to pack his suitcase and returned for the helicopter ride to Olivos, where he met de la Rúa in his office.

In his twenty-eight-year career at the IMF, Reichmann could not recall a more difficult and emotionally charged moment. De la Rúa, a somber, austere man who had won the presidency two years earlier by campaigning on his reputation for being boring but honest, was obviously horrified by the fate he expected to befall his country. He asked Reichmann if he understood what the IMF's decision meant. The mission chief replied that he did.

"We knew that we were losing our last chance," recalled Chrystian Colombo, the cabinet chief, who was also present at the meeting. Reichmann, he added, was "very upset and uncomfortable."

About a half hour into the meeting, a military aide interrupted to inform the group that United could not hold its plane to Washington. The helicopter would have to take Reichmann to the airport immediately or he would miss the flight.

"So nothing can be done?" De la Rúa's tone of incredulity spoke volumes as the IMF official prepared to leave.

Reichmann shrugged wordlessly, raising his palms upward in a gesture of anguish.

The president's head sank to his chest. Reichmann headed to the helicopter.

And the Money Kept Rolling In (and Out)

[CHAPTER 1]

Globalization's Big Bust

THE COLLAPSE of the Argentine economy, which commenced a couple of weeks after the withdrawal of the IMF mission in early December 2001, was one of the most spectacular in modern history. Partly, this was because of the manner in which the country descended into anarchy. First came the scenes of people thronging the Plaza de Mayo banging pots and pans, and mobs looting shops and sacking government buildings all over the country, resulting in so much mayhem (including the deaths of more than two dozen people) that President de la Rúa was forced to resign on December 21. Then came the tragicomic spectacle of a succession of five presidents taking office over a mere ten days, ending on New Year's Day of 2002 when an emergency session of Congress handed the presidency to Eduardo Duhalde.

Equally disturbing was the severity of the economic downturn that beset the country following the government's default on the bulk of its debt and its decision to let the peso sink in early 2002. Like an engine that has seized up for lack of oil, the Argentine economy ground to a virtual halt, as additional restrictions on bank withdrawals led to a breakdown in the system by which people and businesses paid each other, and the bank credit that companies needed for day-to-day commerce dried up. National output shrank 11 percent in 2002, leaving nearly one quarter of the workforce unemployed and a majority of the population below the poverty line, even as prices soared for basic food items such as bread, noodles, and sugar. Average annual income per capita, which in the late 1990s peaked at $8,500—double Mexico's level—sank to $2,800 in 2002. Although that low level was attributable in substantial part to the 75 percent decline in the exchange rate of the peso against the dollar, it reflected the privation felt by millions whose living standards plummeted and personal savings withered in value.

The impact struck Argentines of every social class. One of the country's richest women was forced to auction off paintings by Gauguin, Degas, Miró, and Matisse. Members of the middle class became nervous wrecks over their lost nest eggs; in one widely publicized case, a fifty-nine-year-old woman who could not get her dollars out of her bank account walked into her bank, doused herself with rubbing alcohol, and set herself ablaze. Hardest hit, in general, were people on the bottom economic rungs. Among the most heart-rending tales were those of children suffering in rising numbers from malnutrition, and even dying from it—a shocking phenomenon in a country abounding with cattle ranches and wheat fields. Residents of fashionable Buenos Aires neighborhoods grew accustomed to averting their gaze when hordes of people called *cartoneros* would descend on their streets in the evening, ripping open plastic trash bags in search of anything saleable. In a grisly symbol of the nation's abasement, an overturned cattle truck outside the industrial city of Rosario in March 2002 attracted hundreds of shantytown residents wielding machetes and carving knives, who slaughtered and diced up twenty-two Angus steers on the freeway, then fought over bloody hunks of meat.

Argentina's downfall was especially painful for its citizens to bear—and for outsiders to behold—because during the 1990s the country had seemed at long last to be moving full steam toward its rightful place in the ranks of advanced nations. Argentina is the most Europeanized of Latin American countries, boasting the region's highest education levels and a throbbing intellectual and cultural pulse. The Continental influence is readily apparent to any Buenos Aires visitor who has strolled past the city's manicured parks, Beaux Arts buildings graced by balconies with wrought-iron railings, and bustling cafés that look as if they were transplanted from the Via Veneto or the Champs Elysées. The people of this proud land understandably thought they were leaving behind their history of squandered riches and destructive upheaval when, from 1991 to 1998, the economy grew at an average rate of 6 percent a year, reaching a total gross domestic product of nearly $300 billion, with almost no inflation. That performance marked a drastic departure from the stagnation, bouts of hyperinflation, and repeated currency devaluations that had afflicted Argentina since the mid-twentieth century. Thus the pain was all the more excruciating when these raised aspirations were dashed.

If Argentina's economic unraveling were an isolated case, it might be dismissed as a pitiable curiosity that has little bearing beyond the country's borders. But it came in the wake of financial crises that struck other fast-growing "emerging markets" such as Mexico, Thailand, Indonesia, South Korea, Russia, and Brazil. It offers a case study of a pernicious syndrome that global capitalism has manifested in recent years: A developing nation shows great promise by unleashing the forces of private enterprise; foreign capital streams in, generating an investment boom; amid the ensuing euphoria, the country's economy is puffed up to the point where serious vulnerabilities develop; an economic reversal degenerates into turmoil and panic; and finally, international rescue efforts fail or make a bad situation worse. A good analogy would be the membership process for an exclusive country club, in which hopeful applicants are given tremendous encouragement that they are meeting all of the strict criteria for joining, only to have the club door slammed in their faces and find themselves cast out on the street just as they are nearing the initiation rite. Think of the world's rich nations as the members of this club, and the emerging-market nations as the aspirants for membership who, one after the other, suffer this cruel setback. As an ugly example of the genre, Argentina presents an unsurpassed rise and fall, and the culpability of the international community—both the official and private sectors—is weighty. For believers in the power of globalization to raise living standards in the developing world (and I include myself among them), this dispiriting saga is an eye-opener to the need for systemic change.

Argentina prided itself on following free-market, economically orthodox policies during the 1990s. Few countries if any were so lionized for hewing to the "Washington Consensus," a sort of economic Ten Commandments prescribed by the IMF, the World Bank, and the U.S. government. Among the main elements of this recipe are the eradication of inflation, the privatization of industry, the deregulation of the economy, and the removal of trade barriers, all of which the Argentine government vigorously pursued. The Heritage Foundation, a conservative think tank that evaluates countries according to an "Index of Economic Freedom," rated Argentina in 1999 as tied with Chile for the best policies in Latin America, and almost equal to Australia and Taiwan. (The criteria include the degree of government intervention in the economy, respect for property rights, extent of black-market activity, and so on.) But having been a poster child for the Washington Consensus, Argentina is now a poster child for the growing disenchantment with the model in the developing world.

In the bankrupting of Argentina, the key events of which took place between 1996 and 2001, two sets of actors from abroad belong at the center of the drama—private market financiers and top international policymakers, the latter being principally at the IMF and the U.S. government, the Fund's dominant overseer. By putting human faces on these players, demystifying their operations, and chronicling their actions at critical junctures, I seek in this book to lay bare, in an accessible manner, the uncomfortable story of the international community's role in the Argentine debacle. It may seem obvious that Argentina, for all its own failings, was a victim of misfeasance, nonfeasance, and even malfeasance by foreign money interests, bureaucrats, and political figures. But only by going behind the scenes can the scale be truly appreciated and put in proper perspective. Thorough scrutiny of these events also helps pinpoint the factors that led Argentina over the cliff. Some of the recriminations that have been leveled in the wake of the country's collapse are off-base, and it is important to draw the right lessons from what went wrong.

One crucial (and often ignored) factor in the collapse is the modern system of globalized financial capital. This engine is remarkably powerful but volatile. Just as it would be unwise to put a fourteen-year-old behind the steering wheel of a Ferrari, newly developing economies are not always able to thrive for long with the wild ride of money moving freely across international borders. This is a facet of globalization about which economists harbor growing misgivings. It is one thing to open a country to foreign goods and to investment in factories by multinational firms. It is quite a different matter to open it to the giant flows of international finance, which can be expansive and buoyant during some periods, timorous and flighty in others. At a time when Argentina's indebtedness was mounting in the late 1990s, global markets lauded the country as a paragon of the developing world and poured money in, lulling the government into complacency. The IMF also overlooked Argentina's vulnerabilities, but even when the Fund tried to sound alarms, the markets' optimism rendered the Fund's concerns irrelevant. Nancy Birdsall, president of the Center for Global Development, has coined an apt phrase to describe how Argentina was treated: The country was "the spoiled child of the Washington Consensus."

Globalization is not supposed to work this way. According to globalization's most ardent boosters, international markets reward good, sound economic policies by steering capital to countries that practice them. The influence of the capital inflow makes the government even more disciplined, because policymakers know that otherwise investors may yank their money out. As Thomas Friedman put it in his book *The Lexus and the Olive Tree*, the "Electronic Herd"—the agglomeration of the world's investors—"can impose pressures [for good policy] that few governments can resist. It has a self-interest in doing so and it generates in others the self-interest to comply. . . . The Electronic Herd turns the whole world into a parliamentary system, in which every government lives under the fear of a no-confidence vote from the herd."

That's the theory. In practice, foreign funds numbed Argentine policymakers into minimizing the perils of their policies. The effect was similar to a dose of steroids, giving the economy a short-term boost while insidiously increasing the risk of breakdown in the long run.

Argentina was not a wholly innocent victim—far from it. Democratically elected and appointed Argentine officials made the decisions that led the country down the road to economic disaster. They spent more than they should have, taxed less than they should have, and borrowed more than they should have—all the while keeping a currency system that required much stricter fiscal discipline—because they wanted the political benefits they could accrue from these practices. But in putting their nation's economy on a collision course, they got plenty of help. Argentina will be paying the price for a long time, not only for its own mistakes but for the mistakes of the international community as well.

"It's like a nephew who becomes dependent on a very rich, doting uncle," said William McDonough, who was president of the Federal Reserve Bank of New York until 2003. "Suddenly the uncle dies and leaves the money to someone else, or decides he doesn't love the nephew anymore and cuts him off. You can ask, who's responsible—the uncle or the kid?"

For the markets, doting on Argentina was understandable to some extent, given the great strides the economy was making and the government's commitment to free-market reforms. But fueling the flow of money from abroad were forces that went well beyond the age-old phenomenon of irrational exuberance.

Upon close scrutiny, the conduct of the markets in Argentina is redolent of the scandals that rocked Wall Street following the bursting of the stock market bubble in the United States. Striking parallels can be seen between Argentina's crisis and some of the most notorious flameouts of recent years, such as Enron Corp., WorldCom Inc., and Global Crossing Ltd., in which major brokerage firms pumped up the companies' securities prices, issuing bullish forecasts that were later seen to be tainted by self-interest. In Argentina's case, though, the injured party was not a company or group of stockholders. It was South America's second-largest country, a nation of 38 million people.

The Wall Street firms whose analysts tended to produce the most optimistic and influential reports for investors on Argentina's prospects were generally the same ones collecting fees from bringing Argentine government bonds to market—a business that generated nearly $1 billion for big securities houses during the period 1991–2001. A little over a year before Argentina's default, for example, J.P. Morgan & Co., the firm that brought more Argentine bonds to market than any other, sent clients a report taking issue with pessimists worried that the country was destined for bankruptcy. The report's title was "Argentina's debt dynamics: Much ado about not so much."

Besides optimistic analyses, another factor propelling the excessive amount of capital to Argentina was Wall Street's system for rating the performance of professional money managers. The system created bizarre incentives by rewarding money managers for investing heavily in the bonds of emerging-market countries that already had lots of bonds outstanding. Put more simply, the system strongly encouraged people who controlled huge pools of money to lend to countries with huge piles of debt. Topping the list of those countries was Argentina.

"And the money kept rolling in from every side . . . rollin' on in, rollin' on in," as the song goes from the musical *Evita*.

The complicity of global markets and the IMF in pumping up the Argentine bubble would be less deplorable if the bubble had been gently deflated—that is, if the international community had effectively assisted Argentina in minimizing the impact once its economy fell on hard times and market psychology turned negative. Unfortunately, the international community blew it.

The helicopter ride that Tomás Reichmann took from Olivos in December 2001 marked the end of a rescue effort that only prolonged Argentina's agony and made the crash all the more devastating in the end. The IMF marshaled one major loan package at the end of 2000, and when that failed to pull the country's economy out of its downward spiral, international policymakers—like gamblers doubling a losing bet—tried beefing up the loan a few months later. In the process, they passed up opportunities to confront Argentina's fundamental problems—in particular, the size of its debt—earlier and more proactively. And they ignored warnings that the longer they postponed the day of reckoning, the more catastrophic the result would be. Might Argentina's crisis have ended less disastrously, and might the suffering of the Argentine people been substantially mitigated, had those warnings been heeded? It is impossible to know for certain. But the most plausible answer is surely yes, considering the depth and pain of the collapse that materialized.

Reconstructing these events reveals much about how international bailouts work—or rather, how they often don't work, and make the final outcome worse instead of better. This, of course, was a period when, to quote the song again, the money was "rollin' on out, rollin' on out, on out."

To citizens of rich countries, the implications of what happened to Argentina may seem remote. Crippling crises have been confined to emerging markets; the closest any wealthy nation has come to the cliff was the speculation that forced the British government to devalue the pound in 1992. The idea that an economically advanced country could undergo a setback of the Argentine variety will strike many people living in such nations as preposterous, especially those in the United States. Americans will deem it intuitively obvious that their country's $10 trillion-plus economy is not susceptible to the sort of financial turbulence that wracks their unstable neighbors to the south. And they would have some justification for thinking so, because the rules and practical realities of the global financial system are tilted in favor of wealthy countries, and against those of developing nations, in certain respects.

Perhaps the most important is that political maturity and sheer economic size confer natural advantages that smaller, less mature economies do not enjoy. Markets trust that the leaders of advanced countries will correct major deficiencies in their economies eventually, so investors tend to be patient even when they see policies going astray. They do not give as much benefit of the doubt to developing-country governments. Moreover, the pool of capital held by savers, investors, and financial institutions in rich countries is enormous relative to the amount of securities suitable for foreign investment in emerging markets, a disparity that increases the potential for instability in the developing world. The total assets under management by insurance companies, pension funds, and mutual funds in advanced economies totaled $34.7 trillion in 2001, a sum seven times as large as the value of all the bonds outstanding, plus all the publicly traded stocks, of all emerging markets *combined.* So even modest shifts in the way those trillions of dollars are invested abroad can have an enormous impact—either positive or negative—on emerging markets. This is why some economists have likened global finance to a choppy sea, and the economies of emerging-market nations to small craft bobbing on the waves, all too likely to be swamped or capsized. The economies of rich nations, with their much larger and deeper financial markets, are ocean liners by comparison, capable of steaming through storms.

Another reason emerging markets are more vulnerable to crises than rich countries is that their borrowing abroad is usually conducted in the currencies of other nations; they cannot borrow cheaply in their own currencies. No matter how sound their policies, they suffer from what economist Ricardo Hausman has called "original sin." The governments of Brazil, Poland, and the Philippines may issue bonds to foreigners denominated in U.S. dollars, but if Brazil tries to sell bonds to foreigners that are denominated in its currency, the real, or if Poland tries to sell bonds denominated in zlotys, or if the Philippines tries to sell bonds in pesos, they have to offer considerably higher interest rates, because investors overseas strongly prefer not to be exposed to the risk inherent in such currencies. Major industrial nations, by contrast, can and do borrow in their own currencies (most of Europe uses the euro), and this is particularly true of the United States, whose dollar is the world's main "reserve" currency, widely used around the globe in all kinds of commercial transactions. This gives the U.S. government an extraordinary benefit. Investors in U.S. Treasury bonds can feel totally confident that the government in Washington will never default on its debt, in part because they know that the government has the power to print as many dollars as it likes, and even though printing a lot of dollars might generate inflation, it would be preferable to a default. Argentina's government, by contrast, could not create the dollars (or Japanese yen or euros) in which it borrowed abroad. So it ran the risk of running out of the foreign currency it needed to pay the interest and principal on the bonds, and the danger of an investor panic was heightened as a result.

For all the differences between the rules and practices affecting rich countries like the United States as opposed to emerging markets, some unsettling resemblances to the U.S. situation are evident in the story of Argentina's rise and fall. Most remarkable is the manner in which the flow of foreign capital into the United States has rendered its policymakers complacent about the nation's budget and trade deficits, just as buoyant global markets did in Argentina about the rise in its public debt. The assurances often uttered by officials of the administration of President George W. Bush—that foreigners will continue to provide the funding the United States needs as long as the country remains a good place to invest—bear eerie similarities to the logic employed by Argentine policymakers.

The larger point, though, is that for people everywhere—whether in the First World, Third World, or somewhere in between—the bait-and-switch treatment that is all too often accorded countries aspiring to enter the rich nations' club should be an issue of immense concern. At a time when fundamentalist ideologies and terrorism threaten global order, world peace depends more urgently than ever on offering a path of hope and progress to the great bulk of humanity still mired in poverty and underdevelopment. The Argentine case shows with unmistakable clarity that this path remains far too slippery and unreliable.

Even among foreigners, something about Argentina—the tango, perhaps, or the melodies from *Evita*, or chilling memories of the atrocities committed by the Argentine military in the 1970s—seems to inspire passionate opinions about the country's fate. There are people who insist that Argentines have been inflicting economic and political misery on themselves for the better part of a century, and that the events of 2001–2002 were merely the latest manifestation of the country's penchant for bollixing up its economy. Forces deeply rooted in Argentine society, they suggest, keep the country from breaking through to lasting prosperity, in a manner akin to the "Curse of the Bambino" that purportedly kept the Boston Red Sox from winning the World Series for eighty-six years. A variant on this theme is that the country is so permeated with corruption that it fell of its own rotten weight—a view one can hear expressed on Buenos Aires street corners as well as at dinner parties in Manhattan or Georgetown.

This book is not intended to be a comprehensive history of Argentina during the period leading up to the crisis, so an exploration of the country's pathologies will have to be found in accounts by authors more expert than I on the Argentine national psyche. Corruption is an unavoidable part of the history, but there is strikingly little evidence that it was a significant causal factor in the crisis. It is fair to say, of course, that if Argentina's privatizations of state-owned enterprises had been conducted cleanly—in the same manner that might be found in, say, Switzerland—the government would have reaped more revenue in the early 1990s, which might have made the debt burden less of a critical problem in later years. And if Argentine tax enforcement had been run as honestly as, say, Norway's—or even Chile's—the government could have collected more tax revenue, likewise diminishing the debt. But reprehensible as these problems may be, they were peripheral contributors to the storm that was brewing.

It is crucial to understand how global markets and global institutions helped lay Argentina low. Although the economy revived in 2003 and 2004, the durability of the expansion is open to question, and by many measures the economy is still operating well below 1998 levels. Disdain toward globalization is on the rise in the developing world, in part because many countries that have liberalized their economies have experienced subpar growth, disappointing reductions in poverty, or financial crises. Argentina's implosion, however, is globalization's most stunning bust. It is Exhibit A for critics of global free markets. Globalization's defenders may rightly feel that regardless of what happened in Argentina, lowering barriers to the free flow of goods, services, and investment still offers the most promising way forward for poor countries as well as rich. But globalization will not long survive many Argentinas. Just as Argentines will be better off accepting their own heavy responsibility, the international community will be better off confronting the facts of its role in this story. It began, as the good times started to roll at the opening of what Argentines would regard as their miracle decade, in 1991.

[CHAPTER 2]

"This May Not Be Paradise"

THE ANNOUNCEMENT on January 29, 1991, that Domingo Cavallo would become Argentina's Economy Minister ignited a 30 percent, one-day rally in the Buenos Aires stock market. Partly, this was because Cavallo, a former central bank president and foreign minister, was known to be a well-trained economist with orthodox free-market views. The son of a broom factory owner from the industrial city of Córdoba, he had won a scholarship to Harvard after graduating from college, and he earned a Ph.D. in 1977 under the tutelage of luminaries such as Martin Feldstein, who would later become chairman of the Council of Economic Advisers in the administration of President Ronald Reagan. Partly, too, the markets' enthusiasm reflected the hope that Cavallo's forceful personality would translate into decisive action against Argentina's most intractable problem, the inflation that had driven up prices at triple-digit and quadruple-digit annual rates during the 1980s. Dynamic and mercurial—as a child, his mother nicknamed him "Lightning"—Cavallo was renowned for his damn-the-torpedoes style. "He is so sure about his policies, he has a hard time thinking that things can go wrong,"

Miguel Ángel Broda, a prominent Buenos Aires economist, was quoted as saying shortly after Cavallo's appointment. As the markets expected, Cavallo did not wait long before adopting a drastic approach to quell inflation.

Among the experts Cavallo consulted was Horacio Liendo, a Buenos Aires lawyer with whom he had worked in the past. Liendo had written a doctoral thesis on social and economic emergencies, and he was particularly enamored of the strict monetary rule that Argentina had adopted at the end of the nineteenth century to deal with the turmoil then besetting the country. That system, based on a legal guarantee that paper pesos could be converted into gold pesos at a fixed rate, lasted from 1899 to 1929. "Those three decades," Liendo observed, "were the most successful decades in the history of the country." Argentina should adopt a similar system now, Liendo urged Cavallo, if not by legally linking its currency again to gold then by linking it to a store of value almost as good—the U.S. dollar. After mulling a series of options, Cavallo asked Liendo on a Sunday evening in March 1991 to write a law establishing the principle of convertibility between the currencies of Argentina and the United States. "On Monday at midday, I presented my first draft," Liendo recalled. "Cavallo presented it to the president, and they introduced it in Congress on Wednesday."

With that, Argentina set forth on an odyssey of monetary self-denial, formally putting convertibility into effect on April 1. (Argentines do not observe April Fool's Day, so the inauspicious launch date evoked no wisecracking among the nation's pundits.) The new system was based on a law guaranteeing that the central bank would exchange pesos for dollars at the immutably fixed rate of one peso per dollar. This guarantee, together with other legal strictures on the central bank's freedom of action, would prohibit the monetary authorities from pumping up the money supply—the proximate cause of inflation.

Not everyone was enchanted with the new system, and skepticism ran particularly high at the International Monetary Fund.

Argentina's recent history, after all, was littered with cases of economic initiatives that were unveiled with great fanfare and fizzled shortly thereafter. In 1983 the government had introduced the "peso argentino," a new currency that replaced 10,000 old, badly devalued pesos. Two years later, following months of secret planning, had come the Austral Plan, in which a currency called the austral replaced 1,000 of the new pesos (in other words, 10 million of the old ones), and the government pledged to impose discipline over its budget, monetary, and wage policies. The Primavera Plan, announced in August 1988, had envisioned a loose link between the austral and the U.S. dollar as well as additional efforts at spending restraint. Each of these moves succeeded for only a few months in curtailing the country's chronic hyperinflation. Loan programs negotiated with the IMF during the 1980s to stabilize the economy repeatedly fell apart over Argentina's failure to meet targets for curbing budget deficits, restraining wage increases, and limiting expansion of the money supply.

Although the IMF was not opposed outright to convertibility, both former Fund and Argentine officials clearly remember its lack of enthusiasm. Barring the central bank from inflating the money supply, IMF economists knew, did not necessarily mean that the government was changing its propensity to spend well in excess of the amount it collected in taxes, since the government could still borrow to cover its deficits. Largely for that reason, the Fund feared that the new system would suffer a premature demise, as chronic overborrowing by the government would risk eroding faith in the country's economic underpinnings, leading to a sell-off in the currency. Sterie T. "Ted" Beza, who was then director of the IMF's Western Hemisphere Department, recalled the Fund's reasoning thusly: "To do the kind of exchange rate where you lay down an anchor forever, you need a very good fiscal policy. And for Argentina, that would have represented a marked improvement from past experience." Among IMF staffers, added one of Beza's former colleagues, "Absolutely nobody dreamed that the system would last a decade."

In those days, Argentina was anything but a darling of the international financial elites. In addition to its reputation for haplessness at vanquishing inflation, the country had fallen deeply into arrears in its debt payments to foreign banks. So it was hard to conceive at the time that with the initiation of convertibility Argentina was embarking on a transformation into a role model for the developing world.

But Cavallo was confident that convertibility would work wonders, just as the link to gold had done. "One hundred years ago, Argentina overcame a similar crisis through similar measures and lived through many decades of economic growth and stability," he said at the March 20 news conference announcing the plan.

The urge to rekindle the magic of that period was understandable, for Argentina had been so prosperous then, and it had endured such torment in the interim.

During a halcyon era lasting roughly from 1860 to 1930, Argentina became one of the ten richest countries in the world. Fueling the country's wealth was the fertility of the vast pampas and the arrival of more than 3 million immigrants from 1871 to 1914, most of them from southern Europe (together with some from Ireland, the Netherlands, and Britain), seeking better lives in a land that was being deliberately modeled after Europe and the United States. Industries sprang up in cities around the country, land cultivation burgeoned, and "the Paris of Latin America" blossomed in Buenos Aires, which boasted not only parks and mansions but electric street lights, public transportation, and modern sanitation. National output expanded at an average rate of 6–7 percent a year, led by exports of frozen meat, corn, wheat, flour, and other agricultural products. By 1913 per capita income in Argentina was greater than that in France, Germany, Spain, and Italy. Argentines celebrated the centennial of their nation's 1810 rebellion against Spanish rule basking in praise from their fellow Latin Americans that they were leading the region's march into modernity. "The world looks to this great country of the South," wrote Rubén Darío, a Nicaraguan intellectual. "With its 7 million inhabitants, it rivals, in more than one agricultural or financial enterprise, the other great country of the North, with a population surpassing 80 million."

Argentina's wealth gradually dissipated over a sixty-year period of economic and political convulsions, starting with a military coup in 1930 and the depression that was then spreading worldwide. The country underwent repeated cycles in which populist leaders rose to power, followed by social strife that prompted the military to seize control, then a restoration of civilian rule once the generals' inability to govern effectively had been demonstrated. Most indelible in its impact was the ascendancy of Gen. Juan Domingo Perón, who was elected president in 1946 and galvanized working-class Argentines with his quasi-fascist vision of an "organized community" based on state-dominated cooperation among industry, unions, agriculture, and other interests. Championing the cause of *los descamisados* (the shirtless) and vilifying the wealthy, Perón nationalized many of the nation's enterprises, raised high protective tariffs along with restrictive quotas against imported goods, and issued decrees conferring generous benefits on workers—with special favors going to unions whose support he commanded. The passion he stirred, as evidenced by the throngs who responded rapturously to his addresses, reached its climax in 1952 with the death from cancer of his charismatic wife, Eva, at age thirty-three. But Perón finally took class warfare too far when he raised the specter of civil war against his opponents, and the military toppled him in 1955, forcing him into exile.

The pervasive state control erected by Perón hobbled the economy for years thereafter. For many businesses, success depended less on their productivity than on their skill at extracting start-up permits, import licenses, special bank loans, and other government favors—all of which created a fertile climate for corruption. In the hope of easing social tensions, governments frequently spent well more than they taxed, and the central bank created pesos to cover the difference, with inflation the predictable result. The military's decision to summon Perón back to the presidency in 1973 hardly helped matters; he died the following year, and though his second wife Isabel replaced him, by that time the Peronist movement had divided into left-wing and right-wing factions whose conflicts grew increasingly violent. With the economy in chaos, the military took over again in 1976 and the country descended into its darkest period of all, the Dirty War, in which thousands of union leaders, writers, students, and political activists were tortured and executed at the hands of death squads. "The disappeared" remained largely unaccounted for despite the sympathy aroused worldwide by the Mothers of the Plaza de Mayo, who marched silently in the plaza wearing white shawls that bore the names of their missing sons and daughters. The military finally surrendered power after its attempt in 1982 to seize the Falkland Islands from Britain ended in ignominious defeat. A presidential election the following year, won by Raúl Alfonsín of the Radical Party, restored democracy. But Argentina was then in the throes of a debt crisis that was plaguing much of Latin America. Alfonsín took over a country staggering under a $45 billion external debt, with an inflation rate of 340 percent that would only get worse as the government, seeking to keep the lid on explosive discontent, allowed spending to spiral out of control.

Osvaldo Soriano, an Argentine writer, captured the economic dysfunctionality generated by the rapid price movements of this period, a problem hardly comprehensible to Americans who had reacted with revulsion to inflation rates in the low teens: "In Buenos Aires in 1985, it was no longer possible to buy anything at night for what it had cost in the morning. In the cafés, the cashiers went crazy between the orders of the clients and the demands of the boss, who spent his time listening to the escalation of prices on the radio." When the government launched the Austral Plan in 1985, Soriano noted, "the largest and most coveted bill in the new currency was the red 100 austral, which was worth $185," but the plan's failure was evinced in the fast-changing denominations and exchange rate of the austral: "A little more than twelve months later, the 500 austral bill appeared, which was at first hard to get change for, and finally, by October 1988, the brand new 1,000 austral bill went into circulation, worth barely $70." And by 1989, during which the consumer price index for Buenos Aires soared more than 5,000 percent, Soriano lamented that "while I am writing this article, the cigarettes that I smoke as I sit here in front of my typewriter went from 11 to 13 and then to 14 australs." That year, machines at Argentina's National Mint broke under the strain of printing new 50,000 austral notes, and some wholesalers and retailers stopped doing business on the grounds that they could no longer estimate the replacement cost of their goods.

Although wages were routinely adjusted to keep pace with prices, the unstable economic climate drove living standards steadily lower. On a per capita basis, real gross domestic product—national output adjusted for inflation—declined at an average rate of 2.6 percent annually from 1982 to 1990. One statistic in particular highlights how far Argentina had fallen behind during the latter decades of the twentieth century: In 1950, the nation's GDP per capita had been 84 percent of the average of the world's developed countries; by 1973 that figure was 65 percent, and by 1987, 43 percent. Soup kitchens were feeding 2 million of the 9 million residents of Buenos Aires in the late 1980s. The resulting misery finally exploded in riots over food prices that forced Alfonsín to quit the presidency in July 1989, five months before his term expired. His newly elected successor, Carlos Menem, tried several aggressive anti-inflation measures, shocking middle-class savers by ordering the confiscation of short-term, high-yielding bank deposits and their replacement with long-term bonds. But a few months of relative stability in 1990 ended in yet another inflationary eruption, with the price index for Buenos Aires finishing 1,300 percent above where it started the year.

It was against this backdrop in 1991 that Domingo Cavallo became the fourth economy minister to serve under Menem and established convertibility as the law of the land. Under the law, the

U.S. dollar became fully legal tender, interchangeable with the peso—the theory being that if Argentines had complete freedom to switch to dollars, the government would have a powerful incentive to maintain the peso's equivalence with the greenback. Other countries had fixed exchange rates, but Argentina's system was much more unbending than most. Sometimes called a "currency board" (though it did not meet the strict definition of that term), the system required the central bank to keep enough dollars or gold in reserve to back the total amount of pesos that had been printed, strictly limiting the ability of the central bank to increase the supply of pesos in the economy.

By codifying those rules—in effect forswearing its independent ability to create money—the government was giving up one of the major tools that governments elsewhere use to boost growth during periods of weakness or recession. Unlike other central banks such as the U.S. Federal Reserve or the Bank of England, which can increase or decrease the amount of cash in their nations' banking systems depending on economic conditions, the Argentine central bank was legally bound to put itself on a sort of autopilot. As far as Cavallo was concerned, this was a desirable restraint. In the past the central bank had proved unable to resist pressures for increases in the money supply that had contributed to the nation's inflationary tendencies. Only by credibly tying its hands would the government eradicate inflation and foster the stability necessary for businesses, investors, and savers to start behaving in ways that would make the economy healthy and productive. In a country like Argentina, Cavallo believed, monetary policy was a dangerous instrument, a view effectively endorsed by the Argentine public, which by and large came to see convertibility as a contract locking its undisciplined government into acting sensibly.

At the IMF, wariness persisted about whether convertibility would survive for long, even after the Fund started giving Argentina loans aimed at supporting the system. Few were more dubious than Michael Mussa, the chief economist and director of the Research

Department. Brilliant but eccentric—he once broke into song at a meeting of the IMF executive board—Mussa, a former University of Chicago professor, delighted in making caustic comments at staff meetings or social occasions. At a 1992 farewell party for an Argentine on his staff, Pablo Guidotti, Mussa could not resist the opportunity for a jibe about convertibility, since Guidotti was leaving the Fund to work for his country's central bank governor, Roque Fernández. "Tell Roque to quit while he's ahead," Mussa cracked—a semihumorous suggestion that Fernández ought to resign from the central bank governorship before he could be blamed for convertibility's inevitable rout.

But to the amazement of the skeptics, the system was working according to plan—indeed, far better. Inflation subsided to 17.5 percent in 1992, and then to levels Argentines had not seen in decades—7.4 percent in 1993, 4.2 percent in 1994, and virtually zero for the rest of the 1990s. The benefits of stable prices were felt in ways small and large: Taxi meters, for example, registered fares straightforwardly in pesos, replacing the old system in which meters displayed units that were then converted into fares based on tables that constantly changed with the general price level. As confidence in the currency grew, bank deposits soared, and banks began extending credit on a much greater scale than before; they no longer had to worry about inflation eroding the value of the money they lent. The economy took off, with gross domestic product increasing at more than 10 percent annually in 1991 and 1992—one of the fastest growth rates in the world—followed by 6.3 percent growth in 1993 and 5.8 percent in 1994. The country put the 1980s debt crisis behind it in April 1993 by finalizing an agreement with foreign banks, under the terms of the debt-reduction plan established by U.S. Treasury Secretary Nicholas Brady. The deal replaced bank loans with bonds and trimmed the government's obligations by about $10 billion, to 29 percent of GDP.

All this success sent Cavallo vaulting to the top of the polls of the nation's leading politicians. When he attended a Buenos Aires cattle show with Yair Mundlak, a professor he had known at Harvard, he was mobbed effusively—so much so that Mundlak likened it to the adulation he had seen Israelis shower on Gen. Moshe Dayan for leading his nation's troops to victory over Arab forces in 1967.

The IMF's reservations about Argentina abated further as it became clear how ardently the government was embracing the Washington Consensus. This was especially surprising considering President Menem's background.

La Rioja province, in Argentina's northwestern interior, is one of the poorest among the nation's twenty-three provinces, with many homes lacking electricity and potable water. Carlos Menem served as governor there from 1983 to 1989, running the province in accord with long-standing Peronist principles. Under his stewardship, the public payroll expanded dramatically—from 12,000 to more than 40,000, by one estimate—in a province with a population of roughly 200,000. Some of those hired worked on a program Menem launched to build schools, hospitals, and homes. But many were what Argentines call "gnocchi," typically political loyalists (or their relatives and friends) who have little real work to do, and whose name derives from the pasta they reputedly eat once a month on the day they show up to collect their government paychecks.

To people unfamiliar with Argentina, it may seem puzzling that the governor of a hardscrabble province could afford to provide employment to such a high proportion of the population. The answer to the mystery is to be found in the extraordinary clout wielded by the governors. Thanks to their power, an artifact of the fractious historical relations between the rough-hewn interior and the cosmopolitan capital, the governors oblige the central government to share a large percentage of its revenue with them, so they can spend much more than they raise directly in taxes. During Menem's reign in La Rioja, for example, the provincial government levied taxes equal to only about 5 percent of its outlays, with federal revenue-sharing accounting for much of the rest. One of the major weaknesses of this system is that it gives the governors a major incentive to hike expenditure, since they do not suffer the political cost for raising the money to pay for it. Getting Congress to make a radical change in the system is extremely difficult, because the governors essentially control the selection process for their parties' congressional nominees in their provinces.

Since Menem exploited this system to fund statist policies in his home province, he was widely expected to pursue a similar path when he won the presidency in 1989. Indeed, everything about him reeked of old-school Peronism. The son of Syrian immigrants, he had a raffish manner, accentuated by muttonchop sideburns and a penchant for fast cars and the company of starlets, typical of a *caudillo* (strongman) in the tradition of Perón. As a candidate for the nomination of the Peronist party, he had broken with the party's "renewal" wing, which sought to project a safe, moderate image, and relied instead on the backing of traditional Peronist constituencies, particularly big labor unions.

But after moving into the Casa Rosada, the ornate pink-stone presidential mansion on the Plaza de Mayo, Menem reversed course. Likening himself to Soviet leader Mikhail Gorbachev, he contended that Argentina must shed the policies that had led down the road of stagnation and hyperinflation and adopt the new paradigm of the global marketplace. The end of the Cold War and the triumph of capitalism over communism were giving tremendous impetus to the Washington Consensus throughout the developing world, especially in Latin America. Menem put Argentina in the vanguard of this movement, all the while cloaking himself in the legacy of Perón— who, he said, understood the need for change when he returned from exile in 1973 but didn't live long enough to implement it.

Whether or not Perón would have approved, Menem's government dismantled much of the Peronist apparatus with alacrity. By 1992, Argentina had abolished all price controls, some of which were decades old, and eliminated a host of rules and bureaucratic bodies that regulated the agricultural, wholesale, and retail sectors. The average tariff on imported goods was slashed, from over 40 percent to about 9 percent; and with a handful of exceptions—autos, textiles, and shoes—other barriers to imports were scrapped. On top of this came an aggressive privatization drive, which by 1994 led to the sale of some 90 percent of all state enterprises, including the telephone, electricity, gas, and water utilities; trains; factories; luxury hotels; and even the concession for running the Buenos Aires zoo. The purchasers in many instances were multinational firms—some American, some European—but the investing public also got in on the action with the disposal of the state oil company, which fetched nearly $3 billion in one of the largest-ever initial public offerings of a company's shares.

The abysmal state of the nation's phone system helps explain why free markets were so appealing. While the system was under government ownership, Argentines had become accustomed to long waits for phone lines to be repaired; the waiting time for a new phone line was so protracted that apartment buyers paid premiums for residences in which lines were already installed. Antiquated switching stations resulted in many misdirected calls and jammed circuits. After French and Spanish telecommunications giants took over, the number of lines multiplied rapidly and reliable service became the norm. And telephones were just one example of the overstaffed, inefficient, and money-losing state operations that, once transferred to private hands, provided the government with financial savings while producing substantial improvements in service.

The process of shifting from a cosseted economy to a market-oriented one entailed plenty of pain, however. By 1994 the number of people employed at the privatized enterprises had shrunk by more than half, to 138,000. Bitterness over the fate of those who were laid off was all the keener because of evidence that the privatization process had been bungled in some cases and corrupted in others.

One of the first privatized enterprises, the national airline Aerolíneas Argentinas, was sold in haste to a group dominated by the Spanish airline Iberia. Service became expensive and indifferent, and despite eliminating routes and downsizing its workforce, the company was soon teetering on bankruptcy. Accusations of skimming public funds and steering contracts to cronies tainted the phone system privatization; it did not help that the politician in charge, María Julia Alsogaray, flaunted her wealth by posing in a fur coat, and little else, for a magazine. Ugliest of all was the case of Alfredo Yabrán, a tycoon who was almost unknown to the Argentine public until accusations surfaced in 1995 about his success at enriching companies he secretly controlled that were benefiting from privatization in areas such as customs warehouses and airport services. Yabrán, who had links to military elements associated with some of the Dirty War atrocities, allegedly used mafia-style tactics to stifle competitors and exploited his connections to Menem's top circle to secure legislation tailored to provide him with a postal monopoly. Incredibly, Yabrán's chief accuser was none other than Economy Minister Cavallo, who quit the cabinet in mid-1996. The scandal exploded into violence with the murder of a magazine photographer who had snapped the first picture of Yabrán to appear in the media. In 1998, Yabrán, who had denied all the accusations and filed slander suits against Cavallo, apparently committed suicide as police prepared to arrest him for his role in the photographer's killing.

Still, on the whole, privatization boosted the economy's efficiency and benefited ordinary people in all manner of ways, according to a host of academic studies that have been conducted in the years since. (In one striking finding concerning the privatization of the deteriorating water system, child mortality fell 26 percent in the poorest areas where water services were privatized, because the extension of the water network to poor homes rid drinking water of parasites and other disease-causing agents.) More broadly, the combination of stable prices, a booming economy, and market efficiency improved living standards for millions of Argentines—and not only the elite. Per capita GDP rose from $4,636 in 1991 to $7,501 in 1994. People at the top were faring best, as those with professional skill levels enjoyed an average increase of 46 percent in real monthly incomes over the 1990–1994 period. But the gains registered during this time by those further down the income scale were also appreciable. The average increase in real monthly incomes for skilled workers was 27 percent, and for unskilled workers, 16 percent. The number of people living under the poverty line declined sharply, from 41.4 percent in 1990 to 21.6 percent in 1994.

Oscar Quinteros remembers those years as "the golden age for me and my family." The son of a truck driver and a maid, with a degree from secondary school where he learned technical and mechanical skills, Quinteros worked on the railroad and subways in the greater Buenos Aires area. During the 1980s, he had barely been able to make ends meet; in 1988 his first child was born and a year later his father, who had no health care, fell ill with cancer, requiring the family to spend much of its money on his treatment and medicine. In the winter of 1990, when his father died, "we had no kerosene for the stoves. We froze at home," Quinteros recalled. But not for long would the family have such wants. In 1993, Quinteros, then in his late twenties, got a second job as an inspector on a new subway line, and in combination with his first job on the national railway company, he was earning about $2,500 a month. He bought a used Renault and "a huge audio set with CD player and good speakers because I loved rock and roll," he said. "I gave my wife lots of gifts, especially fancy clothes, cosmetics, and perfume. I bought a computer for the kids as well, and a TV set, VCR, a new stove, a good mattress, an automatic washing machine, and I finished my house," which was located in a working-class district south of the capital. He took pride in his job, which often involved fixing stalled subway trains in an emergency, "being hung up [near the wires that conducted electricity for the trains] with 25,000 volts buzzing close to my head—risking my life maybe, but I was doing what I loved and what I had studied for." He became unemployed in late 1995—as a union delegate, he ran afoul of the leadership by opposing the union president, he said—and for a couple of years he had to work as a carpenter for about $400 a month, supplementing his income with odd jobs such as yard work and masonry. But in 1998, he went back to work on the subways as an independent contractor, helping to install new fiber-optic wiring.

Further up the income scale, Silvia D., a psychotherapist, was a typical example of how professionals flourished during the 1990s. (She asked that, to protect her privacy, her surname not be disclosed.) Divorced and a mother of three children, Silvia had always lived relatively comfortably, because her father owned a successful bazaar in a traditional Jewish Buenos Aires neighborhood, though he nearly went bankrupt in the 1980s. Her therapy practice took off in the mid-1990s when she purchased and remodeled an old house in Palermo Viejo, one of the capital's venerable neighborhoods that was fast filling with trendy restaurants, bars, and boutiques. The house cost $90,000, and she paid an additional $95,000 to have it remodeled into a spectacular blend of the traditional and modern, with nearly everything inside renewed—from the tile floors in the toilets to the state-of-the-art appliances in the kitchen, and a smartly appointed office in which to meet with patients on the upper floor. Silvia got rid of her used 1982 Mazda and bought an elegant new Peugeot, for which she paid $22,000—another luxury she had no problem affording, because she was working up to forty-five hours a week, getting $250 an hour for providing therapy to couples whose ranks included television celebrities and influential politicians. "Many of my patients came to me for therapy because I had an office in the most fashionable district in town," she mused. Despite the burden of supporting her elderly parents, which cost her about $1,500 a month, she was able to travel several times to Europe, where her son was studying art.

For factory workers, life in the 1990s wasn't nearly so cushy, but the economic well-being of many marked an advance over what they had known before. Miguel Machado was an example. In his native Tucumán province, one of Argentina's poorest, Machado spent nine years processing sugarcane in the cane fields until he and thousands of others lost their jobs to machines in the mid-1980s. After moving to Buenos Aires in 1987, he was able to obtain employment at a variety of factories, culminating in a job at a flour mill owned by Morixe, one of Argentina's most venerable flour and wheat companies, where he earned take-home pay of $600 a month. He and his wife started having children—seven in all—and lived in a three-bedroom wood home owned by his wife's mother. The family bought a television, a luxury Machado had never enjoyed in Tucumán. He loved spending time with his kids, going out for ice cream in the evenings and to parks or the zoo on weekends.

All these gains generated by Argentina's new economic model looked as if they might be snuffed out during a few awful months in mid-decade. The reason was the "tequila crisis," the term for the financial jitters sparked all over Latin America as a result of the collapse of the Mexican peso in late 1994. Amid fears that Argentina's currency might follow Mexico's, money poured out of Argentine banks, which lost 18 percent of their deposits, and the economy slumped, with gross domestic product falling by 2.8 percent in 1995. Despite pressure for easy money to combat rapidly rising unemployment, Menem and Cavallo resolutely pledged to protect convertibility at all costs. To demonstrate their commitment to economic probity, they allowed interest rates to shoot up—the prime lending rate peaked at 40 percent—and they even raised taxes, lifting the value-added tax rate from 18 percent to 21 percent. Their grit was rewarded when the economy, having suffered a confidence shock rather than a fundamental setback, recovered smartly in 1996. Economic growth was 5.5 percent that year; in 1997, GDP rose by 8.1 percent, and in 1998, 3.9 percent—with prices still miraculously stable.

At that point, in the aftermath of the tequila crisis, Argentina finally won the IMF's heart. Within the Fund, those who were skeptical of convertibility were on the defensive. In March 1995 an internal staff report had declared for the first time that the Argentines should keep the system. "Argentina's economic history during the 1990s suggests it would be very difficult to keep inflation expectations under control if exchange rate discipline were to be lost," the report said. "For this reason, and in view of the strengthening of policies by the Argentine authorities, the staff supports the maintenance of the fixed exchange rate." The institution's more positive attitude toward Argentina shone through in public comments by Michel Camdessus, the managing director. Speaking before a Buenos Aires audience in 1996, Camdessus recalled how testy the relationship between Argentina and the Fund had been in prior years, when they were split over "important doctrinal differences" concerning matters such as the appropriate role of the state and the importance of fiscal discipline. "Today, there is no longer any doctrinal divide," Camdessus said, adding that Argentina now offered "lessons . . . that we can share with others" about how to prosper. In a return trip to Buenos Aires the following year, the IMF chief raved in a speech over the latest economic indicators showing economic growth sizzling and inflation close to zero. "My friends, this may not be paradise," Camdessus declared. "But the situation is far better than we would have dared imagine not so very long ago."

That enthusiasm was more than matched on Wall Street.

"A Bravo New World." So proclaimed the title page of a report on Argentina and other Latin American markets that Goldman, Sachs & Co. sent to clients in January 1996.

The report hailed Argentina for adhering to the prescriptions of the Washington Consensus and keeping the peso tied to the dollar through thick and thin. "If any country stuck to its original economic program during the worst of the 1995 financial crisis, that country was Argentina," the report's authors stated. "Armed with the belief that most Argentines would rather face unemployment than the well-known cycle of devaluation-inflation-devaluation, President Menem and Finance Minister Domingo Cavallo not only did not retract on their promises, but accelerated their economic reform efforts. For Argentine citizens and for those investors who were willing to believe in those promises, the benefits are now becoming apparent."

As the report's language suggests, this success story translated into a compelling sales pitch for the Street.

A fevered atmosphere for emerging markets had taken hold in the financial world, based on the belief that the fastest growth, quickest profits, and highest yields were to be found in former economic backwaters that were getting with the capitalist program. Seeking to establish themselves as dominant players in the game, firms like Goldman, Morgan Stanley, and Credit Suisse First Boston scrambled to build their presence in Argentina and neighboring countries by dispatching teams of economists and financial experts, who helped send rents skyrocketing in the tony neighborhoods of the region's financial capitals. For firms with pretensions of global reach, it was essential to have a significant Latin American business, preferably with "on the ground" expertise, especially in the big three markets—Mexico, Brazil, and Argentina. Part of their focus was on trading in the region's booming stock exchanges and bringing to market the bonds and stocks of its rapidly advancing companies. But another major line of pursuit was assisting the region's governments, many of which needed to borrow extensively to cover budget deficits. The investment firms competed fiercely for "mandates" to be lead managers of government bond sales, especially in Argentina, whose government was the single largest emerging-market bond issuer. They found plenty of customers for the bonds in the United States and other wealthy countries among professional investors managing the hundreds of billions of dollars held in mutual funds, pension funds, insurance companies, foundations, and other large institutions.

Highlighting the trend was a sale in January 1997, managed by J.P. Morgan and Merrill Lynch, of $2 billion in twenty-year Argentine government bonds. "Every time we finished a meeting [with portfolio managers], the orders would come," marveled Miguel Kiguel, who was then Argentina's undersecretary of finance, recalling a trip he took to the United States to promote the bonds. "People were *desperate* to buy Argentina."

Such openhandedness was especially remarkable in light of Argentina's history of defaults (four of them since the 1820s) and the deadbeat reputation it had acquired during the 1980s. The world's lenders were willing, indeed eager, to let bygones be bygones; Argentina's transformed character was readily apparent in the sterling credentials and polished manner of the Economy Ministry's top officials. Kiguel, for example, was a Columbia University Ph.D. who had worked at the World Bank. Roque Fernández, who had replaced Cavallo as minister, and Pablo Guidotti, who was then serving under Fernández as the ministry's treasury secretary, were both University of Chicago Ph.D.'s who had worked at the IMF.

The bond industry had come a long way from its stodgy origins as purveyors of conservative investments aimed at producing steady, guaranteed streams of income for widows and orphans. Wall Street had turned the marketing and trading of such securities into a business that often required a high degree of mathematical sophistication. Besides plain-vanilla bonds of the sort that Argentina issued in January 1997, which paid a fixed-interest coupon each year and repayment of principal at maturity, the Street's wizards pitched a wondrous array of other products, with myriad features, in the hopes of winning fee-generating assignments from Argentine officials to bring the government's bonds to market. "Step-down bonds" were one favorite (they paid high interest rates in the first couple of years, and lower rates in later years); others included "spread-adjusted floating-rate bonds" and "strippable zero-coupon bonds" (the details of which need only be described as complicated). All of these bonds could be bought or sold through major securities firms, where traders stood ready to eke out profits by skimming a few tenths of a percentage point in price as they flipped the bonds from sellers to buyers. Since the bonds had so many different bells and whistles, their prices depended on myriad factors. But at bottom, all followed the fundamental axiom of bond trading: Prices move inversely with yield. As prices fall, yields rise, and vice versa.*

The river of cash streaming into Argentina and other emerging markets reflected a broader phenomenon—the expansion of globalization into the financial realm. International trade in goods such as shoes and microchips was already substantially free, as was investment in overseas factories by multinational manufacturers. Now national barriers to foreign funds were being rapidly dismantled as well. For much of the post–World War II era, the world's governments had tightly restricted international flows of private capital, fearing a reprise of the crises that had deepened the Great Depression in the 1930s. But rich countries began removing their controls in the 1970s, and in the late 1980s and 1990s developing nations were rushing to follow suit, strongly encouraged to do so by the IMF and the U.S. Treasury. (Argentina completely opened its capital markets in 1989.) The rationale, in simple terms, was that poor countries needed funds to develop, and since rich countries tended to have a surfeit of savings, the less fortunate should not be deprived of financial resources. Moreover, freeing up capital to move across borders would presumably raise living standards globally, because when investors could put their money into investments overseas that offered more attractive returns than they could get at home, the world's overall resources could be used more efficiently.

Just as in the tech-stock boom, which was also starting to gather steam on Wall Street around the mid-1990s, the world of emerging-

---

* For readers who may have seen that axiom in their newspaper business pages but never understood it, consider the example of a bond issued by the Republic of Fredonia with a face value of $1,000 that pays guaranteed interest of 10 percent per annum of the issuing price, or $100. Suppose concerns arise that Fredonia may default, causing the bond's price to fall to $800. For someone buying the bond at the lower price, the $100 annual interest payment provides a fatter yield ($100 divided by $800) than to someone who bought it at its face value ($100 divided by $1,000). Thus, the lower a bond falls in price, the higher its yield; and conversely, the higher a bond rises in price, the lower its yield.

markets investing had its star analysts and strategists, who were often quoted in the press and treated like celebrities at industry conferences. One was a dashing Chilean named José Luis Daza, the head of emerging-markets fixed-income research at J.P. Morgan; another was his counterpart at Merrill Lynch, Joyce Chang, an earnest, superdisciplined woman renowned for her contacts and networking skills. They and their teams often ranked high in the "honor rolls" and "all-star teams" of top analysts published annually by trade publications such as *Institutional Investor* and *LatinFinance*. Among the notable features of the honor rolls was the youth of the honorees, who typically ranged from their late twenties to mid-thirties. (Chang, for example, turned thirty in 1995.) Young though they were, such people "were making money hand over fist in those days," said Stuart Hopard, a recruiter working in the field. According to Hopard and a number of other recruiters, strategists and senior economists at major banks typically earned $350,000 to $900,000 a year, including bonuses, while their bosses, the Dazas and the Changs, received pay in seven figures.

Besides offering advice on where to put money, the analysts' duties included leading trips of professional money managers, who worked for institutions such as mutual funds and pension funds, to Buenos Aires and other emerging-market capitals. These trips were designed to give investors insight into the countries, while also fostering chummy relations between the investors and traders at the Wall Street firms; the traders stood to earn big bucks if the investors chose them to handle the purchases and sales of securities. Participants describe the trips as grueling, with meetings and presentations often starting at breakfast and continuing one after the other throughout the day. But the trips also combined business with pleasure. Moscow was notoriously awash in fleshpots—the best-known being a place called Night Flight where, for investors who were so inclined, their brokerage-firm hosts would dispense wads of cash enabling clients to take their pick among a bountiful selection of prostitutes. As for Buenos Aires, people familiar with the trips there whisper that a fair amount of entertaining went on at Black, a gentlemen's club across the street from the city's most elegant hotel, which featured scantily clad young women dancing on tabletops and snuggling with customers on couches in the hopes of enticing them to pay for sex. (That said, Buenos Aires was less of a sin city than Moscow, and many who participated in trips there swear they never heard of Black.)

On trips to Buenos Aires run by J.P. Morgan, investors typically spent the daytime at meetings with senior Argentine government officials, politicians, and private economists, then followed up with dinner at the city's swankest restaurants and a late-evening tango show. Some of the favorite dining spots were in Puerto Madero, a once-decrepit harbor on the Rio de la Plata where developers had converted warehouse buildings into hip eateries on the waterfront serving thick, juicy slabs of steak; as a symbol of the new, emerging Argentina, the renovation of the area rarely failed to impress. If time permitted, the investors might attend a professional soccer game or polo match, the idea being that "they wouldn't only buy the bonds, but the whole country, the concept," as one former Morgan employee put it. Chang's trips were similar, though in keeping with her reputation for knowing everybody that mattered, the meeting schedules were especially chock-full. "We call it the Joyce Chang dog-and-pony show," said one New York–based fund manager. "They wheel people through the hotel to see you, then there's a big gala dinner. It reminded me of camp, or a teen tour . . . 'You're in bus No. 1; you're in bus No. 2.'"

The investors might have gotten a different impression had they ventured to places like Chaco, Salta, Jujuy, Tucumán, or Formosa provinces in Argentina's impoverished north. Industries such as cotton and timber had once thrived in those parts, but jobs in the private sector were now scarce, especially since factory owners could hire workers at much lower cost in nearby Paraguay, which had a cheap currency. In these areas, provincial governments tended to provide the bulk of the employment, often on corrupt terms, to bolster local political machines and appease the large numbers of unemployed. The legislatures of Chaco and Formosa offered notorious examples of the syndrome; each provincial legislator received well over $1 million a year for "advisers" and other "expenses." Extreme though such cases were—and the northern provinces were much less heavily populated than metropolitan Buenos Aires, home to more than a third of all Argentines—they vividly illustrated how the provincial governments, like the one Menem had run, remained hotbeds of patronage. But such locales were not on the itineraries of most foreign money managers.

One theme on the trips was constant: Argentine officials meeting with the visiting investors almost invariably stressed how firmly wedded the country was to convertibility. When investors voiced concern that the peso was rising in lockstep with the dollar against other currencies, making Argentine goods more expensive on world markets, the response was that undoing the currency system was simply not an option. Officials would explain that this was partly because of the memories of hyperinflation, and partly because such a large percentage of the country's loans were denominated in dollars, which meant that devaluation would instantly increase the debt burden of borrowers, to ruinous levels in many cases. Among the officials uttering a vow of fealty to convertibility was Eduardo Duhalde, then governor of the province of Buenos Aires, who assured a group of visitors in late 1998 that Argentina would "never" abandon the peso-dollar link, according to notes of the session taken by George Estes, a portfolio manager at Grantham, Mayo, Van Otterloo & Co., a Boston investment firm. In recounting the meeting, Estes noted the irony: Duhalde, as president in 2002, would give the order devaluing the peso.

Support for convertibility among politicians, though not unanimous, remained solid despite an increase in poverty, from 21.6 percent in 1994 to 29.4 percent in 1998, and evidence that the new economy's benefits were going disproportionately to the upper classes. Argentines in the professions continued to prosper after the tequila crisis; in 1998 their real monthly incomes were 53 percent ahead of the 1990 level. But for those in the working classes, income gains began petering out and even going into reverse after the decade's midpoint, a major reason being a stubbornly high rate of unemployment (12.8 percent in 1998) caused by the 1995 recession and a flood of imports into sectors such as footwear and textiles. By 1998 the real incomes of skilled workers were still 13 percent ahead of where they had been in 1990, but those of unskilled workers were 2.7 percent lower. In a country that had long boasted one of the least inequitable distributions of wealth in Latin America, the contrasts were growing ever starker between the lifestyles of those who were benefiting from the prosperity generated by the economy's new dynamism and those who were being left behind.

The fortunate ones were dining in Puerto Madero or shopping at places like the Galerías Pacífico mall in downtown Buenos Aires, an airy, lovingly restored nineteenth-century building with murals on the vaulted ceilings and stores featuring the merchandise of Hugo Boss, Lacoste, Ralph Lauren, and Yves Saint Laurent as well as Argentina's top designers. Few such pleasures were in store for the unemployed. Their ranks included people like Horacio Hinojosa, one of the thousands laid off in 1992 from the state-run steel and mining company in Argentina's far north after its sale to a consortium consisting of Citicorp and several other firms. Hinojosa reported in 1999 that the only employment he could find was driving his battered car as an informal taxi, which provided less than half the $13,000 annual wage he had received at the steel company. He was four months behind in the mortgage on his two-room, particle-board house and could not afford to fill a prescription for medicine when he fell ill with pneumonia.

Yet even people suffering such misfortunes counted themselves among the large majorities who appreciated the benefits that convertibility conferred. Recalling the hyperinflation of the late 1980s, Hinojosa said his sister and brother-in-law, who were saving to buy a house, had seen the value of their entire nest egg wiped out in two months because they were not keeping the money in the special accounts designed to protect against rising prices. "Those were ugly days," he said. "Nobody wants to go back to that."

A shadow began to fall over the Argentine bond bonanza when financial crises struck emerging markets elsewhere. Foreign investors bailed out of Thailand in mid-1997, forcing the government in Bangkok to devalue its currency; later that year similar calamities befell Indonesia and South Korea, followed by Russia in mid-1998 and Brazil in early 1999. As these episodes showed, the globalization of financial capital, for all its theoretical advantages, had a dark side—the tendency for investors to succumb to mass panic, pull their money out of countries, and, in the process, inflict punishment out of proportion to the countries' "crimes." Yet Argentina seemed relatively immune. The government continued issuing bonds, offering higher yields to attract investors, who kept on buying. Key to this success was the convertibility system, which was viewed as much more ironclad than the other countries' loosely fixed exchange rates.

The investment firm of Dresdner Kleinwort Benson assured clients that they should not worry unduly about Argentina following countries like Thailand or Indonesia into turmoil. "Argentina has come through the first phase of the Asian crisis with flying colors," the firm said in a June 1998 report, and this was "no coincidence. The economic fundamentals are considerably stronger than three and a half years ago." When the crisis spread to Brazil, knocking Argentine markets for a loop, José Luis Daza wrote in January 1999: "The decade of reform has strengthened Argentina's economic foundations dramatically," and "asset prices should rebound as the market once again is impressed by Argentina's capacity to overcome a difficult global financial period."

Amid all this ebullience, Argentina was sowing the seeds of its own destruction. Regrettably, its interactions with the IMF were not helping much.

[CHAPTER 3]

Who's Afraid of the Molotov Cocktail?

THREE BLOCKS west of the White House stands the IMF's headquarters, a beige limestone building thirteen stories high. On a typical workday, 2,600 employees—roughly one-quarter American, the rest from 141 other nations—pass through the electronic security apparatus, swiping their ID cards as they enter a sunlit lobby to cross a polished marble floor on their way to their offices. Another 117 work in field offices abroad. They hold the status of elite international civil servants and embody one of the most disciplined bureaucracies in the world.

Founded in 1944 at an international conference in New Hampshire, the IMF is like a giant credit union for countries. Its member nations contribute funds to a central kitty, and the money is lent out as needed to the members that are financially strapped. (In 2004, there were 184 member nations, and the kitty totaled about $157 billion.) The money in question is "hard currency"—dollars, yen, euros, pounds sterling, and a handful of others—that can be easily used in international transactions. The distinction between hard currency and other kinds is important, because for the majority of countries, their own currencies can be used only within their borders; hard currency is generally required to purchase, say, a shipment of imported pharmaceuticals or to pay back international loans. Countries often run low on hard currency; in typical cases this is because they have incurred high levels of foreign debt or run large trade deficits. When that happens, they may turn to the IMF for a "program," including loans that can help tide them over so that they can continue importing vital products and keep their economies functioning. (The IMF's loans are thus different in purpose from those of the World Bank, the Fund's sister institution, which lends money on a long-term basis to governments of low- and middle-income countries for projects aimed at economic development and poverty alleviation in areas such as education, health, and transportation.) The loans, which go to the borrowing nation's central bank, come with strings attached—conditions requiring changes in economic policies, aimed at putting the country's economy back on a sustainable path.

Heading the IMF are two officials chosen by rich countries. The senior one is the managing director, by tradition a European; during the 1990s it was Michel Camdessus, the former governor of the French central bank, a man of unrivaled political instincts who had graduated from the prestigious Ecole Nationale d'Administration and risen to the top of his country's powerful civil service. Second in command is the first deputy managing director, traditionally an American; from 1994 to 2001 it was Stanley Fischer, a former World Bank chief economist and former professor at the Massachusetts Institute of Technology, where he had chaired the economics department. Despite his lower rank, Fischer was the Fund's most influential figure during his tenure, in part because of the close ties he enjoyed with officials in President Bill Clinton's administration but also because of his status as one of the foremost economists of his generation. A slender man with oval glasses, Fischer grew up in a small farming village in the British colony of Northern Rhodesia (now Zambia), where his parents, immigrants from Eastern Europe, ran a general store. Most members of the IMF staff revered him for his kindly disposition and the cerebral force of his observations, which he delivered with a dry wit and the pleasing lilt of a southern African accent. But he was viewed warily by some of the institution's economists, who felt he was too inclined to be forbearing and reluctant to say "no" in dealing with developing nations.

The IMF's top officials, powerful as they may be, have political masters—the Fund's twenty-four-person board, which represents the member countries' governments and typically meets several times a week on the twelfth floor of IMF headquarters. Eight board members represent individual countries, and the rest represent groups of countries, with weighted voting based on the size of the countries' contributions to the IMF's war chest. Real clout on the board is wielded by the Group of Seven major industrial countries (the United States, Japan, Germany, Britain, France, Italy, and Canada), which control nearly half the votes, and the G-7 members almost invariably work together as a bloc after reaching a consensus among themselves. Because of the dominance of the United States, both in the G-7 and on the IMF board, the Fund is often viewed as a pawn of the U.S. Treasury—an exaggeration, but not an inordinate one.

On the floors below the board and top management are the offices of the staff, the heart of which is the economists, numbering about 1,250. Most of the economists hold doctorates from the world's leading universities, and they function within an extremely hierarchical organization. They often engage in intense debates over Fund policy toward individual countries, but those discussions are kept strictly confidential, and once a policy is decided—if necessary, with a ruling from the managing director or deputy managing director—staffers are expected to fall in line behind it. Missions that travel to troubled countries must stick closely to their negotiating instructions, which are hammered out in advance among the Fund's various departments; revealing internal differences to outsiders is seriously frowned upon. This method of operation helps the IMF project an image of omniscience, both to the markets and to the countries with which it is negotiating.

In the spring of 1997, an internal IMF memo invited top officials of major departments to an "informal seminar" on Argentina. The April 7 memo came from Teresa Ter-Minassian, who had recently been appointed deputy director of the Western Hemisphere Department with responsibility for overseeing Argentina and Brazil.

Energetic, attractive, and Italian—the Armenian surname is her husband's—Ter-Minassian had been picked for the job partly because of concern among the IMF's top management that the Fund's Latin American specialists were growing too close to the countries they dealt with. (The director of the Western Hemisphere Department, Claudio Loser,* was Argentine.) With a law degree from the University of Rome, a Ph.D. in economics from Harvard, and twenty-six years of experience at the Fund, Ter-Minassian had the background, perspective, and reputation for toughness that her superiors wanted. One of the few of her gender to reach such a high position on the IMF staff, she had spent most of her career in the European Department, where she headed the team that negotiated the Fund's last program for a Western industrial nation, Portugal, in the mid-1980s.

Accompanying the invitation was a briefing paper outlining issues pertaining to a possible agreement between Argentina and the IMF. This proposed arrangement was somewhat unusual, because the Argentine government was only tangentially interested in the IMF's most coveted resource—its money.

In 1997 Argentina was hardly in need of an emergency dollop of hard currency, given all the capital that was flooding in from private sources. The country had been one of the IMF's biggest wards in years past; in fact, it was still borrowing from the Fund under a rela-

---

* Pronounced LOH-ser.

tively small program approved in early 1996 to help ensure stability in the wake of the tequila crisis. But the attendees at the seminar called by Ter-Minassian were being asked to evaluate a different sort of program—a "precautionary" one, that is, a promise by the Fund to lend money if a crisis arose, with the intention that Argentina would never draw the loan. The idea was to provide another kind of benefit that the IMF can confer, a sort of Good Housekeeping Seal of Approval, to reassure markets that the country's policies were on the right track. The program was envisioned to last three years.

The big question facing the IMF was what it should demand of Argentina in return for the Good Housekeeping Seal. Among the Fund staff, plenty of nervousness lingered about how long the convertibility system could last, and some favored pressing the Argentines to adopt an exit strategy for dropping the one-to-one exchange rate between the dollar and peso. The proponents of an exit strategy reasoned that if the economy's underlying fundamentals were strong enough, letting the peso float against the dollar would result in a higher exchange rate for the Argentine currency rather than a lower one. But the Fund was not going to insist that Argentina unshackle its economy from convertibility—and certainly not right away. The authorities in Buenos Aires had reiterated, both publicly and privately, that they would not consider such a move, and under the IMF's articles of agreement, member countries are allowed to choose the type of foreign exchange regime they deem most suitable. As stated in the briefing paper circulated before the seminar:

> The Convertibility Plan has served Argentina well and is widely regarded as a guarantee of stability and symbol of modernization. The generalized support enjoyed by the plan owes much to the still fresh memory of the stagnation and economic disorder of the previous decades and to the fear that a loosening of the strictures of the plan would bring back the chaotic past. Given this background, [the IMF's program] will be based on the assumption that convertibility will be maintained, i.e., that the present monetary

policy and exchange rate arrangement will remain unchanged during the program period, with the expectation that successful implementation of the program may create the conditions for orderly exit from this strategy, if such exit were to be desired.

This was a fateful decision, like that of a ship's crew and superior officers who elect to stay on course despite the possibility that a deadly tempest might be forming over the horizon. The idea of an exit strategy did not gain ground; indeed, the highly tentative proposal for one in the briefing paper would be the last reference to it in internal IMF documents for some time. By failing to exit from convertibility, the Fund—and the Argentines—were passing up a significant opportunity. In retrospect, many economists and policymakers now contend that 1997 would have been the most propitious time for Argentina to slip out of its monetary straitjacket, given the economy's momentum and the market's bullishness. The conditions for a change in the currency regime would be much less favorable in a couple of years with the onset of recession. But this is not to suggest that an exit would have been easy, even in 1997. On the contrary, it is quite understandable why, at the time, the advantages of keeping convertibility in place—and the risks of abandoning it—seemed so overwhelming.

The IMF's basic approach, therefore, was to bolster convertibility rather than alter it. Fund support would be used to induce Argentina to take the measures necessary to ensure the system's survival. So what did Argentina need to do?

One step, favored by the IMF for years, was to reform the nation's labor laws, which since the days of Perón had boosted union bargaining power and made it difficult for employers to lay off workers. Argentine companies that fired employees were legally required to make costly severance payments. If negotiations with a union failed to produce a settlement within a specified time, companies were obliged to abide by their existing contracts, which meant unions could drag their feet to preserve anachronistic work rules.

Moreover, the law required companies to negotiate with unions on an industrywide basis, which undercut the ability of smaller, newer enterprises to bargain for lower-cost wages than those paid by big, established firms.

Such laws were incompatible with the fixed value of the peso, in the IMF's view, because Argentina needed a flexible labor market to compensate for the rigidity of its currency. After all, with every upward tick of the dollar against other major currencies, the peso was rising too, so Argentine industry was coming under increasing danger of losing competitiveness as its goods increased in price compared with foreign products. Predictably, Argentina's powerful unions opposed changing the labor laws—legislation to that end was then bogged down in Congress—and with the unemployment rate above 13 percent, the unions had a potent argument against any measure that might ease the way for more layoffs. But the rebuttal from the Fund, along with many mainstream economists, was that the old rules were contributing heavily to the high jobless rate by discouraging promising enterprises from adding new employees.

Labor market reform thus became one major condition of the IMF program. But even more important was fiscal policy. "Fiscal policy will play a key role in buttressing confidence in the continued viability of the Convertibility Plan," declared the IMF's briefing paper. Today, remorse runs deep at the IMF on this point, and many economists' postmortems agree: Fiscal policy was one of the crucial junctures where Argentina went wrong.

An oft-repeated joke about the IMF is that its initials stand for "It's Mostly Fiscal." The humor stems from the Fund's seeming obsession with bludgeoning countries into cutting spending or raising taxes, as if there were no economic problem that a lower budget deficit or (better yet) fatter surplus wouldn't cure. During the Asian financial crisis, the IMF would be accused—with considerable justification—of pushing countries such as Thailand and Korea too far in the direction of budgetary austerity, driving economies that were already headed for trouble even deeper into recessions. Paradoxically, in the case of Argentina, its pride and joy, the Fund's pushing would be too weak.

On the surface, Argentina's fiscal accounts in the mid-1990s looked as if the government had overcome its earlier penchant for spending beyond its means. In 1997, a fairly typical budget year, the federal government was running a deficit of $4.6 billion, equal to just 1.6 percent of GDP; with the provinces added in, the overall government was $6.05 billion in the red, or 2.1 percent of GDP. Moreover, the entire deficit that year, and a bit more besides, could be attributed to government interest payments. So on a "primary" basis—that is, excluding interest—the government was running a small surplus.

For most countries, a budget deficit of those proportions would be of little concern; in fact, the European nations that used the euro as their common currency had set a deficit ceiling of 3 percent of GDP. Just as in the case of a company that borrows to finance a new plant showing promise of increased profits, a government may sensibly borrow to fund a deficit on the theory that increased growth will generate the higher tax revenue needed to pay its creditors. No major problem should arise as long as the total debt stays under control—that is, as long as the debt stays comfortably within the government's ability to keep paying interest and principal as obligations come due.

But Argentina had a special reason to exercise extraordinary prudence in its budgetary policy: the cherished convertibility system. Like a person prone to heart attacks who must maintain a much healthier lifestyle than the average individual to reduce the risk of a fatal seizure, Argentina needed to be ultradisciplined about fiscal matters.

There were two reasons for this. First, Argentina was borrowing mainly in dollars, and although that is a common practice in developing countries because of the interest rate advantage, it raised the danger of a financial conflagration that could destroy the dollar-peso link. If the government's debt started looking excessive, markets would worry that the government lacked the dollars required not only to pay its creditors but also to exchange pesos with all comers at $1 each. The result would be a rush to exchange pesos for dollars that would exhaust the central bank's dollar supplies and wreck the underpinnings of convertibility. In sum, Argentina needed to keep its debt ratios in check, especially the closely watched ratio of debt to GDP.

The second, related reason for fiscal caution was that Argentina needed to maintain more than the usual amount of reserve ammunition in case of a recession. Since the government had forsworn use of the monetary printing press, it had to be sure it could respond to slumps with other types of stimulative measures—that is, by cutting taxes or boosting spending. The only way it could prepare itself for such an eventuality was by adopting a highly responsible budget policy, preferably sizable surpluses, during boom times. Ideally, the government would achieve what economists call "balance over the cycle," meaning that the surpluses generated when the business cycle was headed upward would offset the deficits generated when the cycle turned downward.

In the mid-1990s, one economist in particular—an Argentine—was sounding the alarm that the government's fiscal policy was far too loose. Mario Teijeiro, a University of Chicago Ph.D. who headed a small Buenos Aires research institute, was well known to the IMF because he had worked at the Fund in the 1980s. In a July 1996 paper, Teijeiro accused the government of grossly understating the size of the deficit, especially by excluding factors that were adding substantially to the government's debt. Principal among these were large sums that the government was paying, mostly in the form of bonds, to pensioners and suppliers, many of whom had won court orders declaring them entitled to receive amounts that were past due. Teijeiro also argued that Argentina needed to aim for balance over the cycle. "In the presence of [international] capital volatility that can give rise to booms in consumption and temporary income growth, the basic principle of fiscal policy [should be] conduct that accumulates surpluses in favorable cycles and falls into deficits in adverse periods," he wrote.

"People at the IMF knew what I thought," Teijeiro recalled. "They didn't want to speak to me very much. They knew I was sort of a single voice speaking out against what was happening."

IMF economists say they agreed in principle that balance over the cycle would be best for Argentina. But they had never been able to persuade Argentine officials that it was necessary to go that far, and the evidence shows that Fund officials at the top were not inclined to push very hard either. In August 1996, for example, Fischer, the first deputy managing director, wrote in the margins of a staff memo on Argentina: "Budget balance in [19]97 is less important than finding or agreeing on a financeable deficit that will be attained given reasonable growth performance." Still, the IMF's basic approach was that at the very least, it could move the Argentines in the right direction.

The IMF briefing paper circulated in April 1997 identified grounds for concern about Argentina's fiscal policy. It noted that the government's total debt had risen rapidly in the past several years, approaching 40 percent of GDP (in part because of the issue that concerned Teijeiro, the bonds given to pensioners and suppliers in court rulings). To pay principal and interest coming due on that debt, the government would have to borrow an additional $10 billion to $13 billion annually over the next several years—"amounts that are perceived as giving rise to considerable risk" because of the possibility that the markets might turn negative on the country and refuse to advance more cash. Accordingly, "the ability of the public sector to incur deficits should remain constrained," the authors recommended, the idea being to "reduce, or at least stabilize, the debt-GDP ratio."

Reduce, or at least stabilize, the debt-to-GDP ratio: The importance of this goal would become apparent in years ahead. To get there, the IMF in 1997 intended to press for a package of deficit-reduction measures, including a tax-reform plan the Argentine government was already considering plus reforms in the national social security and health insurance system for retirees. According to the Fund's projections, adoption of such measures would lead to a "desirable fiscal scenario" in which the deficit would steadily shrink close to zero by 2000, with the total debt burden receding to 34 percent of GDP that year. Those figures would serve as targets that Argentina would be required to meet in exchange for its Fund program.

That sounds reasonable. Trouble is, it was based on a fairy tale— an Argentine economy that would continue to perform beautifully for years to come. A table in the back of the IMF briefing paper showed how the "desirable fiscal scenario" was to be achieved; it was based on the assumption that Argentina's GDP would grow at a rate of 5 percent or more well into the next decade. There was no provision for the possibility that a recession might hit, which would cause tax revenues to fall, the deficit to balloon, and the fiscal scenario to turn anything but "desirable."

The error is painfully apparent, with the full brilliance of hindsight. While the sun was still shining brightly in the spring of 1997— a year in which the economy would grow more than 8 percent—Argentina would have been well advised to make loads of hay. Fund officials should have been browbeating Argentine officials to embark promptly on a major fiscal tightening that could armorplate the economy against a crisis. Since such an approach would undoubtedly have aroused political resistance from whichever groups lost benefits, the Fund might have counseled that Argentina must exit from convertibility if it were unable to clamp down sufficiently on the fiscal front. Unfortunately, the opportunity to take this tough stance was lost, as the IMF and the Argentines moved at a leisurely pace toward adopting the targets set in the "desirable fiscal scenario."

The IMF has not tried to deny its mistake. "The Fund clearly took too accommodating a position with regard to Argentina's fiscal targets . . . during the [1990s]," wrote Mark Allen, a high-ranking Fund economist, in a paper published in 2003. "[Argentina] should have run a surplus if it was going to have room for fiscal stimulus in the event of a downturn." An official IMF staff retrospective on the Argentine crisis published in March 2004 acknowledged that the Fund had backed Argentina "on the basis of a policy package that was ultimately inadequate," in which "the most glaring omission was in the fiscal area." The IMF's Independent Evaluation Office, in a report published a few months later, reached similar conclusions, and senior IMF staffers generally endorse a withering critique in a book authored by Michael Mussa in 2002 after he left the chief economist's position. Mussa pointed out that from 1993 to 1998, Argentina's debt rose from 29 percent to 41 percent of GDP despite the economy's overall splendid health. "This was clearly not an adequately disciplined or sustainable fiscal policy," he judged. Furthermore, the Fund failed to suspend its program with Argentina, or take other punitive actions as it had in other countries' cases, when the Argentine budget deficit overshot targets that had been agreed initially, according to Mussa, who gave this explanation of his former colleagues' motives:

> With the Fund under widespread criticism (rightly or wrongly) for its involvement in Asia, it was particularly gratifying to be able to point to at least one important program country where the Fund appeared to be supporting successful economic policies. In this situation, there was probably even more than the usual reluctance for the Fund to be the skunk at the garden party, by stressing the accumulating failures of Argentine fiscal policy.

Did members of the IMF staff voice concerns during the period in question, as well as after the fact, that the Fund was being insufficiently rigorous with Argentina? Nobody claims foresight that was nearly as keen as hindsight, but internal Fund documents show that a number of staffers were voicing dissent, with fiscal policy being only one of the issues. The critics were almost invariably economists from outside the Western Hemisphere Department, from departments such as Research, which Mussa headed, and Policy Development and Review (PDR), a powerful department that plays a coordinating role over the other branches of the Fund staff. This is a common pattern at the Fund: Staffers in area departments, though viewed as harsh taskmasters by people in the countries they negotiate with, are often derided by colleagues from other departments as being susceptible to "clientitis."

In the days after the seminar called by Ter-Minassian, for example, a memo to top IMF management dated April 28, 1997, reported that three departments, including Research, PDR, and Fiscal Affairs, "raised serious doubts about the adequacy of the proposed reform agenda for an extended [three-year] arrangement," and they urged a shorter program. But as for Western Hemisphere, "we believe that the reform agenda proposed in the briefing does constitute a minimum critical mass that can merit support," wrote Claudio Loser, the department's director. Six months later, when the executive board was about to approve the $2.8 billion precautionary program along the lines outlined in the aforementioned briefing paper, the Research Department declared in a memo that the program "is not ambitious enough to warrant Fund support in the form of a high access extended arrangement," and other departments also "expressed strong reservations about the scope of both the fiscal adjustment and the structural reform agenda that are being proposed," according to a memo written by Loser. Those departments, he explained, "feel the program falls short" of what is needed, adding that the Western Hemisphere Department "shares these concerns, but believes that, on balance, the risks are still acceptable." Loser would have good reason to regret his assessment of those risks.

The 1998 award for "Issuer of the Year," bestowed by *LatinFinance* magazine, went to Argentina, reflecting the government's remarkable capacity to sell large quantities of bonds even in difficult international markets. Were it not for Argentina, the magazine said, many emerging-market investment bankers "would probably have been twiddling their thumbs" that year, because the currency crises in Asia and Russia had caused capital flows to dry up to the markets they usually served. "Argentina above all other issuers, both sovereign and corporate, was the bankers' saving grace in 1998," the magazine said.

Beneficial though it may have been for financiers, the gusher of private capital that Argentina was tapping posed a problem for the IMF, by limiting the leverage that the Fund could exert. The IMF can usually push countries around by threatening to cut off their loans. But during much of the late 1990s the program for Argentina was only precautionary, and warnings from Fund officials sounded less urgent to the Argentines at a time when investors were delivering such a resounding vote of confidence. "They would say, 'The markets trust us,'" said Ter-Minassian—a complaint widely echoed by others in the Fund who worked on Argentina at the time.

Former Argentine policymakers acknowledge that foreign money made the government less concerned than it should have been about its debt burden and more inclined to treat admonitions with indifference. "Once you know the markets are there, and there is financing, you behave as if financing will be there forever," said Miguel Kiguel, who was undersecretary of finance and chief adviser at the Economy Ministry. Agreed Rogelio Frigerio, who served with Kiguel at the ministry as undersecretary for regional programming before becoming secretary of economic policy in 1998: "You can say to the politicians, 'We need fiscal balance.' But if you get the money so easily, as we did, it's very tough to tell the politicians, 'Don't spend more, be more prudent,' because the money was there, and they knew it."

Blaming the markets for the errors of others should not be carried to an illogical extreme. To repeat: Nobody forced the Argentine government to borrow as much money as it did. The Argentine authorities chose not to confront enough powerful interests to ensure the adoption of a more prudent fiscal policy.

When the IMF tried to issue wake-up calls to the Argentines, however, the markets sometimes thwarted the effort. An example was the Fund's attempt to instill discipline in one of the most worrisome and politically sensitive aspects of Argentina's fiscal policy—spending by the provinces, which totaled about 10 percent of the nation's GDP. Although the provinces' finances were technically separate from the federal government's, in practical terms they were not, because if a province went into default—especially a big one—the pressure for a federal bailout would be enormous, and the markets would seriously question the creditworthiness of the federal government.

The IMF wanted to secure major changes in this area. Kiguel and Frigerio recalled that Ter-Minassian often badgered them to exercise control over provincial borrowing (which would have indirectly capped spending) and reform the system by which the federal government was obliged to share much of its revenue with the governors. Not all governors were getting as much largesse from the federal government as Menem had in La Rioja, but on average a bit more than half of their revenue was coming from the central government.

Argentine economic policymakers first fended off Ter-Minassian's admonitions with the explanation that, under their nation's federal system, they had no control over provincial spending and deficits. When she continued to pursue the matter, they presented a harder-to-refute argument concerning the biggest and most powerful province of all, Buenos Aires, which accounted for the lion's share of the provincial deficit problem, with spending soaring from $4.1 billion in 1991 to $10.7 billion in 1998.

Trying to impose fiscal responsibility on Buenos Aires would not work, the Argentines contended, because the provincial government could—and often did—take advantage of the giddy atmosphere in international markets by issuing bonds, just as the federal government did.

"We said, '*Maybe* we can force the other provinces [to limit spending], but not Buenos Aires, because they can go to the markets,'" said Frigerio, whose job involved overseeing relations with the provinces. "Buenos Aires was out of our control." With that, the IMF was stymied.

"The Argentine economy contains a sort of Molotov cocktail. There are no warning alarms to avert a speculative attack. You have to make a preventive adjustment."

Those remarks, carried in Argentine newspapers, were attributed to Ter-Minassian during a visit she made to Buenos Aires in the first six days of April 1998. As the words suggested, apprehension about Argentina was rising fast at that time—at the IMF, if not in the markets. Instead of huddling with economy ministry and central bank officials as Fund officials typically do while on mission, Ter-Minassian met with a wide range of policymakers and private-sector representatives, including congressional leaders, employer associations, and trade unions, using uncharacteristically blunt language to convey the message that Argentina needed to protect itself against the financial flu that had raged through Asia. She also handed a letter to top economic policymakers that was leaked to the press. "There are clear risks that market sentiment may change in the months ahead if . . . the authorities are perceived as unwilling or unable to take appropriate corrective actions," the letter said

What lay behind the Fund's newfound disquiet? One major factor, although Ter-Minassian was too diplomatic to say so publicly, was costly maneuverings by Menem to bolster the political standing of the Peronists and, more specifically, himself. As explained in an April 7 memo that Ter-Minassian sent top IMF management, an alliance led by the Radical Party appeared to be gaining the upper hand against the Peronists in the jockeying for the 1999 presidential election, and this was prompting Menem to consider seeking a third term, which would require a constitutional amendment. "The consequences of these renewed ambitions of President Menem are evident, among other things, in his yielding to unions' pressures in the labor reform, in promises of large salary increases for teachers, and in the unveiling of a mammoth new highway construction project," Ter-Minassian wrote.

Menem's wheeling and dealing threatened to halt progress toward meeting the terms of Argentina's IMF program, including the conditions concerning another deficit—the one in trade. Imports seemed set to exceed exports by as much as $8 billion in 1998, Ter-Minassian fretted in her memo, and the current account deficit (a term roughly equivalent to a trade deficit though broader) was likely to breach substantially the ceiling set in the program. Large and growing current account deficits had been one of the triggering factors in the Asian crisis, and they were worrisome in Argentina for reasons similar to budget deficits. To buy more goods from abroad than they exported, Argentine consumers and businesses had to borrow dollars from foreigners, and if the indebtedness seemed to be getting out of hand, a sell-off of pesos might result that would destroy convertibility.

Ter-Minassian and her colleagues proposed a way to insulate the economy from such dangers. In their letter to top Argentine officials, they wrote, "There is a clear need to accelerate the pace of fiscal consolidation envisaged in the program"—that is, to shrink the budget deficit faster than the Argentines had already pledged to the IMF. One purpose of doing so was to cool down the economy, thereby reducing imports and the current account deficit.

But the advice was firmly rejected. At a cabinet meeting, President Menem told the IMF to stop meddling in Argentina's affairs and devote attention instead to the situation in Asia, "which was its own doing"—remarks that were promptly relayed to the press. In a more polite vein, Economy Ministry officials contended that the Fund was simply wrong to get so exercised about the current account figures. "Our view is that the current account deficit doesn't represent a threat to Argentina," Kiguel told a group of investors at a Deutsche Morgan Grenfell conference during the IMF mission's visit. "It represents the success of Argentina." This was a defensible argument; a country can run such a deficit only if foreigners are willing to provide the money used for purchasing imports, and in any case much of Argentina's imports consisted of machinery that could help boost productivity. Confident that the markets also perceived scant grounds for worry, Treasury Secretary Pablo Guidotti told audiences, "in the end it is investors who will decide." That confidence proved justified, for the markets shrugged off the IMF's warnings, with a report by Credit Suisse First Boston deriding the Fund for "crying wolf."

Ter-Minassian's mission likewise got nowhere on the issue of labor market reform. This was a matter of intense frustration for the IMF staff. As one of the main conditions of the Fund program, the Argentines had agreed to enact sweeping revisions in the laws protecting jobs and unions. But the bill making its way through Congress in mid-1998 was significantly watered down from what had been promised.

The IMF thus faced a potentially momentous choice. It could lower the boom on Argentina and sever its program on the grounds of noncompliance with the conditions, or at least suspend the program for a while by refusing to complete regularly scheduled reviews. That is what the Fund does when it wants to send a stern disciplinary message to a country, and Argentina was arguably in sore need of such a message. Alternatively, the IMF could let Argentina off the hook. The danger of taking too strong a stand was that it might prompt jittery markets to abandon Argentina and add the country to the already long list of the crisis-stricken. On the other hand, some at the Fund thought that the markets would probably pay little notice to the suspension of a program that did not involve any real money anyway.

The IMF threw down a gauntlet to the Argentines in late July, when Ter-Minassian led another mission to Buenos Aires. The mission "made it clear" to the Argentines that the IMF program would be suspended—that is, that the pending review would not be completed—until congressional passage of the labor-law changes the

IMF wanted, according to a memo written by Ter-Minassian dated July 29.

The timing could hardly have been worse. A crisis that dwarfed Argentina's problems was on the verge of erupting, and in the process, the staff's concerns about developments in Buenos Aires would be subordinated to other goals—including the need for global capitalism to showcase a success story.

On August 17, Russia defaulted on much of its debt and devalued the ruble, knocking financial markets worldwide into one of the worst tailspins in memory, with a particularly nasty slide in Latin America as panic spread from one country to the next. So even though the labor reforms were still not enacted, the IMF abandoned its effort to confront Argentina for fear of throwing the country to the dogs of financial contagion. A change in Argentine economic policy that was supposed to be central to the IMF program would be delayed indefinitely. The dejection that hard-liners felt over this turn of events was reflected in a September 3 memo signed by Paul Masson, a senior adviser in the Research Department, to Ter-Minassian:

We realize that management opted for completing the review despite the staff's suggestion . . . that it be conditional on legislative approval of an amended draft of labor market reforms, which has not occurred. We see merit in the argument that the current turmoil in international markets justifies the continuation of Fund support, but, on the whole, we think that a weakening of conditionality in the area that has been widely perceived and publicized as the cornerstone of this Fund arrangement is a mistake. This decision will signal to the markets (and to the authorities) that there is only a remote possibility that the Fund will ever let this arrangement go off-track—even for a few months. The Fund's credibility will be further weakened as a result.

Credibility was not high in the minds of the global economy's high command at that moment. The following days brought even more frightening developments, as the Russian default led to the crash of a giant Connecticut-based hedge fund, raising fears among senior U.S. officials about a breakdown in the normal functioning of the U.S. financial system. At the same time, a plethora of signs suggested that Western-style capitalism might be slipping into reverse after its decade-long advance. In Russia, old-style socialists returned to power. In Malaysia, the government slapped on controls strictly limiting the amount of money investors could take out of the country. Throughout the developing world, voices proclaiming a loss of faith in the free market were growing louder.

Amid the gloom, Argentina provided a beacon, a reassuring case study of the benefits that could be reaped by developing nations from implementing the Washington Consensus under the IMF's tutelage. An opportunity arose to make that beacon glow brightly during the exceptionally dismal annual meeting of the IMF and World Bank in fall 1998. At a press conference on October 1, Camdessus confirmed that Menem would address the meeting's plenary session; the Argentine president would be the only world leader to be accorded that honor besides Bill Clinton, the head of the host government. Asked whether this meant that Argentina should be regarded as a "leading case," the managing director replied affirmatively, explaining:

> [I]n many respects the experience of Argentina in recent years has been exemplary, including in particular the adoption of the proper strategy at the beginning of the 1990s and the very courageous adaptation of it when the tequila crisis put the overall subcontinent at risk of major turmoil. . . . Notable, too, are the efforts of Argentina since that time to continue its excellent compliance with the performance criteria under our arrangements and much progress in implementation of the structural reforms.
>
> So clearly, Argentina has a story to tell the world: a story which is about the importance of fiscal discipline, of structural change, and of monetary policy rigorously maintained.

According to IMF staffers, Camdessus made the decision to invite Menem without consulting them. He certainly took a different tone in his news conference from the worries that Ter-Minassian had expressed publicly about Argentina's weaknesses a few months earlier. And he did not mention that the Fund's staff had just threatened to withdraw the institution's support because of Argentina's reform transgressions. Argentina was back in the Fund's highest graces. It was needed there, for the world's sake if not its own.

Argentina had skirted around a squall—the crises afflicting Asia and Russia. But the place in which it had taken shelter was about to be struck by wave after wave of bad news.

At his desk in the minister's office at the Ministry of Economy on the morning of January 13, 1999, Roque Fernández was perusing a book on the genetics of cattle, a subject of fascination to him, when Guidotti interrupted with word that Brazil had just devalued its currency, the real, dropping its semifixed exchange rate just as Thailand, Indonesia, Russia, and others had done before. Fernández listened placidly to the news and went back to his book. The minister had been expecting for some days that Brazil would be forced to devalue, and although he knew that Argentine financial markets would undergo some turmoil, he believed Argentina would weather the storm just as it had the tequila crisis four years earlier.

Fernández's calm reaction was well founded, at least in terms of the impact on markets. The Brazilian crisis did not spread beyond that country's borders. But Brazil's woes produced serious economic problems for Argentina. Brazil was an important market for Argentine exports, purchasing nearly one-third of the products Argentina shipped abroad in 1998. That market became much less receptive to Argentine goods when the real depreciated sharply, because competing Brazilian products were suddenly much cheaper. The result was a 28 percent drop in Argentine exports to Brazil in 1999.

Although that problem by itself might have been manageable, it was far from the only shock to hit the Argentine economy around that time. The worldwide prices of grain and other commodities that Argentina exported declined by 20 percent in 1998. Meanwhile, the U.S. dollar was rising on foreign exchange markets, pulling the peso upward with it, which made Argentine goods of all kinds less competitive on world markets. Exports fell not only to Brazil but to other countries as well, by 10.5 percent in 1999; and cheap imports were decimating some Argentine industries, such as shoes and clothing, just as they were in richer markets like the United States. Worse, interest rates were rising on loans of all sorts to emerging markets following Russia's default.

Argentina's boom was ending. Recession was setting in. Vanishing with the good times was the country's best chance to put its economy on a sound footing. Once a downturn got under way, efforts to rectify the government's fiscal problem would become much more difficult politically and injurious economically. In other words, the country's economy was not sheltered, it was stranded, and at the mercy of the fates as the new millennium approached, with all the attendant rumblings about the impending apocalypse.

Up to that point, the markets had demonstrated a remarkably sanguine attitude toward Argentina—excessively so, in fact, the result being a major disservice to the country. The factors influencing the markets' behavior merit investigation.

[CHAPTER 4]

Enronization

DESMOND LACHMAN was older than most of his counterparts at major Wall Street firms. Born in South Africa in 1948, Lachman, who was chief emerging-market economic strategist at Salomon Smith Barney, had a background at the IMF rather than on the Street. (In the late 1980s, he was responsible for Argentina as chief of the IMF's River Plate division, which also included Uruguay and Paraguay.) Reserved in manner but strong in his convictions, Lachman also distinguished himself from other analysts in another important respect: Long before Argentina's collapse, and long before his competitors at other firms, Lachman foresaw that the country's economy was bound to hit the wall one way or another. Many people in the emerging-markets business vividly recall that in the months following the January 1999 Brazilian devaluation, Lachman became convinced that Argentina would be forced to default, devalue, or both.

Lachman's key insight as Argentina's economy slumped was that the country lacked the instruments for lifting itself out of recession. Pumping up the supply of pesos was forbidden under the convertibility system, as was lowering the exchange rate of the peso to boost exports. Stimulating the economy with a major spending program or tax cut was also out of the question, because the resulting increase in the deficit would panic the markets that the government's debt was getting out of hand. Paradoxically, cutting the deficit substantially to improve the fiscal picture would not work either, because it would only exacerbate the recession.

The result, Lachman realized as the recession dragged on, was a country standing in the way of a hurricane. The downturn would depress tax revenues, widening the deficit. That would arouse alarm about the government's ability to service its debt, leading markets to pull capital out of the country, which would drive up interest rates, deepening the recession even more—and so on, in a vicious cycle. Lachman stuck with his gloomy assessment throughout 2000 and 2001, even during periods when most of his competitors were predicting an Argentine recovery and the country's markets were rallying.

But Lachman's views on Argentina were not spelled out in research reports published by Salomon. He conveyed his pessimistic opinions to clients in private conversations. Therein lies a tale about a serious problem on Wall Street: the reluctance of big firms like Salomon to offend major issuers of securities for fear of losing business.

Salomon (which renamed itself Citigroup Global Corporate and Investment Banking Group) was a "sell side" firm, meaning that it brought to market the bonds and stocks of corporations and governments. During the 1990s, Salomon was the fifth-largest sell-side firm in Argentine government bonds, serving as lead manager for $5 billion worth of bond sales, for which the firm earned $53 million in fees from the government. The purchasers of these securities, naturally, are referred to as the "buy side," and they can include anyone from individual investors to professionals managing money for mutual funds, pension funds, endowments, and the like.

Sell-side firms employ legions of analysts like Lachman, who cover industries or regions and write research reports that are supposed to help the buy-side investors decide where to invest. This arrangement is fraught with potential conflicts of interest, because an analyst's work may cover the same companies or governments that pay fees to his firm's investment banker colleagues for bringing bond or stock issues to market. As readers of U.S. business news sections are well aware, a national scandal erupted over these sorts of conflicts of interest in 2001 when revelations began to emerge about analysts who had strongly recommended the stocks of companies such as Enron that were investment banking clients of their firms. One of the most infamous cases involved Jack Grubman, a Salomon colleague of Lachman's. Federal and state investigators found that Grubman had been under pressure from Salomon's investment bankers to issue positive evaluations of telecommunications stocks that later collapsed, and that he had fattened his multimillion-dollar pay by helping the bankers win deals to handle stock issues, flagrantly disregarding the "Chinese wall" that is supposed to separate research from banking. In one e-mail that prosecutors unearthed, Grubman privately called a company he was publicly recommending a "pig." Other firms also rewarded their analysts handsomely for their contributions in getting investment banking business from companies the analysts covered, and some Wall Streeters even paid rival firms to issue positive reports on stocks they were underwriting.

Similar dynamics, albeit less extreme, were at work in the business of financing emerging markets, according to numerous people who were involved, and of course this included the country that had won the 1998 "Issuer of the Year" award from *LatinFinance* magazine. "The time has come to do our mea culpa," Hans-Joerg Rudloff, chairman of the executive committee at Barclays Capital, told an audience of fellow bank and brokerage executives in London in 2002. "Argentina obviously stands as much as Enron" in showing that "things have been done and said by our industry which were realized at the time to be wrong, to be self-serving." Miguel Kiguel, who was the Economy Ministry's point man with the markets from

1996 to 1999, recalled: "I think that wit. ..i the banks there was some censorship, to avoid offending us. If they had something negative to say, they toned it down in public. It came out perhaps in oral conversations, but not in public." Kiguel added that he did not pressure sell-side firms to issue positive reports, in part because doing so proved unnecessary. "We were big issuers in the market. They wanted to have good relations with us," he said. "My view is, these people are not fully independent or objective."

By all accounts, Salomon's Lachman was able to state his views about Argentina straightforwardly in his talks with clients. But the fact that his prognostications were kept out of print was important. A written research report carries much more clout than an opinion expressed verbally. Although buy-side emerging-market investors say they are well aware of the biases among sell-side analysts, many are still heavily influenced by published research. In some cases that is because they lack the resources to do their own analyses, or the importance to command personal attention from analysts. Even for portfolio managers who know the countries involved, "You need to be able to show in your files why you did what you did," said Eric Hermann, president of FH International Financial Services, a Harrison, New York, money management firm. "It's a lot easier for me to invest when I can show in my files two or three research reports saying, 'This is the greatest thing since sliced bread.'"

Officials at Argentina's Economy Ministry knew that Lachman was describing the country's prospects in bleak terms. They continued to include Salomon among their underwriters anyway, but told the firm to "make sure you have a variety of views" besides Lachman's, a former Argentine official recalled. Indeed, research by other Salomon analysts, whose work was published, tended to be much more optimistic about the country's chances for pulling through. Even in the turbulent months leading up to the default, the firm's reports featured relatively bland wording on Argentina's predicament. "The Argentine government may find it increasingly difficult to meet its financing needs unless domestic confidence can be restored quickly," said one such report published in April 2001.

Lachman, who left Salomon in 2003 to become a scholar at the American Enterprise Institute, declined to be quoted. Asked why his negative assessment of Argentina was not published, Arda Nazerian, a spokeswoman for Salomon, cited Salomon's merger with Citibank in the fall of 1998, which created a firm with an abundance of analysts, enabling Lachman to spend more time privately with big clients. "The expansion of our emerging-markets research team reduced Desmond's responsibilities for writing on individual countries," Nazerian said. But Lachman published reports frequently on other subjects, and I can remember that when I contacted him in the past to get his views about troubled emerging-market countries, he often shared his opinions only on condition that his identity be withheld, because of concerns about his firm's relationships with the country in question.

That's the way it goes for people in those sorts of positions on Wall Street. "It's a lot of self-censorship," said Federico Thomsen, the former chief economist in the Buenos Aires office of ING Barings, another securities firm. "It's like, if you have something good to say, you say it, but if you have something bad to say, just keep your mouth shut. With the fees involved, the investment bankers will kill you. If the Minister of Economy of Argentina is mad at you, that could mean a lot of business lost, and even if your comment is not the reason, the people in your firm might blame you for not getting the business. You don't want to be in that position, especially when bonus time comes."

That attitude does not mean the research reports emanating from Wall Street failed to take note of problems facing Argentina. As the economy's woes intensified, the reports became markedly less bullish. They harped on the need for fiscal discipline and labor reform, lamented the government's shortcomings on those issues, and acknowledged that worries were mounting among investors about the possibility of default and devaluation. But in general, reports presented Argentina as a country going through a rough patch that it would be able to surmount, and they frequently played down risks of a cataclysm.

J.P. Morgan's September 2000 report, "Argentina's debt dynamics: Much ado about not so much," was an example. The basic thrust of that report, a product of José Luis Daza's research team, was that fixing the fiscal problem was essential but that a modest adjustment would enable the country to avert default. In March 2001 another Morgan report—the chief author of which was Joyce Chang, who replaced Daza after a merger—said: "The government's capacity to service its debt this year is not in question. . . . We believe that the fears of abandoning convertibility are overdone and point out that devaluation is not a policy option due to the limited benefits." Another sell-side firm, ABN-AMRO, assured its clients at the end of June 2001: "Argentina has neither devalued its currency nor defaulted on its debt obligations and we continue to believe that neither scenario is in the cards."

It is surely no coincidence that the one analyst who most loudly and publicly issued early warnings of Argentina's impending doom was Walter Molano, head of research at BCP Securities, a Connecticut-based firm that does no underwriting of government bonds. Molano began peppering his reports on Argentina with dire comments in early 1999. "A full-blown economic crisis may still be a year away, but it seems like the die has been cast," he wrote in April of that year, and in a report dated October 23, 2000, he advised investors: "Argentina is on the verge of insolvency." Some of Molano's competitors accuse him of taking such strong stands for the sake of garnering publicity, and despite his general bearishness, he occasionally veered toward the wildly bullish in his Argentina prognostications. (Even though his firm did not underwrite Argentine bonds, it did trade them and thus stood to benefit from pronounced swings both upward and downward.) But whatever Molano's motivation, the contrast between his fearlessness and that of his sell-side competitors is instructive. Having once headed the research department at a sell-side firm, Molano knew the constraints that his rivals labored under, and he delighted in pointing them out, as he did in this sarcastic passage from a December 15, 2000, report:

> Why was the Street so positive on Argentina a year ago when the Menem government was the picture of complacency? Why did the Street forgive all of Argentina's excessive borrowing between 1997 and 1999? Why did the Street ignore Argentina's lack of fiscal discipline during the past four years? It probably has nothing to do with the fact that Argentina was one of the biggest bond issuers in the world during that same time period.

The sell-side's rebuttal to comments like Molano's is that such cynicism is grossly misplaced. With indignation, many sell-side analysts of emerging markets maintain that their overriding objective is to serve investor-clients well by providing the best advice possible; and although they may have been overly optimistic on Argentina in retrospect, their mistakes were honest, not venal, because they genuinely believed what they were writing. Others point out that analysts and strategists are often judged by how well they predict very short-term swings in markets, and that Argentine bonds staged significant rallies on several occasions during the 2000–2001 period, which meant that taking a consistently bearish view would have been professionally foolhardy.

"My incentive is to be able to predict what will happen," said Siobhan Manning, emerging-markets strategist at Caboto USA. "If I can predict accurately, hopefully I gain credibility, and the firm does, and I'm able to make money."

It seems fair to say that the conflicts of interest in the emerging-markets world—at least the ones I have been able to detect without benefit of government subpoena power—have been much less egregious than the practices that have come to light concerning the sell-side's activities in technology stocks. Although a few emerging-market sovereign bond analysts relate stories of being called on the carpet when their reports caused heartburn among their investment banking colleagues, the pressures on them to engage in hype were not as intense as in other areas of research where more money was at stake. Still, pressures and conflicts existed.

"When you're working at a big firm, and I was chief emerging-markets strategist at a big firm, clearly the investment banking business is up for grabs, and it definitely influences the kind of research you feel you're able to write," said Peter Petas, who worked at Deutsche Bank during much of the 1990s and later joined Credit-Sights, a much smaller outfit specializing in research. "Do I think it's as bad as the stock guys? No. Generally nobody is going to come down and scream at research for putting an 'underweight' [recommendation] on a country's bonds like they might for saying, 'Sell Intel,' or whatever. But there's also going to be some realization that some significant portion of your firm's revenues come from the investment banking business. To say otherwise is a bit silly."

At the heart of the problem is Wall Street's hoary system of using annual bonuses to provide a substantial portion of the compensation earned by its professional employees. The methods of distributing bonuses differ greatly from one sell-side firm to another, and details about how individual bonuses are decided is a matter Wall Streeters are loath to discuss. But this much is clear: Because research departments do not earn revenue—they incur costs that must be apportioned to other parts of their firms—the committees deciding bonuses for emerging-market analysts in many cases have included top investment bankers as well as the research department bosses.

"Your salary will only be about one-third of your compensation in a decent year, so your bonus is everything," said Christian Stracke, who covered Latin American economies at Deutsche Bank and also moved to CreditSights. "You'll never know what percentage of that bonus came from the recommendation of Debt Capital Markets [the investment banking department responsible for sovereign bond underwriting], but you do know that without the recommendation of Debt Capital Markets, your bonus is just not going to be very big. Analysts for their own sake want to be good and make the right calls, of course, but analysts are bankers too. They're in it for the money. If they were in it to be smart, they'd be professors."

Moreover, the fees that Wall Street firms are paid directly for bringing bonds to market are only a portion of the revenue they can secure by winning a "mandate" from an issuer like Argentina. A firm that underwrites a new issue gets to control trading in those bonds for a period of time, so it earns trading commissions. Once the bonds are salted away in investors' accounts, the firm that sold those bonds knows who owns them, so it is most likely to get trading business from future buyers as well. This helps explain why firms vie so fervently for mandates, and why any analyst is likely to be mindful of the benefits that come when investment banking colleagues win deals.

Accordingly, many emerging-market analysts have willingly breached their firms' Chinese walls to help their banking colleagues secure business. In the spring of 2001, for example, Lacey Gallagher, director of Latin American economics for Credit Suisse First Boston (CSFB), worked with her firm's bankers on a major Argentine government bond swap that CSFB was managing. During the few weeks Gallagher was working on the deal, she was barred under CSFB rules from publishing opinionated reports on Argentina, to avoid the appearance of conflict of interest. But soon after she returned from being "over the wall," she was allowed to resume her regular duties as an analyst.

Even at firms where research and investment banking were kept at a healthier distance, analysts knew that the more deals their banking colleagues got, the bigger the pool of money available for funding their bonuses. "If your department makes $50 million, you get paid well; if your group makes $2 million, you don't," said Michael Pettis, a former managing director in the fixed-income capital markets group at Bear Stearns.

Small wonder, added Pettis, who later became a professor at Columbia Business School, that so much of Wall Street's research on

Argentina looks rosy in retrospect: "We all have this amazing tendency to believe what's in our best interest to believe."

Some Wall Streeters insist nonetheless that they cannot be accused of going soft on Argentina. Their evidence is the "underweight" recommendations they issued on the country's bonds. Throughout much of 1999–2001, Salomon recommended that its clients hold underweight positions in Argentina, except for a few months when the recommendation was "neutral," the firm's spokeswoman pointed out. Likewise, Joyce Chang observed that since she left Merrill Lynch in mid-1999, the firms where she has worked have "not ever [issued] an overweight recommendation on Argentina," and throughout 2000 and 2001, her recommendation on the country's bonds was most often "underweight."

But what does that mean—to recommend an "underweight" position? Not much. Here, the problem is on the buy side—and here, the story of how global markets malfunctioned in Argentina takes a mind-boggling turn.

Anyone who has heard marketing pitches by mutual funds or other investment firms knows their most potent selling point: "We beat the index." If they manage stocks, they boast that during bull markets the shares they picked rose higher than, say, the Standard and Poor's 500-stock index or the Wilshire 5,000 index, and during bear markets their portfolios fell less than those indices.

The emerging-markets world has its own indices that many portfolio managers are expected to outperform if they want to keep their jobs and earn tidy bonuses. For the buy-siders who were purchasing Argentine government bonds, the most commonly used by far was the Emerging-Markets Bond Index-Plus, or EMBI-Plus, which was developed by J.P. Morgan.

The EMBI-Plus tracks on a daily basis the prices and yields of bonds issued by various countries such as Mexico, Poland, South Africa, Malaysia, and Lebanon, which rise and fall based on news developments and interest rate trends. Each country in the index has a percentage "weighting"—say, 10 percent for Russia, 6 percent for Venezuela, 2 percent for Bulgaria, and so on—that depends largely on the amount of bonds it has issued compared with the total issued by all the countries combined. The index has a variety of functions: Individual investors might use it to decide whether a mutual fund specializing in emerging markets was well run. Or the administrator of a pension fund might use it to evaluate how skillfully the portfolio managers he had hired were managing their emerging-market investments. These managers could expect to have their performance measured against the index every quarter or even more frequently in many cases.

"Perverse" is a word used repeatedly by people in the business to describe the way the index works. Beating it often involves a great deal of gamesmanship—and in Argentina's case, the way the game was played exacerbated the problem of the country's being led down the primrose path to bankruptcy.

The perversity stems from the fact that the countries with the heaviest weighting in the index, the ones to which investors are obliged to direct the most money, are those with the most bonds outstanding—that is, the greatest indebtedness. During much of the period 1996–2001, Argentina had the heaviest weighting of any nation, averaging 23.3 percent (the number fluctuated, peaking at 28.8 percent in late 1998)—not because of its economic size but simply because its government had issued so many bonds. (Brazil, with an economy more than double Argentina's size and a population more than four times greater, had the second-largest average weighting during this period, followed by Mexico, Russia, Venezuela, and Poland.) Being "underweight Argentina" thus did not necessarily mean that a portfolio manager held a tiny amount of Argentine bonds; it simply meant that the portion of Argentine bonds in his portfolio was less than Argentina's weighting.

The result was that bizarre logic would be played out at investor panels and conferences, recalled Mohamed El-Erian, who managed emerging-market bonds at Pacific Investment Management Company (PIMCO), the giant West Coast investment firm. When asked for their views and investment strategies concerning Argentina, portfolio managers "would say, 'negative, negative, negative,'" El-Erian said, and they would also say they were "underweight." But soon it would emerge that enormous proportions of their funds were invested in Argentine bonds anyway. "The dreaded third question would come: 'How *much* underweight?'" El-Erian said. "They would say, 'It's 22 percent of the index. I can't possibly be more than 5 percent underweight.' So they'd have 17 percent of their money in Argentina."

The habit of cleaving to the index, in other words, virtually forced these investors to lend vast sums to Argentina even if they feared the country was likely to default in the long run. Although default would hurt their portfolios, they would still lose less than the index as long as they were a bit underweight Argentina. At the same time, they didn't dare be *too* far underweight. Money managers who shunned Argentine bonds completely, or held only small amounts, were taking a huge risk, because in the event that Argentine bonds rallied for some unforeseen reason, their portfolios would almost certainly underperform the index for a period of time, a potentially disastrous blow to their careers.

Illustrating this mode of thinking was a report by Deutsche Bank published in March 2001 warning clients that despite the country's problems "it is risky to be underweight" in Argentine bonds, since the bonds might well rise in price. Such concerns had an impact on investors like Tom Cooper, manager of the $1 billion GMO Emerging-Country Debt Fund, who in July 2001 told the Bloomberg News wire service that he had "more than 10 percent" of his fund's assets in Argentine bonds, even though he was bearish on the country's prospects. "We measure ourselves not only on absolute return but relative to our peer group and to the index," he explained.

Dissatisfaction with index-based performance measurement runs high among financial market participants, and people have been aware for some time of its particularly warped results in emerging markets. In November 1998 an article in the *Emerging Markets Debt Report* said that investors and analysts "generally agree" that the EMBI-Plus "poses some serious problems," including "the irony of the fact that by relying on the EMBI-Plus, the market is being encouraged to lend to those countries that are the most heavily indebted." An amusing analogy, provided by Michael Pettis of Columbia Business School, likens the system to "a bizarre AA program in which you remove booze from the homes of people who are reducing the amount they drink and put it into the homes of people who are drinking more every day." Despite the obvious drawbacks, nobody can come up with a satisfactory alternative. Pettis added, "It's like these college ratings systems. Everyone knows they suck. But if you don't play the game, you're screwed."

Paradoxically, one of the leading critics of the EMBI-Plus was Joyce Chang—that is, before she became head of emerging-markets research at Morgan in late 2000. "Why hold more of a country because it has more debt?" she was quoted as saying while she was still at Merrill Lynch. After moving to Morgan, Chang began trying to convince investors to switch to another Morgan index, the EMBI Global Diversified, which caps individual country weightings. (Mexico was the biggest in mid-2003, at a little over 12 percent.) But the new index does not solve all the problems of the old one. Moreover, it has taken several years to start catching on; many portfolio managers have established long performance records using the old index, and historical comparisons with a new index are difficult.

Peter Marber, president of The Atlantic Funds, a New York money management firm, lamented "the reality that so many decisions on Wall Street are driven by this methodology of money management," but observed that the index is completely logical from the Street's standpoint. "If you have a multibillion-dollar pension fund and you're farming it out to be managed, the index separates the gunslingers from skillful managers," Marber said. "But you end up with situations like Argentina."

Professional money managers, of course, are sophisticated investors with a pretty good sense of the dicey game they were playing in the market for Argentine bonds. The same could not be said of some other players.

Felicia Migliorini, a divorcée who lives north of Rome, sank her life savings, about $135,000, into Argentine bonds in March 2001. Giacinto Innocenzi, a retiree, invested about $94,000 in Argentine bonds around the same time. About 400,000 of their fellow Italians did likewise; together with other individuals, most in Europe and Japan, they ended up holding about $24 billion in claims on the bankrupt Argentine government.

Migliorini was forced to put her apartment up for sale because her losses left her unable to afford the condominium fees and other expenses. Innocenzi, who was planning to pay for his daughter's wedding and help her buy a house with her future husband, lost his nest egg and was forced to postpone the wedding. Like thousands of other Italians in this situation, they are incensed at their banks, which sold them the bonds. "They told me [the bonds] were good, stable, guaranteed, and that since they were obligations they had to be paid back," Migliorini said.

European retail investors like Migliorini and Innocenzi were an attractive market for the syndicates selling Argentine bonds. Professional money managers in the United States, more aware of the potential risks, were often reluctant to buy at the yields the Argentine authorities were willing to pay. So the syndicates tailored a number of their offerings to Europe, in currencies such as the Italian lira, the German mark, and, after its establishment in 1999, the euro. One attraction of the European market was that regulations protecting small investors are less strict than in the United States. (American individuals were investing in Argentine bonds too, but mostly indirectly, via mutual funds.) Another factor that made the Europeans receptive was the sharp decline in yields available on their own governments' bonds. Innocenzi's banker, for example, told him he could earn only 3–4 percent on Italian bonds—a fraction of the yields he had grown accustomed to—but that he could double his return by choosing Argentine bonds instead.

Italian banks, which had to defend themselves against numerous lawsuits after the Argentine default, rejected claims that they acted in bad faith, arguing that the higher yields on the Argentine bonds provided an obvious clue that the investments were risky. "There may have been a few very unsophisticated investors who didn't know what they were getting into, but the great majority could not have not noticed the difference" in yields, said Nicola Stock, the head of the Association of Italian Banks. "Nobody questioned [the banks] when things were going well." More important from a legal standpoint, the banks distributed prospectuses to investors that included warnings about the possibility of default; whether these documents were even glanced at, much less heeded, is another matter.

The juicy returns on Argentine bonds that foreign investors found so irresistible had a counterpart, of course, in the interest cost Argentina had to bear on its debt. To quantify that cost, market pros use a special term—"country risk," or in Spanish, *riesgo país*. As Argentina's crisis intensified, *riesgo país* became a regularly reported statistic on Argentine news programs, like the daily temperature. People who didn't know exactly what it meant, even children, knew this much about it: The lower the number, the better for Argentina. The higher the number, the worse.

The phrase refers to the amount of extra yield investors demand as compensation for the riskiness of holding a country's bonds. Specifically, it is based on the "spread" between the yields on U.S. Treasury bonds—regarded as the safest investment in the world— and the yields on comparable bonds issued by another country. For example, if the yield on ten-year U.S. Treasury bonds is 5 percent, and the yield on Argentina's ten-year bonds is 9.5 percent, then Argentina's *riesgo país* is 450 (the 4.5 percent difference is expressed in hundredths of a percentage point, thus 450). Every day, the number changes as market participants deliver their verdicts on economic and political developments, driving yields up when they sell and sending yields down when they buy.

During Argentina's headiest days, its *riesgo país* was quite low, dipping below 300 in 1997. That was a boon for the government, which could sell bonds yielding only 3–4 percentage points more than Treasuries. But as the decade advanced, so did *riesgo país*. It spiked above 1,000 during the crisis surrounding the Russian default, and although it subsided fairly soon thereafter, it stayed well above the pre-Russia levels, ranging mostly from the high 500s to the 700s during 1999 and the first half of 2000. That meant the government was having to borrow at interest rates of 6–7 percent above the rate for Treasuries. Further, the government had to borrow sizable sums, upward of $20 billion a year, to cover its budget deficit and pay off old debt that was maturing.

This crunch put Argentina in a position analogous to that of an individual with a hefty credit card balance who suddenly finds the credit card companies no longer willing to offer low promotional interest rates on their cards. It hurt not only the government but also private Argentine companies, which saw their borrowing costs rise commensurately—and with inflation at zero or even below zero at times, the cost was particularly steep, since firms could not easily recoup their borrowing costs by raising prices. By early 1999, real interest rates (that is, rates adjusted for inflation) were 5 percentage points higher than they had been in early 1998, with the prime rate on peso loans at around 13 percent and dollar loans at around 11 percent.

Why did this happen? Amid all the forces that were still pumping money into Argentina—the generally positive assessments of Wall Street analysts, the obligations of index-bound money managers to apportion much of their portfolios to Argentine bonds, the desire of European retail investors to diversify out of their own governments' low-yielding paper—a counterforce was building: Cash was being withdrawn, in considerable amounts.

*   *   *

It was a stealth operation, carried out as quietly as possible so as to avoid tipping off others in the markets. Players have no other option when they are attempting a major reshuffling in one of the biggest aggregations of capital in the world.

The brains behind the maneuver was Mohamed El-Erian, who moved from London to Newport Beach, California, in April 1999 to oversee the emerging-market portfolios at PIMCO, a firm that managed about $170 billion worth of bonds of all types including U.S. Treasuries, municipals, and corporates. The son of an Egyptian diplomat father and a French mother, with an undergraduate degree from Cambridge and a doctorate from Oxford, El-Erian was a former colleague of Desmond Lachman, both at the IMF and at Salomon Smith Barney's emerging-markets research department. He and Lachman shared not only similar work experiences but also similarly downbeat views on Argentina well before the perspective became commonplace. Soon after arriving in his new buy-side job, El-Erian began questioning the wisdom of keeping the $2 billion-plus in Argentine bonds that then accounted for about 40 percent of the firm's total emerging-market bond holdings. "He started banging the drum within the investment committee, literally within weeks or months of being on board," said Paul McCulley, another senior PIMCO fund manager.

Those were transformative times in the world of emerging-markets investing. The shock of the default by Russia, a country once assumed to be too geopolitically important to fail, had driven many investors to abandon their bets on developing countries. "Crossover investors"—large pension funds, insurance companies, and other institutions that had allocated a few percentage points of their assets to emerging markets during the heyday of the mid-1990s—were switching back to safer, blue-chip havens. "Dedicated investors," such as mutual funds established for the specific purpose of investing in emerging Asia or Latin America, were suffering demands for redemptions among their customers. The result was a sharp drop-off in demand for emerging-market securities of all kinds. Private capital flowing to major Latin American countries (Argentina, Brazil, Chile, Colombia, Mexico, Peru, and Venezuela), which had totaled about 5 percent of their collective GDP during the boom period of 1997 to mid-1998, shriveled to less than 1 percent of their GDP by mid-1999. This was the main reason that Argentina was having to pay more costly interest rates to attract foreign funds; a substantially higher *riesgo país* was the fate of all emerging markets.

As bad as that was for Argentina, El-Erian saw other problems specific to the country that raised concerns about its creditworthiness—in particular, the difficulty it faced in recovering from recession. Like Lachman, with whom he talked occasionally, El-Erian believed Argentina had fallen into a hole from which it had no easy means of escape because of its fiscal bind and self-imposed monetary rigidity. "Given the [convertibility] system," he wrote in an e-mail to PIMCO portfolio managers on May 4, 1999, "the country's only adjustment instruments are (a) additional fiscal tightening and (b) competitiveness-enhancing structural reforms. The former will impose further contractionary pressures.... The latter cannot compensate in any meaningful manner in the period ahead for the significant real effective exchange rate appreciation"—that is, the rise in the value of the peso, which was hurting exports.

Accordingly, PIMCO began steadily reducing its exposure to Argentina, eliminating its holdings of the country's bonds entirely by the end of 2000. The process was lengthy because with a position of such immense size, PIMCO could not afford to let others in the markets detect its strategy lest they "run ahead" and sell their Argentine bonds first, which would lower the price at which PIMCO could sell. "There were times when the markets rallied against us," El-Erian recalled, "and we would just step up our sales at that point."

To make sure the decision to unload the Argentine position was sound, El-Erian continued to visit Argentina every three to six months—usually on his own, rather than as part of a big investor trip. Developments in Argentina generally reinforced the bleakness of his perspective.

The economy had contracted by 3.4 percent in 1999, and the fiscal picture turned more worrisome. This was partly because of the damaging impact of the recession on tax revenue, but it was also because the presidential campaign of 1999 engendered something of a government spending spree. The main offenders were Buenos Aires Governor Eduardo Duhalde, the leading Peronist candidate for president, and President Menem, who was considering a third consecutive term though he ultimately gave up the quest. Duhalde showered funds on roads and schools and raised the salaries of public employees in his province; Menem sought to build political support by funneling resources to governors in other provinces. The federal deficit that year was $7.1 billion, and the overall deficit including the provinces widened to $11.8 billion, helping to drive the total debt of the public sector to 47 percent of GDP, up from 41 percent the year before.

The final stage of the Menem administration also highlighted how far the country still had to go in stamping out corruption and instilling the rule of law to match its progress on other fronts. Although privatization had eliminated many of the opportunities for corruption, it created others, and the Argentine press in the 1998–1999 period was unusually full of headlines about government officials engaging in bribe-taking, siphoning government funds, and selling illegal arms. Suspicion also abounded—though no tangible evidence was offered—that Menem was improperly enriching himself. The president was building a Spanish colonial mansion in his remote home village with a gym, sauna, soccer field, tennis court, and pool. Nearby was an airport under construction, with a runway long enough to accommodate jets, which Menem said was financed by donations from business leaders.

Hopes rose that the country might be headed in a new direction when voters, disgusted with the rot in the Menem regime, elected Fernando de la Rúa to the presidency in October 1999. De la Rúa headed a somewhat tenuous alliance led by his own Radical Party that had joined with a left-wing party for the purpose of ousting the

Peronists. In personal terms, he was Menem's polar opposite; he was a man of old-fashioned virtue, who had written textbooks on legal procedure and enjoyed taking Sunday strolls after church with his family. But he staunchly endorsed convertibility and the overall free-market policies of his predecessor, and he launched a determined effort—with backing from a new IMF precautionary program—to curb the deficit upon taking office, securing a $2 billion tax increase and a $1.4 billion spending-cut package.

Those moves, unfortunately, served only to suck more oxygen out of the economy. By mid-2000, with unemployment rising above 14 percent, social unrest in the countryside and labor strife in the cities were becoming increasingly common, especially after de la Rúa's government ordered an additional round of spending cuts that reduced salaries of national government workers by 12 to 15 percent. A symbolic barometer of pessimism about the country's future was the growing lines of Argentines seeking to emigrate who queued at the Italian, Spanish, and U.S. embassies; the Italians dispensed 7,000 passports in the first half of 2000, the same number as in all of 1999.

The cycle took more vicious turns as GDP fell for a second straight year in 2000. Tax revenue continued to stagnate, and the government's interest bill continued to burgeon—the cost of a high *riesgo país*. The overall deficit thus stayed high ($6.9 billion for the federal government, $10.3 billion overall), adding to the public-sector debt, which by the end of 2000 topped 50 percent of GDP.

There seemed no reason to believe that the situation was going to improve, El-Erian concluded in 2000 during his trips to Buenos Aires and his meetings with Argentine officials visiting the United States. He and his PIMCO colleagues coined the term "immaculate growth" to refer to the mysterious force that Argentine officials, and some in the markets, seemed to think would lift the nation's economy back to health. "They did not know how recovery would happen, but just thought it would," El-Erian recalled. "The only way to generate growth was to issue more debt, which itself was a time bomb."

All the while, the Argentine government continued to raise

money on international markets. El-Erian's wholesale shift out of the country was unusual, if not unique, among market pros. Lured by the tantalizing yields that Argentina was offering, many buy-siders, both professional and unsophisticated, added to their holdings of Argentine bonds in 2000. From January to September of that year, the Argentine government borrowed nearly $6 billion by selling dollar-denominated bonds, at interest rates ranging from 11 3/8 percent to 12 percent. It borrowed another $4 billion-plus by selling euro-denominated bonds, mostly to European retail investors, paying annual interest of 8 1/8 percent to 10 1/4 percent.

This borrowing kept Argentina going. It allowed the government to fund its budget deficit, pay interest on existing bonds, and pay off old bond issues that were maturing. But as the economy staggered into the latter months of 2000, with no firm signs of recovery, market buzz was growing louder that the vicious cycle—recession, wider deficits, market jitters, higher interest rates—might finally spin out of control.

A tipping point came on October 6, when a political development raised market anxiety several notches, and out-of-control began to seem more of a distinct possibility. On that day, Vice President Carlos Álvarez quit in outrage over reports that several senators had taken bribes to vote for a government-backed labor reform bill. Álvarez headed the left-wing faction in the governing coalition, so his resignation underscored the fragility of de la Rúa's government and heightened the difficulties it faced in securing passage of legislation in Congress, where it lacked a majority in both houses. At risk was the government's 2001 budget, which included a number of unpopular spending cuts; as a result, investors became fixated on the fiscal problem and the broader issue of the nation's ability to pay its debts. Of particular concern was the question of how the government would be able to cover both its budget deficit and $14 billion in principal payments that were coming due in 2001. The markets, which had set *riesgo país* in the 500–700 range during most of the year, drove it above 800 by mid-October.

To some observers, it was becoming increasingly apparent that the financiers who had continued to lend Argentina money had done the country no favor—because the longer the economy was kept going as it was, the worse the nation's eventual plight would be.

Guillermo Gonzales, the Argentine ambassador to the United States, had never heard the word "haircut" used in an economic context— that is, not until one day in October 2000, shortly after Álvarez's resignation, when he found himself in an unusual meeting at his country's embassy in Washington.

The occasion was a visit from Charles Calomiris, a forty-two-year-old Columbia University economist. Calomiris's main area of expertise was banking, but he knew a fair amount about Argentina, having done some consulting for the government on its banking system and worked on a World Bank analysis of the country's financial sector in the late 1990s. Accompanied by Walter Molano of BCP Securities, Calomiris delivered a grim prognosis: At some point, the Argentine government would be unable to service the debt it had incurred because of the viciousness of the cycle the country was falling into, and delaying the recognition of that reality would only lead to catastrophe. The most sensible approach was thus for the government to administer a haircut to its creditors—that is, force them to accept a reduction in the amounts they were legally owed.

"He presented a very bleak future for Argentina, although actually, he turned out to be optimistic," Gonzales recalled. "I have to admit, my reaction was one of disbelief."

Calomiris's proposal might sound as if it would most logically come from a left-wing populist, or from a member of activist groups such as Jubilee and Drop the Debt, which had campaigned for a cancellation of the obligations incurred by sub-Saharan African nations and others among the world's heavily indebted poor countries, or HIPCs. There were some parallels between Calomiris's argument and those of people advocating debt forgiveness for the HIPCs, but there were important differences too, because extremely poor countries such as Uganda, Laos, and Honduras owed nearly all their debts to official, taxpayer-financed creditors—the U.S. Agency for International Development, for example, or the World Bank—rather than to the private sector. Calomiris was no left-winger; he was well known in Washington circles as a conservative, and unlike the drop-the-debt activists, he was not basing his argument concerning Argentina on humanitarian grounds or on doubts about the legitimacy of Argentina's debts. He reached his conclusion from a different perspective—the need for preemptive action to preserve as much as possible of the nation's economic fabric, especially its banking system.

His reasoning went as follows: Argentina's debt, over $130 billion by October 2000, was unsustainable. The double-digit interest payments that markets were demanding on new borrowing were substantially in excess of the country's likely growth rate. That was a recipe for a debt burden that would inflict an endlessly mounting drain on the economy. This phenomenon, a prominent feature of previous crises, notably Russia's, is called "exploding debt dynamics." It refers to an ever-increasing debt-to-GDP ratio, with higher interest payments and low growth driving the ratio inexorably upward with the passage of time. Foreign investors were bound to reach a consensus sooner or later that the debt was unpayable, Calomiris warned, and when they did, they would cut the country completely off from the fresh capital it needed just to keep paying interest and principal on old debt.

Accordingly, the government would be foolish to postpone a default that was inevitable anyway, Calomiris argued, and by continuing to honor its obligations in full, Argentina was setting itself up for a bigger fall. This argument reflected a well-established financial truth—that serious debt problems left unaddressed almost invariably mushroom. During the late 1980s, for example, U.S. policymakers had tried to paper over the bad loans issued by savings and loan institutions, only to end up with a much more expensive fix because the S&Ls—desperate for profits to escape their predicament—took greater and greater risks.

In Argentina's case, the debt would become an increasingly explosive problem because of what would happen to the banking system, Calomiris predicted. Argentina then had one of the soundest banking systems in the developing world, with healthy capital cushions and relatively prudent supervision. But as foreigners' willingness to invest in Argentine bonds diminished, the cash-starved government would surely use its power over the banks to pressure them into buying more and more of those bonds, Calomiris feared; that pattern had materialized in other developing countries. So when default finally came, the banks would be laden with assets that were plunging in value, creating the conditions for runs by depositors and a complete financial breakdown.

"The point I was arguing was, 'You've got this wonderful thing here called the banking system. You're going to destroy it, and when you do, it will destroy you,'" recalled Calomiris, who at the time was making his case for a haircut privately. (He would generate controversy by advancing it publicly about seven months later.)

Banks, after all, are inherently fragile institutions, as well as being essential to modern commerce. They accept deposits from the public and lend the money out, keeping only a fraction of the funds in their vaults to meet the daily demands of depositors who need access to their cash. If depositors suddenly turn up at the door in large numbers clamoring to withdraw their funds, banks have no practical way of meeting those demands without calling in the loans they have made, which in turn means shutting down businesses. If the government responds by limiting withdrawals, people will have problems obtaining the cash they need to make payments—and that, too, will severely constrict the functioning of commerce, as one individual's inability to pay causes a financial squeeze for another individual, and so on down the line.

The best way forward for Argentina, according to Calomiris, was to do a haircut promptly, while keeping convertibility intact, before the government's debt problem became totally unmanageable. Creditors might be unhappy at first, he acknowledged, but they would soon recognize that they would be better off in the long run by accepting lower claims because they would have a greater certainty of being repaid. Calomiris was not claiming that debt reduction by itself would solve Argentina's problems, because if the country failed to address other weaknesses, it would just end up in the same fix down the road. He proposed combining the haircut with substantial cuts in spending, including at the provincial level, along with trade, labor, and tax reforms. But he viewed a haircut as essential, because it would give Argentina resources to grow, and he urged that it be used as the linchpin of a "shared sacrifice" plan in which foreign creditors, government employees, workers, and taxpayers would all contribute in a concerted fashion. His estimates of the precise amounts required were admittedly of the back-of-the-envelope variety; partly for illustrative purposes, he suggested a 10 percent haircut, a 10 percent spending cut, and proportionate sacrifices in other areas.

The ambassador promised to discuss Calomiris's proposal with officials in Buenos Aires—who, the Columbia professor subsequently heard, dismissed it out of hand. Their negative reaction was hardly surprising. For a government to renege on its debt is a matter of considerable gravity. By stiffing its creditors, Argentina would destroy the good name it had worked so diligently to build in credit markets during the 1990s, impairing its ability to borrow in the future. It would undermine another of the decade's great accomplishments—the increase in respect for the sanctity of contracts and property rights—because if Argentines saw their government disregarding its contractual obligations, confidence in other contracts surely would diminish. In Argentina's case, faith in one of the government's most important contracts—the convertibility system—would definitely be shaken, and quite possibly shattered.

Calomiris did not think the consequences of a haircut for Argentina would be all that horrific, but the main issue, he thought, was whether the country would be better off taking the hit sooner rather than later. And the sooner the debt problem was tackled, the greater the likelihood that convertibility could survive.

"Everyone wants to delay," Calomiris said. "If you can delay something [bad] for six months, maybe it won't happen on your watch. Maybe you'll get another job." That typical mind-set of government officials, he said, "is often what you're up against when you're making an argument about long-run sustainability."

Argentina's bondholders had played a major role in getting the nation's economy into the mess it was in, and now the country's best hope of averting a catastrophic outcome lay in making the bondholders take their lumps as soon as possible. In recommending such a step, Calomiris may have been cavalier, but in the months that followed, the nightmare scenario he had sketched out began to unfold more or less as forecast.

[CHAPTER 5]

Show Me the Money

THE SMALL Washington-bound plane that departed Montreal on the evening of October 25, 2000, was loaded with members of the world's economic policy elite, who had been attending a meeting of officials from major industrial and emerging-market nations. Among those on the flight were Lawrence Summers, U.S. Treasury secretary; Alan Greenspan, chairman of the Federal Reserve Board; and Horst Köhler, managing director of the IMF. So distinguished was the passenger manifest that others on board could not help cracking a joke or two about the importance of a safe landing for the stability of the global economy.

Another passenger, less widely known, was Daniel Marx, Argentina's finance secretary, a former banker who, in a career of shuttling between the private and public sectors, had established a reputation as one of Latin America's ablest economic policymakers. Before boarding, Marx encountered Summers, whom he had asked to meet in Washington. Secretary Summers suggested they sit together and arranged for his Secret Service bodyguard to move to another seat. As Marx squeezed in next to Summers, they shared a chuckle over the fact that they were wearing almost identical ties.

Serendipitous as the matching ties may have been, it was no coincidence that Marx was approaching Summers. During Summers's eight years at the Treasury Department, where he moved from undersecretary for international affairs to deputy secretary and finally to secretary, he had played a central role in mobilizing giant international rescues for crisis-stricken countries in the 1990s, actively wielding America's influence as the IMF's number-one shareholder to shape the size and terms of Fund loans. Now it looked as if Argentina might be next to require assistance from Washington. The skittishness sparked by the resignation of Vice President Álvarez in early October was worsening. Deposits were draining from the banking system (to the tune of $789 million that month), and Argentine bond investors were turning tail, due to the concerns about the weakness of the de la Rúa government and its capacity to service the nation's debt, both in the coming year and in the more distant future. The day Marx and Summers flew to Washington together, Argentine government bonds plummeted by an average of 3 percent, with the benchmark bond closing at 85 cents on the dollar. That sent *riesgo país* shooting up to nearly 900; the markets now deemed Argentine securities so risky that, by comparison with U.S. Treasuries, an extra 9 percentage points of yield was required to make them worth buying. In Latin America, only Ecuador's bonds were trading at higher country-risk levels. Even Colombia and Venezuela, two countries with ample political problems, were deemed safer than Argentina.

Up to that stage, Argentina had been relying on precautionary IMF programs, not actual loans. But the nervousness besetting the markets in October was such that the government felt a large, straight loan from the Fund would be necessary. "We're at the point," Marx told Summers, "where we're in a show-me-the-money mode."

Thus began discussions that would lead to the first IMF-led rescue for Argentina in the year prior to the economy's collapse. The Argentine government would give the bailout a name—*blindaje,* or "armor." The label, obviously intended to convey the impression that the country was shielded from danger, had a touch of bravado to it, for similar IMF rescues had shown an unfortunate tendency to work more like sieves than protective gear.

The IMF's initiatives to save emerging markets from crises in the 1990s, although varying from country to country, followed a basic formula. The Fund would give a country a sizable loan package, substantially in excess of its normal lending limits, in the expectation that this would calm markets and dispel immediate concerns about the country's running out of hard currency; the idea was to give the country time for a change in policies that would put its economy on solid footing. IMF rules specify that a member country may borrow no more than 300 percent of its "quota"—the country's contribution to the Fund's kitty. But the rules allow for lending more in "exceptional circumstances," and as crises struck during the 1990s, exceptional circumstances seemed to arise time and again. Often, loans from institutions other than the IMF—including the World Bank and rich-country governments—helped fatten rescue packages even further. Countries receiving such aid, of course, had to agree to conditions negotiated with the Fund for revamping their economic policies.

The results had been mixed at best. Sometimes rescues succeeded in restoring countries' financial health relatively speedily, with Mexico's recovery from its 1995 meltdown being perhaps the best illustration. But in a number of cases—prominent examples including Russia, Indonesia, and an initial attempt to save South Korea—IMF-led loan packages had provided only brief respites from market storms and failed to stop mass sell-offs. Lucky investors and financial institutions took advantage of those respites to pull their money out before currencies crashed; in effect, the dollars furnished by the IMF enabled these foreign market players—and rich locals as well—to cash in their chips. When such fiascoes occurred, the Fund typically blamed borrowing countries for failing to fulfill their reform pledges.

But another important factor was the huge increase during the 1990s in the size, speed, and volatility of private capital moving across oceans, continents, and national borders. With traders in financial centers able to unload their holdings with a few computer keystrokes, a stampede by the Electronic Herd could overwhelm international rescues, even ones involving loan packages in the tens of billions of dollars.

The cost of these botched bailouts could be steep, so would-be rescuers had an obligation to consider carefully the likelihood of success—a point often stressed by Robert Rubin, the previous U.S. Treasury secretary, who favored the term "probabilistic" to describe his mode of thinking about such matters. Rubin's point was that provided all the costs and benefits and probabilities were appropriately weighed, the decision to launch a rescue was not necessarily wrong just because it ultimately failed. Yet at the same time, policymakers were duty-bound to refrain from offering loans if the odds against success appeared too long. For one thing, the IMF risked squandering its credibility, because a major part of the Fund's value to the international community stemmed from its ability to instill confidence among bankers and investors, and a rescue gone bad could seriously diminish its capacity to instill that confidence in the future. On top of that is the potential cost to the country involved, because the IMF's assistance comes in the form of a loan that must be repaid, an added burden—often of significant dimensions—on the country's taxpayers. Fund loans cannot be restructured or forgiven; countries that breach their promises to repay the Fund—whose ranks mostly include failed states like Sudan and Somalia—risk being treated as total financial pariahs, with no chance of obtaining other forms of international aid. Moreover, a rescue may cause a recession to become more wrenching. That is especially true when the conditions agreed by the IMF and the recipient country are excessively harsh, but apart from that issue, an IMF loan that allows a government to defer necessary action will simply cause problems to fester and grow—and as Calomiris had observed concerning Argentina, a country's long-term interests are poorly served when that happens.

In Argentina's case, the loan under consideration would beef up the country's precautionary program to $14 billion, or 500 percent of quota, well above the $9 billion that would be allowed under the normal limit. The purpose was to assure markets that the government would have the funds it needed to fulfill its debt-payment obligations for at least a part of the coming year, and during that time, the authorities in Buenos Aires could take steps that would curtail future indebtedness and restore creditworthiness. Then, once investors had regained confidence in Argentina's medium-term prospects, the government could resume tapping private markets as needed. Or so the theory went. This sort of IMF loan, typical of many rescues, is called "catalytic," because the money is aimed at catalyzing private markets into restoring financing to the country at reasonable cost.

Whatever the aid might be dubbed, the need for some sort of action became increasingly urgent in the early days of November 2000, as the sell-off of Argentine bonds turned into a rout. When the government held a sale of treasury bills on November 7, it was forced to offer yields of 16 percent on one-year bills, a huge jump from the 8.89 percent it had paid on bills auctioned in mid-July. On six-month bills, it had to pay 14.51 percent, compared with a yield of 8.64 percent offered on similar bills in mid-October. At interest costs like those, Argentina's debt dynamics were clearly explosive, and depositors stepped up their withdrawals from banks in November. Pressure was mounting on the IMF to move quickly, as was clear from a memo sent by Ter-Minassian to her superiors on November 20, which cited the danger of "a collapse of confidence, a drying up of financing to the government, [and] a massive flight of deposits from the banking system." Such a scenario was "unlikely" over the next couple of weeks, according to the memo, but there was a strong caveat: "If, however, there is no clear prospect of an international support package materializing soon, things could start to unravel around the middle of December," because at that time, "large government debt [payments] come due, and the Treasury's cash on hand will have dwindled to near zero."

The crisis loomed as the first major test for Horst Köhler, a former top official of the German finance ministry who had become the IMF's managing director the previous May at age fifty-seven. Sandy-haired and blue-eyed, Köhler had spent most of the period since his appointment on trips to fifteen countries in Asia, Africa, and Latin America (including Argentina), getting to know some of the Fund's major borrowers and learning about the powerful institution he now led. The Fund staff, meanwhile, was getting to know their new boss, and one thing was abundantly clear: Köhler was in most respects a very different sort of leader from his predecessor, Michel Camdessus.

For starters, there was Köhler's temper. He was not shy about upbraiding subordinates in the presence of their colleagues, and he often showed impatience for the elaborate arguments that the Fund's Ph.D.'s tended to advance in internal debate. His penchant for taking people to task publicly and vehemently was a jarring contrast to Camdessus, who—although icily formal—had always kept his cool, even when conveying his displeasure. The new managing director stood apart also in the gruff manner he sometimes used in dealings with countries' officials, showing little of the diplomatic flair for which Camdessus had been renowned. Acknowledging Köhler's deficiencies in this area, Jack Boorman, who headed the IMF's Policy Development and Review Department, said that although the managing director was a genuinely good-hearted person, "He and Camdessus could say more or less the same things, deliver the same message, and authorities would walk out of the meeting with Camdessus feeling they had been bolstered, and walk out of meetings with Köhler wondering what had hit them." Köhler's blustery approach struck many people within the IMF as the sign of a poor manager with deeply rooted insecurities. But some preferred his style to Camdessus's, noting that the Frenchman's honey-eyed tone sometimes masked unfriendly intentions, while Köhler's raised voice always let people know where they stood—and Köhler usually apologized later when his anger got the better of him.

Köhler was a farmer's son born in what is now Poland during World War II. His family fled to East Germany as the Russians advanced, and then to West Germany in 1953. Young Horst spent considerable time in a relocation camp, and years later he would reminisce fondly about the Care packages he received from the United States at Christmas. He earned his Ph.D. in economics and political science from the University of Tubingen, then joined the German economics ministry. Upon rising to the post of deputy finance minister in 1990, Köhler played a major role in helping to negotiate the unification of East and West Germany, and after five years in the mid-1990s as head of the German Savings Bank Association, he was named in 1998 to the presidency of the European Bank for Reconstruction and Development (EBRD), the London-based institution established to aid Eastern Europe's transition from communism to capitalism. His appointment to the top job at the IMF was less than a glorious triumph, for it came as the result of insistence by the German government that its turn had come to choose the European who would run the Fund. When the U.S. government objected to Berlin's first choice, German officials put forward Köhler instead.

Köhler and Camdessus did hold one thing in common: Though they outranked Stan Fischer, both shone dimly by comparison with Fischer in discussions over economics. The stature of the first deputy managing director was greater than ever with the staff following the crises of the 1990s, during which he had demonstrated a capacity to juggle multiple emergencies with aplomb. Still, Köhler was determined to put his stamp on the institution. In speeches after assuming office, he acknowledged the validity of some of the criticism that the IMF's detractors had raised, notably the complaint that the Fund had imposed reforms on reluctant governments without ensuring that the countries "owned" the policies they were adopting.

He also gave notice that under his leadership, the Fund would redouble its efforts to prevent its loans from bailing out rich lenders and enabling governments to perpetuate policies that were doomed to fail. The problem he was addressing is known among economists as "moral hazard," which refers to the phenomenon that saving people from their mistakes often makes them unduly inclined to take risks. Auto insurance offers a simple example; a car owner who is fully covered for accidents may be more prone to drive recklessly. Likewise, in emerging markets, investors may throw money around imprudently, and governments may adopt unsound policies, if they assume the IMF can be counted on in a pinch to provide rescue packages.

"Creditors and borrowers must know that the Fund's resources are, and should remain, limited," Köhler declared in a speech at Washington's National Press Club on August 7, 2000. "The Fund is not an institution which can produce money by printing money. . . . It's good that the Fund has only limited resources, so that there can be no doubt that creditors and borrowers must assume responsibility for the risks they take, and that taxpayers' money will not be easily available to protect them against the consequences of misjudgment."

In Argentina, those lofty principles would be subjected to trial by fire.

"Where will the growth come from?"

Köhler raised that question repeatedly at the numerous meetings IMF officials held in late autumn 2000 to fashion a rescue for Argentina. At times hectoring, at times challenging the Fund's staff to think in new ways, he pressed the Ph.D.'s to design a program that would jump-start an economy that had been moribund for two years. To some on the staff, this was evidence of Köhler's lack of background as an economist; he sounded as if growth could result from the push of a button rather than happening as the natural consequence of a country getting its policies right. Still, Köhler had good reason to worry about growth, because in its absence, Argentina stood no chance of breaking out of its vicious cycle, and the Fund's rescue would be for naught. Moreover, the economy's torpor was poisoning Argentina's political atmosphere and undermining the country's ability to deal with fundamental economic problems. The de la Rúa government was under attack from many of its own allies in Congress for its failure to reverse conditions that had driven unemployment above 15 percent and the poverty rate above 32 percent. Militant demonstrations were on the increase, especially in poorer provinces where crowds were blocking roads to protest joblessness and cuts in benefits.

The most commonly cited drag on Argentina's growth was the convertibility system, because of the impact of the peso-dollar equivalency exchange rate on the competitiveness of Argentine goods. Köhler expressed considerable unease in private conversations about the problems caused by convertibility, according to former Argentine officials with whom he spoke, and Fischer also reraised the question of whether the Argentines ought to be looking for a way out.

But the Argentine negotiators, led by Economy Minister José Luis Machinea, had strapped themselves to the mast of convertibility, and many within the IMF agreed that the currency system was not the country's main problem. Under convertibility, exports had surged every year until 1998, and the decline thereafter could be attributed at least partly to lower world prices for commodities Argentina exported, such as wheat. The most recent data suggested that Argentine industry remained competitive; exports of manufactured goods had risen 11 percent in volume terms in the first half of 2000.

Most important was the fact that letting the peso fall against the dollar would have enormous and potentially crushing consequences. The IMF had been studying the implications of such a scenario since the recession had deepened in 1999, when people from a cross-section of departments began meeting regularly in a group that came to be known as the "Argentina task force." Although some staff members revived the idea in 1999 of pressing the Argentines for an exit strategy from convertibility, the task force had consistently concluded that scrapping the system raised significant risks of reigniting hyperinflation; even if that did not happen, the country would face a huge mess sorting out the losses resulting from the sudden disparity between the currency people earned and the currency they had promised to repay others. Nearly 80 percent of all bank loans were denominated in dollars at that time, along with many business contracts and utility prices, so exiting from convertibility "would be extremely difficult, if not chaotic," stated an August 1999 memo from the Western Hemisphere Department—a finding repeatedly endorsed in subsequent analyses. With those realities confronting the IMF's managing director, "I think Köhler understood that to abandon convertibility would be very damaging," said Mario Vicens, who as Argentina's treasury secretary was one of the Economy Ministry's top negotiators with the Fund.

Thus the question remained: Where will growth come from? Thanks in substantial part to Köhler's dogged pursuit of that issue, the IMF chose an approach on fiscal policy that, once again, contravened its image for being hard-nosed on budget matters.

Already in 2000, the Argentines had greatly exceeded their budget-deficit ceiling. The IMF and the de la Rúa government had agreed on holding the federal government's deficit for 2000 to $4.7 billion, the theory being that since the markets were worried about the country's burgeoning debt, a tight fiscal policy—and less government borrowing—would bring interest rates down from their punishingly high levels. As the recession continued to take a toll on tax revenue during the first half of the year, however, by late autumn it was clear the gap between spending and revenue would exceed $6 billion.

Instead of being told that they must try again to cut the deficit in 2001, Machinea and his team—who had been seeking looser fiscal targets—were pleasantly surprised to hear from the IMF that the federal budget gap for the coming year could stay at around the current year's levels. In fact, Machinea recalled that when he proposed a $6 billion target for 2001, Fischer told him "you can do a little more"—and they agreed on $6.5 billion.

To compensate for the high deficit in the near term, the government promised to take a number of measures that would substantially shrink the budget gap in future years. These included overhauling the pension system to reduce payments for some retirees, deregulating the health care system, and capping the amount of money the federal government shared each month with the provinces. But here, too, the Fund agreed to a more relaxed target than before; the nation's Fiscal Responsibility Law, which had mandated a balanced budget by 2003, would be amended to extend the deadline year for a zero deficit to 2005.

A number of Argentine economists consulted privately by the IMF warned that the Fund was making a grave mistake. Giving Argentina the go-ahead to run a $6.5 billion deficit, they predicted, would lead to an even larger deficit because the government would exceed that target too, shredding its credibility further. Within the IMF staff, there were many doubters as well. "We have serious concerns about the viability of this program," said Peter Heller of the Fiscal Affairs Department in a mid-November 2000 memo to Ter-Minassian. From the Policy Development and Review Department, Jesús Seade agreed, writing that the proposal to achieve budgetary savings in the long run "risks stretching the credulity of market participants, coming as it does with only the promise of consolidation at a future date," and he warned that with high interest rates likely to continue deterring business spending on plant and equipment, the economy would not revive, "and Argentina will remain entrapped in its current vicious cycle of low growth, low revenues, low confidence, high interest rates, and low growth." Miguel Savastano, an economist in the Research Department who had long been one of the staff's greatest skeptics on Argentina, wrote that "the program may soon become hostage to political developments" as Argentine politicians rejected the longer-term budget reforms.

But Köhler wanted an answer to his question about where growth would come from, and he had a powerful ally in Fischer on the fiscal issue—so the $6.5 billion target stuck. Not that the managing director regarded the plan as a surefire success; given the social strains caused by the recession, he was especially worried about the government's ability to deliver on its promises for changes in pensions, health, and provincial spending, Argentine officials recalled.

Köhler had another big question: What about extracting something from the private sector—the foreign bondholders and Argentina's other private creditors? Weren't the extremely high rates of interest they were earning supposed to reflect a commensurately high degree of risk? Could any rescue work with money coming only from official sources like the IMF? Shouldn't the private sector be contributing in some way as well?

Ultimately, these questions raised the possibility that the IMF and the Argentine authorities should consider something like Calomiris's "haircut" proposal for forcing creditors to accept reduced payment of their claims. Amid strict secrecy, a few Fund staffers were busily examining what might happen if Argentina had to take that option, which was dubbed "Plan Gamma."

The idea of "involving" private lenders in a rescue—bailing them *in* instead of bailing them *out*—was hardly novel. During the debt crisis of the 1980s, the IMF had insisted that if taxpayer money was going to help save indebted countries from defaulting on their loans to major international banks, the banks would have to pony up too, by providing fresh loans or rescheduling old ones. This sort of approach was not as practical during the crises of the 1990s, because the creditors in most cases were bondholders rather than banks, numbering in the hundreds of thousands, who were impossible to gather in meetings for the purpose of pressuring them as had been done with bankers in the 1980s.

Still, the appeal of bail-ins had gained ground as disenchantment rose with large, catalytic loans that so often failed to rescue countries from turmoil. When opportunities presented themselves, the IMF and G-7 had sought to wring some concessions from private creditors. One prominent example was South Korea's crisis in late 1997, where after the failure of the IMF's first rescue, a second rescue package succeeded by including a worldwide coordinated effort by government officials to prod banks into maintaining their credit lines to Korea. Later in the decade came the cases of Pakistan, Ecuador, and Ukraine, where the IMF granted loans on condition that the governments obtain the broad consent of their bondholders for a debt restructuring—an exchange of old bonds for new ones, aimed at stretching out the maturity dates, or reducing interest and principal payments, or both.

Needless to say, members of the financial community were not pleased about this trend. They tended to view sovereign bonds as a country's sacred obligation, since most such bonds contained indentures promising to pay in full and on time, with no ifs, ands, or buts. They were exhibiting a sense of militancy, including threats of litigation, against any attempts to force them into accepting less than the full amount owed. "Many bond investors, particularly in the U.S., are beginning to stand up for their contractual rights to receive payment—no matter what the IMF and its main shareholders decide is right," declared Arturo Porzecanski of ABN-AMRO Securities in an October 2000 report. Suing a foreign government is usually unrewarding, because the government's overseas assets are generally modest in size, or completely protected from litigation in the case of embassies and other diplomatic facilities. But as Porzecanski noted, in one recent case an aggressive legal strategy had paid off for Elliott Associates, a New York–based "vulture fund"—a fund that buys the bonds of troubled debtors at distressed prices. Elliott had bought a substantial amount of Peruvian government bonds for $11.8 million in the mid-1990s, then filed suit against Peru's proposed restructuring, and, after winning a judgment in a Belgian court, forced the government in Lima to settle in September 2000 with a cash payment of $55 million. The case "sent a powerful warning shot" and "will encourage other investors to resist future bond restructurings," Porzecanski cautioned.

The IMF had fired a warning shot of its own, however, at its annual meeting in Prague in September. A communiqué issued by the Fund's top policy-setting body, the International Monetary and Finance Committee, which consists of finance ministers from member countries, attempted to codify the policy concerning when large catalytic loans would make sense and when they would not. In effect, the policy stated that when a country had no reasonable prospect of paying its private debts in accord with the contractual terms, an IMF loan would be granted only if the country restructured those debts to sustainable levels.

This policy left some big questions unresolved, which IMF economists were wrestling with as they crafted Argentina's rescue plan. The biggest was how to decide when a country really has no reasonable prospect of paying its debts. This is essentially the same sort of dilemma any commercial bank faces in deciding whether, say, a struggling company can survive over the long haul. Maybe the company just has a liquidity problem—a shortage of cash, which if addressed would put the firm on the road to profitability. But maybe the problem is one of solvency—an insurmountable surfeit of liabilities over assets, which an emergency loan would alleviate only temporarily. Making such an assessment about a company is often quite difficult; when the debtor in question is a country, the judgment is even more an art than a science. If one assumes a healthy level of growth, declining interest rates, and government willingness to embrace budgetary austerity, the country's debt dynamics will appear stable. If one assumes a low growth rate, high interest costs, and limitations on the government's ability to impose fiscal discipline, the country's debt dynamics will appear certain to explode in the future, with an ever-rising debt-to-GDP ratio.

In Argentina's case, the IMF seemed to have a marked tendency toward rosy scenarios in projecting the country's debt dynamics. As recently as 1997 the Fund had judged that public-sector debt would shrink to 34 percent of GDP by 2000; instead, it had risen to 50 percent, in large part because economic growth and interest rates had proved so much worse than the Fund had assumed.

In 2000 the IMF was again projecting that its program for Argentina would cause the debt-to-GDP ratio to recede rather than explode, and again it was basing that projection on optimistic assumptions. The Fund assumed that a recovery would begin in 2001, that growth would pick up to a 4.3 percent annual rate for 2003–2005, that interest rates would subside, and that the government would enact the long-term fiscal measures it had promised. But within high official circles in late 2000, a few other voices were expressing the view—in private, of course—that on the spectrum between insolvency and illiquidity, Argentina was much further toward the insolvency end.

One of those voices belonged to the British Treasury. As a member of the G-7, Britain has a seat on the body that often controls major IMF decisions from behind the scenes. On economic issues in general, and financial crises in particular, the G-7 strives to maintain a united voice to avoid spooking markets. But that unity sometimes masks scrappy internal debates, and the British took the unusual step of sending a private letter to the U.S. Treasury and the other G-7 finance ministries advancing the argument that the chances of failure for a conventional IMF program in Argentina were very high. "If growth doesn't return, there is a real risk that a payments interruption will become inevitable, and [convertibility] will become untenable," the British stated in the November 10 letter.

Even more negative about a conventional IMF loan, and more insistent on bailing in the private sector, were the Bank of England, the Bank of Canada, and Germany's Bundesbank, which as central banks play only a supporting role in the G-7 debate compared with the finance ministries. Top officials of the British and Canadian central banks had been making the case for several years that an entirely new approach was needed to replace catalytic IMF loans as the instrument of choice in handling financial crises. In their view, the Fund ought to aid countries facing large-scale investor panics by backing a decision to impose "standstills"—temporary suspensions of debt payments that would give the country and its creditors time to work out a restructuring of claims. The argument was crystallized in a remarkable sentence in a paper circulated to other policymakers: "The problem historically has not been that countries have been too eager to renege on their financial obligations, but often too reluctant." Argentina at the end of 2000 was another such case, in the opinion of these central bankers. Like Calomiris, they believed the government in Buenos Aires was avoiding the hard truth that it could not service its debts, for fear that making such an admission would cause an economic perturbation that might induce a change of political leadership. Furthermore, delaying this recognition would mean that the Argentine people would suffer more in the long run.

The IMF was all too aware that a large loan might fail—and that was the reason for Plan Gamma.

Plan Gamma was outlined in a November 20 memo labeled "Secret" (as opposed to "Confidential," the usual classification on internal Fund documents), a status that reflected its extraordinary sensitivity and the tight circle in which it was discussed. The memo stated: "[T]he authorities might decide to abandon the catalytic approach to mobilizing financing and resort to concerted techniques"—that is, a forced debt restructuring, or haircut. But doing so, the memo warned, would be fraught with peril.

The danger, as the memo's authors saw it, was that a debt restructuring might trigger a series of reactions that, like a set of dominoes toppling one after the other, would knock the economy flat. A government decision to deny creditors some portion of the amounts they were due would undermine confidence in financial contracts generally in Argentina; moreover, it would raise concerns about the soundness of the country's banks. Although the system was in general good health (as Calomiris had claimed), in the Fund's view the banks were already vulnerable to the shock of a restructuring, because they held, on average, 17 percent of their assets in government bonds. "There would be a major risk that the inevitable pressures on the banking system would get out of control," the memo's authors stated, referring to a possibility that depositors would pull massive amounts of their savings out of banks. As the banks handed over dollars to satisfy depositors' demands, they would tap the central bank's reserves for more dollars, and the reserves would quickly dwindle. This would pose a mortal threat to convertibility, since convertibility was based on the promise that the central bank would maintain enough dollars in reserve to back the supply of printed pesos. And if convertibility were abandoned, chaos would reign amid a broad inability by debtors to meet their obligations.

A forced restructuring would not *necessarily* lead down such a road, in the IMF's view. The Plan Gamma memo envisioned a relatively benign outcome, which it called "Scenario I," in which the government would restructure the debt, bank runs would be contained, and convertibility would survive. Under this scenario, the IMF could extend fresh loans to help the government maintain stability "if the crisis were successful in promoting a political consensus on a new set of policies worthy of Fund support." But it was impossible to guarantee against a slide into "Scenario II"—the outcome involving major bank runs, the collapse of convertibility, and the imposition of a wide range of financial controls that would stifle the economy.

In light of those risks, and with the prospect that a traditional rescue loan might be successful, the overwhelming sentiment among top IMF officials in late 2000 was in favor of extending a loan without forcing Argentina's creditors to submit to a haircut. That corresponded with the wishes of senior Argentine policymakers, who likewise feared the injury that would result from a bruising confrontation with creditors. At the U.S. Treasury, a similar debate was taking place and reaching similar conclusions—though at least one participant was making the case for a more radical approach.

Born in Turkey to Iranian Jewish parents, raised in Italy, and educated at Bocconi University in Milan and at Harvard, Nouriel Roubini was something of a celebrity in the community of international financial-crisis experts. As an economics professor at New York University in the fall of 1997, Roubini had created a website, the Asia Crisis Homepage (later renamed the Global Macroeconomics and Financial Policy Site), where he posted important documents, news articles, and academic papers—and for people interested in the subject, the site became a cyberspace version of the place to see and be seen. After spending a couple of years in the late 1990s at the Council of Economic Advisers and the Treasury, by late 2000 Roubini was working at the Treasury only part-time as a consultant. But the argument he was advancing about Argentina in the Treasury's lively internal debates was noteworthy for its hardheaded realism.

After two years of recession, Argentina was still mired in economic stagnation and would almost certainly remain so, especially considering how overvalued the peso was, Roubini contended. He perceived the country as at least borderline insolvent, given its combination of a rising debt burden, high interest rates, and slow growth. Thus, a catalytic IMF loan would most likely succeed only in postponing default and devaluation, he predicted. The best solution in the long run, in his view, was for Argentina to bite the bullet now—let the peso float downward and impose a debt restructuring, perhaps with an IMF loan to help moderate the impact.

Roubini was under no illusions that moving in this direction would be painless. But he saw it as preferable to buying time with IMF loans and trying to stave off a crisis that was bound to occur eventually. It would be better to face the situation promptly and squarely, and return the country as quickly as possible to competitiveness, growth, and solvency, he asserted.

Just as Plan Gamma struck most IMF officials as an unacceptably risky option, however, the same was true at Treasury for the approach Roubini was suggesting. For one thing, political developments in the United States at the end of 2000 militated in favor of a conventional IMF rescue and against moves that would risk upsetting the international financial system. The Clinton administration was on its way out, and legal battles were raging over whether Texas Governor George W. Bush or Vice President Albert Gore had won the presidency. As one former Treasury official recalled, "People were not entertaining very radical ideas at that moment."

Beyond that, Larry Summers's Treasury team believed that the odds of success for a large IMF loan were substantial enough to justify the attempt. "People knew it was high risk," said Ted Truman, who was assistant secretary of the Treasury for international affairs. "We managed to convince ourselves that the debt dynamics were sustainable. That was probably a mistake, but it was a serious effort. We looked at a number of analyses and did some of our own." A more serious error, Truman added, was that "there should have been a clearer message [to the Argentines] that the next step would be Plan B, not more of the same"—in other words, a solid understanding that if the IMF program failed to improve Argentina's economic situation fairly quickly, the country would have no choice but to restructure its debt and, if necessary, change its currency policy as well. "That message," Truman said, "was not conveyed as firmly as it should have been by any of the parties."

This was indeed a crucial omission. The case for giving a rescue loan in late 2000 may have been hard to resist, because the Argentines had done so many things right, and the chance that they might save themselves did not appear remote. But considering the odds that the program would fail, a concrete plan for pulling the plug should have been devised and agreed with the Argentine authorities. In fact, a January 2, 2001, memo sent by Western Hemisphere Department head Claudio Loser to IMF management said: "[I]f activity were to continue to stagnate over the next six months, and market concerns were to intensify, closing off Argentina's access to external borrowing, the whole strategy of the program would need to be rethought." But no such policy was put into practice.

All the attendees knew pretty much how events would unfold when the IMF's executive directors convened on January 12, 2001, to consider the program for Argentina. As they normally do several times a week in fulfillment of their duties as representatives of the Fund's member nations, the directors made their way from their offices to the twelfth-floor boardroom, an oval chamber sixty feet long and two stories high with plush blue carpeting and suede-and-wood paneling, decorated only by large portraits of past managing directors. They settled into their gray swivel chairs around a horseshoe-shaped table with microphones at each place, and staff members took seats a few feet away from the table.

With the U.S. Treasury behind it, the *blindaje* was set for approval. The British Treasury and the central banks had laid aside their objections, and the G-7 had fallen into line. That outcome is common in these situations, as European and Canadian officials ruefully admit, because once Washington favors giving an IMF rescue to a country, other G-7 members cannot make the case with absolute certainty that the rescue will not work, and they do not want to dissent openly for fear of undermining the effort. The IMF and Argentina had publicly announced on December 19, 2000, that Köhler would recommend that the board approve the program, and the managing director never makes such an announcement without having informally ascertained that he will have the support of a board majority. In fact, most board decisions are taken by consensus, with an abstention being the strongest act of dissent.

Thus there was no doubt about the outcome: Argentina would receive a $14 billion loan, of which $5 billion would be disbursed by January 2001, with the remainder scheduled for disbursement later in 2001, 2002, and 2003. Additional pledges of about $6 billion in loans were coming from the World Bank, the Inter-American Development Bank, and the government of Spain. The rescue was being advertised as adding up to $40 billion, because it also included some flimsy, ill-defined pledges by Argentine financial institutions and pension funds to continue buying government bonds. The purpose of those pledges, which amounted to only feeble private-sector involvement, was mainly to make the "headline" number look more impressive, as a number of officials who were involved later acknowledged.

But just because all attendees intended to endorse the program formally did not mean they were going to remain silent about their doubts within the private confines of the board discussion. In fact, several of the twenty-four directors, including two G-7 members—the British and the Canadians—stated that the *blindaje* had a very slim chance of success, mainly because of the size and probable explosiveness of Argentina's debt burden.

In a confidential statement circulated to other board members for the meeting, Thomas Bernes, the Canadian director, focused on a figure that was also worrying many in the markets—the fact that Argentina's combined public- and private-sector debt owed to foreigners was roughly five times as large as the country's exports. Paying debt service on those foreign obligations in the coming year would consume all of the hard currency Argentina was expected to earn from selling goods abroad, Bernes noted. "This level of debt service is clearly not sustainable," he warned, and the burden "is unlikely to ease." In other words, Argentina would not be able to generate sufficient hard-currency reserves for all of the payments it would have to make to foreign creditors, and that problem would become more glaring, "thereby exacerbating market participants' concerns, and potentially contributing to a vicious cycle" as investors became increasingly reluctant to keep their money in the country. He dismissed the staff's projections that a rapid rise in exports would help solve the problem, arguing that it was based on "a much more rapid rate than what we have seen over recent history," and for good measure he repeated his main point: "Argentina's debt servicing costs are unsustainably high."

Success for the program depended on the Argentines' winning over the markets by demonstrating perfect compliance with the conditions, but that already looked like a shaky assumption, Bernes and others observed. Congress was resisting the long-term fiscal savings that the government had promised, and although de la Rúa had started to implement them by presidential decree, the decrees were subject to legislative and judicial challenge. That problem raised serious questions about whether the government could fulfill its pledge to balance the budget by 2005, an issue that worried the Fund staff as well. "Concerns about ownership of the program by the political class have been confirmed by the attitude of Congress, which in the end refused to support the government in some of the essential but politically more difficult elements of the program," Ter-Minassian wrote in a December 29 memo to management.

Nonetheless, the board, including all the doubting Thomases, dutifully supported the program. Even the more enthusiastic directors said they perceived substantial risks and fretted that it was based on optimistic assumptions. But Argentina got its $14 billion suit of IMF-fortified armor, together with the rhetorical assurance the Fund traditionally bestows—that fidelity to its prescriptions would work wonders. A statement issued after the board meeting declared: "It will be important that the authorities at all levels of government adhere firmly to the economic program so as to restore market confidence, return the economy to a higher growth path, and protect the country's convertibility regime."

January and early February—midsummer in the Southern Hemisphere—are typically vacation periods in Argentina. So Tomás Reichmann had to wait before he could telephone anyone at a senior level in the Economy Ministry from his IMF office in early February 2001. But his call was urgent, and as soon as he could he contacted Mario Vicens, the Treasury secretary.

Reichmann, who had worked on Argentina in the Fund's West-

ern Hemisphere Department for a number of years, now held overall responsibility for the country, having taken over from Ter-
Minassian right after the New Year when she was promoted to head
another department. Just a month into his new job, and just weeks
after the board's approval of the *blindaje,* trouble was afoot. "Mario,
have you seen the January numbers?" Reichmann recalled asking
Vicens, referring to the federal government's budget figures for that
month. When Vicens explained that he had just returned from holiday and had not had the chance to see the figures, Reichmann
replied, "You'd better look at them. They're massively off track."

The numbers showed that the federal government deficit for the
month of January alone would total nearly half of the $2.1 billion
target the IMF and the Argentines had agreed for the first quarter.
By itself that was of little consequence, and the problem stemmed
mainly from small amounts of overspending by a number of ministries, with the rest attributable to another shortfall in tax revenue.
But since the government was expected to generate even more red
ink in March than January, and future quarterly targets were lower,
the data were an ill omen suggesting that Argentina was going to
bust the IMF's deficit target for the year once again, lax though the
target may have been. Vicens, for his part, was worried about what
he saw as an even bigger problem—increasingly fierce attacks by
members of Congress against the government's proposals for savings
in the pension, health, and provincial spending areas, which were
further dimming hopes about the government's long-term budget-
balancing pledge.

These developments threatened to reverse the enthusiastic reception that financial markets had initially given to the *blindaje.* Thanks
in part to surprise interest rate cuts in January by the U.S. Federal
Reserve, which heralded relief from high borrowing costs, the
Argentine government had auctioned three-month treasury bills at
yields of 6.75 percent on January 23, the lowest in over a year, and
overall *riesgo país* dipped into the 600s. But now, events appeared to
be vindicating the pessimists who had worried that the program

would not hold together. Evidence was mounting that the recession-weary country could not muster a political consensus for either short-term or long-term fiscal restraint. *Riesgo país* rose back into the 700s in the second half of February, climbing above 800 at month's end.

Stupefied, officials in Washington watched as the situation in Buenos Aires deteriorated still further. Economy Minister Machinea, whose efforts to rein in spending had drawn obloquy from many politicians in the ruling alliance, resigned on March 2 after Congress rejected the long-term pension and health reforms. His replacement, Ricardo López Murphy, a burly, University of Chicago–trained economist who had been serving as defense minister, sought to regain the confidence of the markets by proposing a new package of deficit-reduction measures worth $2 billion. But the initiative stood no chance amid the antipathy of the populace toward further austerity. Among the proposals was an end to free university education; this was a commendable idea, given that taxpayer-funded college degrees constituted a subsidy to rich and middle-class Argentines, but it was wildly unpopular, and it helped bring a jarringly quick end to López Murphy's tenure. With de la Rúa unwilling to back him after six top officials quit the government to protest his program, López Murphy was forced out on March 19, having lasted less than three weeks. Such a rapidly revolving door at the Economy Ministry was a forewarning of the disintegration that was to come.

As these events unfolded, a debate was intensifying within the IMF about what Argentina should do if it were forced to capitulate on convertibility. Spirited discussions were held among members of the Argentina task force, who began meeting with increasing frequency in Stan Fischer's office as the issue assumed new urgency in February and March 2001.

One option was dollarization, in which the dollar would completely replace the peso as the national currency. Argentine officials had toyed with this idea for years, repeatedly stopping short of adopting it because it entailed a total surrender of sovereign control over their currency and monetary system. Dollarizing the economy had one huge advantage: It would spare the country the trauma of delinking the peso from the greenback, because people and companies who had borrowed dollars would not suddenly be faced with a steep rise in their debt burdens compared with their earning power. But for all of dollarization's short-term benefits, critics of the idea viewed it as a sham panacea with many long-term drawbacks—specifically, it would leave Argentine industry just as uncompetitive as ever, and the government just as deeply mired in debt as before. Accordingly, many at the Fund believed that the only viable option for Argentina in the long run was to let the peso float downward according to market forces. In between these two options was a third, in which Argentina would first devalue the peso to a fixed rate—to 85 cents, say, or 75 cents—and then dollarize at the lower exchange rate. As attractive as the in-between option sounded, it too had drawbacks, because once the $1-per-peso peg was broken, people would question how long the government could stick with the new fixed rate, and they might ship so many of their dollars overseas that the economy would lack sufficient currency to function.

No consensus emerged among the twenty-odd economists who at various times attended meetings of the task force. Beyond widely concurring that the convertibility system was well worth trying to preserve as long as it was viable, Fund staffers could not agree on which replacement system would be best should one be needed. Fischer played devil's advocate, forcing people to defend their positions, but even within departments, IMF economists took strong issue with one another on this question. In some cases, they switched sides; Reichmann, for example, first favored a floating peso, then became enamored of dollarization for a while, and then returned to the floaters' camp.

Members of the group were churning out papers, assessing in detail the costs and benefits of each option and the likely impact on the economy; by the time of default and devaluation, more than forty reports would be produced. None of them would be shared with top

Argentine policymakers, useful though they might have been in helping the Argentines prepare for the worst. The rationale was that all the options posed major difficulties, and although the Fund wanted to be ready to offer well-reasoned analysis should Buenos Aires request it, such a weighty choice would have to be Argentina's.

"Amazingly, we kept this confidential," Reichmann said. "Imagine the reaction in the markets if it had leaked. But it never did."

By February and March 2001, members of Jonathan Binder's team at Standard Asset Management in Miami were focused on Argentina's prospective economic demise. Developments in Buenos Aires were providing ample grounds for firms like Binder's to speculate on a bad outcome, and more were starting to do so, often using that favorite technique of market bears, "short-selling."

Short-selling involves placing bets that the market will fall, or more specifically, that the prices of certain securities will decline. Whereas ordinary investors usually bet on higher prices and thus try to buy cheap in hopes of selling dear, short sellers aim to first sell dear and buy cheap later. To do so, they engage in a variety of transactions, all of which boil down to the same function of selling while prices are higher than they will be down the road. (Mechanically, a short-seller borrows bonds or other securities and promptly sells them at the current price in the expectation that the price will fall, and if that expectation proves correct, he can buy the bonds later at a low price and repay the loan, collecting a tidy profit in the process.) Many professional buy-side investors are forbidden to engage in this sort of trading; a typical manager of pension fund or mutual fund assets who takes a bearish view of an individual country's prospects can act on those instincts by selling the country's bonds—in other words, reducing exposure—but not by selling short. Those constraints do not apply, however, to hedge funds, whose clients have substantial net worth and, in most cases, will allow fund managers to invest their money in high-risk, high-return ventures.

The hedge fund for which Binder worked, headquartered in the Bahamas, was part of South Africa's Standard Bank Group, and its clients were mostly wealthy Europeans and Latin Americans. After cutting its holdings of Argentine bonds at the beginning of 2001, the fund began taking short positions in the bonds, having identified Argentina as an emerging market that was likely to underperform other countries; it balanced that stance by maintaining a "long" position in Russia. "We made pretty good money—not as much as we could have, but we certainly made money where most people lost," Binder said.

Though sometimes reviled as speculation of the most unproductive sort, short-selling can help markets function more efficiently by sending early signals of investor pessimism and by ensuring that enough sellers are around to match buyers. In Argentina's case, the nature of some of the short-selling added a dash of irony to the practice. According to a number of market insiders, the short-sellers included some of the proprietary trading desks at big Wall Street firms, which invest and trade their firms' capital for the firms' own accounts. Having made money during Argentina's boom period by bringing the country's bonds to market, those same firms—albeit different departments—were profiting again by speculating on the bonds' decline.

Whoever the short-sellers were, there was no disputing their impact. The greater their trading activities, the further Argentine bonds fell, driving *riesgo país* ever higher. By mid-March, at the time of López Murphy's resignation, all the market gains generated by the *blindaje* had been lost, with yields on Argentine bonds back to where they had been before the package. The economy was still showing scant signs of life, and the chances seemed more remote than ever that the government could make the fiscal adjustments necessary to achieve debt sustainability.

Even some of the market players who had once toasted Argentina's reforms were now talking as if the country had been an obvious train wreck all along. One prominent example was José Luis

Daza, who left his job at J.P. Morgan in early 2001 to become Deutsche Bank's chief debt strategist for emerging markets.

"For several years now it's been very clear that Argentina's government spending has been growing at a pace that is unsustainable and growing mostly funded by debt," Daza said at an event sponsored by the Americas Society in New York on April 6. "But those who used to finance that spending are no longer willing to do it."

[CHAPTER 6]

Robbing Pedro to Pay Pablo

FOR SOMEONE who is trying to make the case that a new day is dawning, breakfast can be a favorable time to hold a meeting. The early morning atmospherics worked well for Domingo Cavallo when he first met Paul O'Neill, the new U.S. Treasury secretary, on April 4, 2001, during a gathering of finance ministers from thirty-four Western Hemisphere countries in Toronto.

Cavallo, the father of convertibility, was back as Argentina's economy minister. In an electrifying move aimed at resurrecting the country's sagging fortunes, de la Rúa had named Cavallo—one of his rivals in the 1999 presidential race—to replace López Murphy on March 20 and entrusted him with sweeping authority. Brimming with the self-confidence for which he had become known when he launched his plan in 1991 to quash hyperinflation, Cavallo wanted everyone—the Argentine public, the markets, international economic officials—to know that he expected to perform the same sort of miracle again.

That was the message he brought to his breakfast with O'Neill. Referring to a presentation O'Neill had made to the group the night before about his long involvement with the global economy, Cavallo told the Treasury secretary: "You've always lived with globalization. I've always lived with crises." He then recited a litany of crises he had handled during his public career, including the hyperinflation of 1990–1991 and the tequila episode in 1995.

O'Neill asked the obvious question: How did Argentina's current crisis compare with the others Cavallo had dealt with? "Much easier," Cavallo replied.

By all accounts of people who were present at the meeting, O'Neill seemed thrilled by what he heard from Cavallo. The Treasury chief was especially pleased with Cavallo's assertion that he intended to quell the crisis without seeking any additional money from the international community beyond the loans pledged in the *blindaje* program. O'Neill told reporters later that day that he was "enormously impressed" with Cavallo, and at one point described him as "a hero."

It was a promising start to an important relationship between two of the most headstrong policymakers in the world.

After nearly a quarter century in the top executive ranks of corporate America, O'Neill had become convinced that just about any seemingly intractable problem could be resolved by individuals who refused to let themselves be restrained by artificial limits. His own life was a testament to the boundlessness of human possibility: His father was an Army sergeant who became an attendant in a Veterans Administration hospital, and the family lived in homes lacking running water and indoor plumbing. A graduate of California's Fresno State University with a master's degree in public administration from Indiana University, O'Neill went to work in 1961 as a systems analyst at the Veterans Administration and rose through the civil service ranks to become deputy director of the White House Budget Office during the administration of Gerald Ford. He moved to the private sector in 1977, first at International Paper Company, where he became president in 1985, and then at Alcoa, the Pittsburgh-based aluminum giant, whose board appointed him CEO in 1987 at a time when the company was floundering financially. Although O'Neill knew next to nothing about aluminum when he took the helm, his tenure at Alcoa transformed the corporation. He decreed that the elimination of workplace injuries would become the firm's top priority—because, as he told his managers, a focus on safety was the best way to show employees that they were valued as human beings, and thus the best way to win their cooperation for the improvements in productivity needed to restore a healthy bottom line. By the time he retired as CEO in 1999, Alcoa was not only the most accident-free major industrial company in the United States but also one of its most profitable.

Appointed at age sixty-six to the Treasury secretary's job on the strength of recommendations from former Ford administration colleagues such as Alan Greenspan and Dick Cheney, O'Neill encountered difficulties in adjusting from his role as a captain of industry despite his previous experience in Washington. His quirky perfectionism became a subject of ridicule following media reports that he was devoting large amounts of time to reducing workplace accidents in the Treasury's vast bureaucracy. Capable of using wit and sarcasm to great effect, he was soon creating a stir both in markets and in Congress with tart-tongued comments that reflected the delight he took in debunking conventional wisdom. Acknowledging that years of slavish repetition by Treasury chiefs about their devotion to a "strong dollar" meant little in policy terms, he told a German newspaper that what really mattered to the value of the greenback was the fundamental strength of the U.S. economy—an utterly sensible observation that nonetheless sent the dollar plunging. Deriding Wall Street traders as "people who sit in front of a flickering green screen," he told the *Wall Street Journal* that they "are not the sort of people you would want to help you think about complex questions."

But it was the subject of financial crises and IMF bailouts that seemed to elicit the most irascibility from O'Neill, who was unsparing in his criticism of the Clinton administration for the multibillion-dollar IMF loans it had engineered for emerging markets. "The IMF rides in on its horse and throws money at everybody, and the private sector people get to take their money out," he blustered in an interview with the *International Herald Tribune*. His undersecretary for international affairs, John Taylor, had once advocated the abolition of the Fund while a professor at Stanford University. The media was soon using the term "tough love" to describe the administration's views, because O'Neill and his colleagues suggested that countries and financial markets, like wayward children, sometimes needed harsh discipline rather than rescue. The IMF, O'Neill told members of Congress, had been "too often associated with failure," and in an April 19 speech, he declared: "As we in the finance ministries of the world talk glibly about billions of dollars of support for policies gone wrong, we need to remember that the money we are entrusted with came from plumbers and carpenters who sent 25 percent of their $50,000 annual income to us for wise use."

His new Argentine counterpart was no less reticent about speaking his mind. Since leaving President Carlos Menem's cabinet in 1996, Cavallo had formed his own small party and, in books and lectures, delivered withering blasts at the venality and muddled-headed policies he saw as threatening the economic legacy he had bequeathed. The more he watched Argentina's fortunes sink, the more openly he let his belief be known that the country's salvation depended on returning him the levers of economic power. "I am a legend," he told a group of foreign investors at a dinner speech in March 2001 shortly before his appointment to head the Economy Ministry. The power of his intellect, his incorruptibility, and the sincerity of his desire for his country's well-being were undeniable; the only question was whether he had a sense of proportion about himself.

Upon his return as minister, Cavallo spoke and acted as if it would be but a short time before Argentina's problems would melt away, with convertibility intact and the government's debts honored in full. "In just a couple of months, years at most, the whole topic of debt in Argentina will be like it is in Australia, or Canada, or any European country, where nobody even talks about it," he told *La*

Nación on March 25. A few days later, he told the *Financial Times,* "You are going to begin to see results in the next few months. 2001 is going to be very similar to 1991, in terms of economic development."

Even though the government was overshooting the deficit target for the first quarter by about $1 billion, Cavallo vowed that he would meet the $6.5 billion budget-deficit target for the year. To do so, he said, he would eschew spending cuts of the sort envisioned in the *blindaje* or the ones championed by López Murphy; rather, he would focus on spurring growth and raising more tax revenue. Within ten days of taking office, he won extraordinary powers from Congress that allowed the executive branch to change business regulations by decree. Lawmakers also approved his proposal for a tax on financial transactions, plus reductions in tariffs on imported equipment (to aid industrial companies), which were offset by increases in tariffs on imported consumer goods. Reflecting his dominance of the nation's political scene, the cover of the magazine *Noticias* portrayed him as Hannibal Lecter, alongside this caption: "Voracious and insatiable, his ambition could save the country."

But the markets did not respond. *Riesgo país* hovered in the high 800s to low 1,000s in late March through mid-April, reflecting the increasingly widespread view that the country's debt burden was simply too large, its economy too torpid, and its chances for escaping its trap too remote. As Cavallo charged ahead, reminding audiences of the "Lightning" nickname his mother had given him, even some of the top policymakers at the Economy Ministry were disconcerted by his overweening behavior. "He had this very simplistic idea, 'I did this kind of thing in the 1990s, and it was a success, and I will do it again,'" said Nicolas Gadano, a former undersecretary of the treasury, whose comments were typical of a number of ministry officials. "I was thirty-three then. Cavallo was like a myth for me. In April 1991, I was finishing a master's in economics. Cavallo was ... *Cavallo.* When he asked me to stay in the government, I said, 'Of course.' But he would say, 'I know you don't believe me, but the economy will grow ten percent this year.' He expected just his face on TV sets to produce results. Sometimes we thought, this guy is out of his mind."

The phone rang at Tomás Reichmann's suburban Maryland home on the afternoon of Saturday, April 14. As Reichmann and other IMF officials were about to learn, weekends could be especially hectic under the Cavallo regime, because that was when the economy minister tended to spring surprises.

The call was from Stan Fischer, who needed "ammunition"—and quickly. The IMF's first deputy managing director explained that Cavallo had just informed him that he planned to make an announcement that evening, which Fischer wanted to talk him out of for fear that it would generate another damaging bout of market turmoil.

The announcement concerned a proposal to modify the convertibility system at some point in the future so that instead of being linked purely to the dollar, the peso would be linked to a blended average of two currencies, the dollar and the euro. In strictly economic terms, the idea had some merit. The peso's worrisome strength stemmed from its link to the dollar, which was more than a little artificial, because only about 15 percent of Argentina's trade was with the United States, while nearly a quarter of it was with the European Union. Before taking office, Cavallo had made speeches suggesting it was time to alter the convertibility formula, and under his proposal Europe's common currency, which was then trading at about 89 cents per euro, would be used in setting the peso's value once it reached a one-to-one parity with the dollar.

But the idea was anathema to the IMF, which, despite its own reservations about convertibility, feared that any tinkering with the system would undermine the one major benefit it conferred, namely the markets' faith in the government's resolve to stay the course. Knowing that Fischer understood the point well, Reichmann suggested that Cavallo should be told to let sleeping dogs lie—to avoid any move that would sow doubts and confusion about convertibility. But nothing could dissuade Cavallo, who forged ahead with his announcement at a news conference a couple of hours later.

Whatever the validity of the arguments, the episode was typical of a pattern that emerged as the year wore on: Cavallo would unveil major initiatives, often late on Fridays or during weekends, and often with very short notice to the IMF or with little consultation. This method of operating "irritated the hell" out of Horst Köhler in particular, recalled Claudio Loser, who as chief of the Western Hemisphere Department witnessed a number of their interactions. "The chemistry between the Latin Cavallo and the Germanic Köhler was terrible." Compounding the Fund's unease was word from within the Economy Ministry that in some cases, Cavallo's own aides were being kept in the dark about his moves, and their last-minute objections unheeded—a particularly worrisome example being Finance Secretary Daniel Marx, for whom Fund staffers had high regard.

"Cavallo's view of economic policy is, it is the responsibility of the country, and the IMF decides whether to support it. He won't ask permission," said Guillermo Mondino, who was chief economic adviser during Cavallo's reign at the ministry. "We called them [the IMF] before [making announcements], but sometimes maybe just half an hour before. The IMF was justified to respond the way they did. They felt, 'These guys are fucking up, they don't ask us, they don't tell us, and they ask us to go to the board and defend this program?'" But often, he added, the seemingly impulsive behavior of Cavallo and his team was fueled by the hesitancy of Reichmann and his colleagues. "You're trying to put out a fire, fighting a bank run or whatever, dealing with a bureaucrat saying, 'Well, I don't know,'" Mondino said, using a timorous voice to mock Fund staffers.

For his part, Cavallo justified his methods by citing the remarks Köhler had made upon becoming IMF managing director emphasizing the importance of countries "owning" their policies. Cavallo heartily approved of Köhler's views on this subject; he had published a magazine column praising them, and he recalled that when he became economy minister he sent a copy of the column to Köhler, as a way of breaking the ice. But Cavallo's view of "ownership" struck IMF officials as taking the concept to ridiculous extremes—something closer to "sole proprietorship," as one grim joke among Fund staffers had it.

"It may be that the staff of the IMF, and maybe also Köhler, thought that I did not offer them explanations well in advance of implementing moves," Cavallo told me. "I don't think Stan Fischer would say that, because I had discussions with him often. But one aspect of dealing with crises: You cannot take a long time to explain what you are going to do."

In any event, neither Cavallo's mystique nor his maneuvers were having the desired effect on market sentiment, to his immense frustration. On April 23, he released "An Open Letter to the Markets," in which he wrote, "To be honest, I am a bit surprised by how little credit we have been given for getting the fiscal numbers back on track." He also took aim at pessimists like Calomiris, who in an op-ed article in the *Wall Street Journal* titled "Argentina Can't Pay What It Owes" went public with his proposal for the government to take the haircut route. "I have thought a lot as to why honest people may dare write a recommendation as to how Argentina may default," Cavallo wrote. "Who could conceive such a destructive idea for a country, and be bold enough to propose it? . . . There is a complete misunderstanding (almost omission) of the costs that a compulsory restructuring of our debt would have." In an op-ed he authored for the *Financial Times,* Cavallo vowed that "Argentina will not be lured by the call of the sirens" who were calling for a restructuring. "Property rights are a basic principle of a well-organized economy and debt contracts are most certainly a fundamental aspect of this," he wrote. "It is ludicrous to think that a program that will build on market principles, structural reforms and an effective insertion in international markets will begin with debt restructuring."

But evidence was already mounting to support the concern

Calomiris had raised about what would happen if the country bulled ahead in trying to ensure that it could honor its full obligations. The government, unable to raise cash in international markets, was turning increasingly to the nation's domestic banking system to obtain the funding it needed. That very month, in fact, the Economy Ministry had pressed some of the nation's biggest banks into buying about $3 billion in government bonds, at yields substantially below prevailing market rates. To entice the bankers into accepting the bonds, Cavallo engineered a change in banking regulations enabling the banks to count the bonds as part of their legally required cash reserves. (The move escalated a clash between Cavallo and the respected central bank governor, Pedro Pou, who was forced to resign and was replaced by a man close to Cavallo.) This was one of several instances in which the government would use its powers of "moral suasion" over the banks in 2001 to induce them into providing financing. "We were pressured," said the CEO of one Argentine bank. "I'm not saying, government officials called and threatened, 'We will close your bank.' But there were a lot of calls, more than normal," mostly from the Economy Ministry.

Whatever influence Cavallo had over the banks, the limitations on his ability to beguile investors at large became starkly clear the same day his letter to the markets was released, when the government was forced to cancel a treasury bill auction for lack of investors willing to buy at acceptably low interest rates. *Riesgo país* remained in the 980 to 1,200 range through mid-May.

At those levels of country risk, Argentina's chances of pulling through were getting very slim. There is no magic figure, of course, at which country risk is so high that bankruptcy becomes inevitable. But in Argentina's case, if it were to stay above 1,000 for a sustained period of time, the debt dynamics were explosive using any reasonable set of economic assumptions. The commensurately high rates of interest for the Argentine private sector would snuff out growth, and to reduce its debt burden, the government would have to run an extraordinarily austere budget policy—so austere as to be both politically inconceivable and economically damaging to a country already in recession. To be sure, the possibility that *riesgo país* might come down to more moderate heights could not be ruled out. But that would require a monumental shift in market sentiment. Thus, the fear of default, as reflected in the high yields on Argentine government bonds, looked more and more like a self-fulfilling prophecy.

Michael Mussa, the IMF's chief economist, was as frank as a Fund official can be in public when he was asked about Argentina at a news conference on April 26 during the IMF–World Bank spring meetings. "It is going to be very difficult to get the domestic economy moving forward if interest rates remain a thousand basis points above U.S. Treasuries," Mussa said. Köhler, by contrast, put a brave face on the situation, telling reporters the next day: "No doubt, there is some concern about the situation in Argentina, but indeed, I do think that everything is in place to find a good solution to overcome the problems." And the Fund disbursed a scheduled $1.2 billion tranche of its $14 billion loan on May 21 with a press release quoting Köhler as saying, "Continued strong implementation of the program should restore macroeconomic stability . . . the Argentine authorities have responded promptly and effectively in difficult circumstances."

Internally, the Fund's assessment was much less optimistic. "The probability of a full-blown crisis in Argentina has increased," the Argentina task force wrote in a memo to management in late April. "The avoidance of such an outcome seems unlikely, though not impossible."

Bleak as the outlook was, some of Argentina's old "friends" on Wall Street still had a card to play.

David Mulford, a man with TV news-anchor looks and a sonorous voice to match, was the sort of financier who enjoyed private access to top economic policymakers around the globe, and on the evening of March 20, on his way home to London from a meeting in Chile, he flew into Buenos Aires for an important rendezvous. The next day Mulford, who headed the international business of Credit Suisse First Boston, was ushered into Cavallo's office. It was the first day after Cavallo's triumphant return as economy minister.

The two men had a long history of dealing with each other. During much of Cavallo's previous tenure as economy minister, Mulford had been U.S. Treasury undersecretary for international affairs, and he had devoted considerable attention to Argentina in his capacity as architect of the Treasury's plan for reducing the indebtedness of Latin nations. Their relationship had deepened when Mulford joined CSFB, which handled the privatization of Argentina's state oil company in 1993 and became a major underwriter of Argentine government bonds.

Now the silver-haired Mulford had an idea for a deal that would dwarf the ones that had come before. He proposed a debt "swap," in which Argentina's bondholders—hundreds of thousands of investors, holding dozens of different issues—would be given the opportunity to exchange their old bonds for new ones, on a purely voluntary basis. The purpose was to eliminate a problem that was disturbing the markets—the large amounts of interest and principal payments Argentina was required to make during the 2001–2005 period. Under the swap, the payments would be stretched out so that much more would fall due in the years after 2005. In this way, Argentina would gain time to recover and avoid default.

Bond transactions are not usually the stuff of great passion. But the *megacanje,* or megaswap, as this one would come to be known, ranks among the most infamous deals that Wall Street has ever peddled to a government—and with good reason: For CSFB and a half dozen other Wall Street firms, the megaswap would be a bonanza, earning them more than $90 million in fees paid by the Argentine government. For Argentina, it would be a bust, rendering the country's solvency even more questionable than it was already.

Swaps of this sort were fast becoming the bread and butter of firms like Mulford's. No longer were Wall Streeters minting money in emerging markets by bringing to market the securities of governments and corporations. Now they were looking for new kinds of transactions. According to an article in the September 2001 issue of *LatinFinance*:

> These are lean times for investment bankers, especially those working in Latin America. It is years since business has been this bad. Fees have crumbled ... Wall Street firms are under pressure to keep deals flowing to cover their large overheads. As Rick Liebars, head of origination at Cabot, says: "Some banks have very large teams—not just on the origination side, but in research, trading and back office as well. If we're not seeing desperation now, give it a couple of months and we certainly will." In the words of another banker, the biggest players have a lot of mouths to feed and even a deal at half the price it was is better than none at all.

The new name of the game was "liability management"—that is, arranging for debtors to stretch out or reduce their debt burdens, as another article in the magazine *Euromoney* explained around the same time:

> Such banks as J.P. Morgan, Goldman Sachs, Salomon Smith Barney and more recently CSFB have been aggressively pursuing liability management transactions to prop up dwindling margins from emerging debt underwriting. "Frankly, if we are going to make any money, we have to be in this liability management stuff," says a banker at one of the top firms. ... When new issue work is thin, liability management transactions are also a good way of justifying large emerging market sales, trading and research infrastructure.

In most cases, these types of deals were used by countries with firm market standing to save money. Mexico and Brazil, for example, had used swaps to retire a few billion dollars worth of old, high-interest bonds that for technical reasons were difficult to trade, offering in their stead new, lower-interest bonds that were easier to trade. Argentina's situation, however, was different. The Argentine government in 2001 was in a position not terribly dissimilar from a small businessman so desperate for cash to meet the immediate demands of creditors that he agrees to borrow at usurious rates from a loan shark. Not that Wall Streeters like Mulford were going to send thugs around to break Cavallo's legs if Argentina failed to pay its obligations, but the deal Mulford was proposing would increase Argentina's debt costs rather than decrease them; that was the price the country would have to pay to postpone its debt payments.

There was an important distinction, after all, between the sort of transaction Mulford was proposing—in which investors would *voluntarily* exchange their bonds—and a haircut in which the bondholders would be forced to accept less than the full amount due. As a general rule, bondholders will not voluntarily agree to a substantial reduction in the value of their claims. They will not accept a lower or stretched-out principal payment, for example, unless offered some kind of compensation such as higher interest payments; and they will not accept lower interest unless offered some other form of compensation or threatened with some sort of penalty. They may recognize that a country cannot afford to pay all its debts, and that as a group bondholders would be wise to accept, say, 70 cents on the dollar instead of 100. But as individuals, each bondholder has the incentive to hold out for 100 cents and hope that the other bondholders settle for less—a phenomenon economists call the "collective action" problem. Thus if a deal is voluntary and involves no coercion or threat inducing bondholders to go along, bondholders must be offered a deal that entitles them to as much or more than the one they already have.

When Mulford first approached Cavallo with the megaswap proposal on March 21, the minister's initial reaction was that he might consider it later. He saw no need to embark on such a scheme right away since, with all the optimism that goes with the first day on a new job, he was anticipating that the economy and market confidence would quickly begin recovering. But after seeing for several weeks that his policies were not having the market impact he was counting on, he agreed to let Mulford proceed, along with bankers from J.P. Morgan who were working on a similar idea, and plans for the swap were unveiled in early May.

The appeal the deal had for Cavallo was obvious. Mulford's basic message to him was that for reasons unrelated to his stewardship of the economy, Argentina was facing a liquidity crisis, with more than $80 billion in principal and interest coming due in the next four and a half years that the government would be hard-pressed to pay in full. There was no need to default or impose a haircut; investors would be happy to reschedule $15 billion or so of the amount to be payable later, with much of the relief coming in 2001 and 2002. Once that was accomplished, markets would start to settle down, giving Cavallo the leeway he needed to work his magic. To promote the swap, the two men embarked on a "road show" to the world's financial capitals in May 2001. The deal "shows a new way for the future," Mulford told an audience of investors at the St. Regis Hotel in New York. "It is large, it is bold, it is broad, but it is unique in the sense it is a private market exercise." To reporters in Buenos Aires, he asserted that the swap was "essential to long-term success in restoring Argentine growth."

Ridicule from a number of quarters greeted this line of reasoning as the swap's terms became clear. Desirable as it might be to reduce near-term payments, critics said, the cost was far too high because of the huge amount of additional debt that Argentina would owe on the new bonds in the years 2006–2030 and the heavy burden of paying interest on them. The calculations were complex, because the swap involved replacing old bonds with five new ones of different maturities (one maturing in 2006, two maturing in 2008, one in 2018, and another in 2031). The 2018 bond illustrated the delayed costs: Although it required no interest payments until late 2006, interest was payable thereafter at an annual rate of 12.25 percent, and the deferred interest would be added to principal, making its total yield equivalent to 15.24 percent.

"The Argentine Exchange: Robbing Pedro to Pay Pablo" was the headline on the swap in a June 5 report by the independent research firm CreditSights. "The unambiguous winners from the exchange are the investment banks," said the report, written by Peter Petas. "The losers, ultimately, will be the Argentine people and whatever investors are unlucky enough to be holding Argentine debt when the music stops (and it will) and the country is forced into a coercive exchange or outright default." In a like vein, Walter Molano of BCP Securities told his clients, "The swap is akin to a modern Treaty of Versailles, with Argentina moving closer to insolvency and the brink of disaster."

The IMF, though not directly involved in the transaction, had kind words for it in public. Jack Boorman, head of the Policy Development and Review Department, attended the presentation for New York investors where he said that the Fund viewed the swap as "an important complement to the authorities' program of economic stabilization and reform." But behind the scenes at the IMF, the swap drew scorn from the Research Department, whose director, Mussa, was then in his last days as the Fund's chief economist. (Köhler had asked him to leave, a request Mussa said he was happy to oblige.) After the swap was completed, Mussa's anger boiled over in a table-pounding, finger-pointing exhibition in front of the managing director concerning a paper prepared by other departments that assessed the swap's impact in a generally positive light. Mussa's staff had calculated that the transaction would save $12 billion in debt payments from 2001 to 2005 while adding $66 billion in payments from 2006 to 2030—and at an effective interest cost of 16 percent for lengthening the maturities, well above the economy's potential growth rate even under the best of circumstances. To borrow so much at such high cost made no sense for a country that was already having grave difficulty convincing the markets of its ability to pay its debt, in Mussa's view. Other Fund officials disputed his calculations, and contended that the megaswap was necessary to buy time even at a high long-term cost. But a number of those who challenged Mussa have since acknowledged that he was basically right even if his figures may have been exaggerated. Mussa correctly saw that the megaswap "would just prolong the agony," Reichmann recalled. And in a report written in 2003, the Fund staff conceded that the deal, far from buoying the markets' spirits, "contributed to concerns about [Argentina's] solvency."

The swap's champions proclaimed the deal a triumph when the final results were tallied on June 3, 2001, showing that bondholders owning $29.5 billion worth of securities—considerably more than initially expected—had swapped their bonds on the terms offered. "We have beaten those who were betting against Argentina," Cavallo declared, with de la Rúa at his side. Mulford, meanwhile, predicted that "the market will now recover," with yields falling so that "future financing will be done at substantially lower rates." In response to concerns about the increase in Argentina's long-term debt burden, Mulford retorted that the country first had to get itself out of its financial squeeze by reducing its near-term money-raising requirements, and it could curtail its high interest costs later, perhaps by buying back some of the bonds. "If they are growing and successful and so on, they can take into consideration various operations that would address that [high interest] problem," he said.

The critics were not impressed that a large number of bondholders had elected to participate in the swap. The important issue, after all, was not whether bondholders found the deal attractive but whether it left Argentina better able overall to service its debt and whether it reassured markets on that score. Among the skeptics were economists at Bear Stearns, who saw the swap as "dramatically" increasing Argentina's long-term debt burden despite the near-term relief. The markets, Bear Stearns predicted in a June 4 report, would experience "a short honeymoon period, and then a renewed focus on the still-recessionary economy."

That turned out to be right on the money. Government bond prices gained about 7 percent by June 12. But by the following week, the bonds were back in the tank, driving *riesgo país* close to 1,000. Once again, Argentina's hopes for salvation were going unfulfilled.

The markets' disappointing reaction to the megaswap is subject to conflicting explanations, none of which can be proved. Mulford and other bankers involved in the deal have blamed the Argentines, accusing them of making two market-rattling mistakes. First, the government continued auctions of treasury bills in which local banks were reportedly pressured to buy, upsetting market participants who had thought such policies were to be halted. Second, Cavallo sprang another weekend surprise that some analysts interpreted as undermining convertibility. On June 18 he announced that a subsidy would be paid to exporters, and a duty would be charged to importers, to help stimulate competitiveness in the manner envisioned by his proposed dollar-euro mixed peg for the peso. The measure was akin to a 7 percent devaluation of the peso for trade purposes, and Cavallo had difficulty convincing experts that he was sticking religiously to the principle of one peso per dollar.

Although these moves were unhelpful, it is a stretch to call them the cause of the letdown that followed the megaswap. The markets bounced back quickly from the initial drubbing they took in response to Cavallo's tinkering with peso valuation, and then they resumed falling a few days later. In sum, the swap did not produce the miraculous effects that Mulford had predicted, and it arguably made matters worse.

This bitter pill was all the more unpalatable in light of the disclosure in mid-June that the seven Wall Street firms managing the swap were getting $137 million in fees thanks to the large number of bondholder participants. The fees were divided into three installments, and therein lies one small solace: The firms received only the first two installments, because the third came due after the government's default. Thus the payments the firms actually received totaled a mere $90 million.

First the *blindaje,* then the *megacanje,* and still Argentina was in dire straits—a ship with a cracked mast, a sputtering engine, and a hurricane continuing to bear down on it. Efforts to restart the engine had failed, and hoisting a new set of sails had only rendered the vessel less seaworthy.

By late June and early July, the markets were in full flight, with the megaswap fast receding into memory. The chief cause was a fount of dismal news about the country's inability to generate either economic growth or a political consensus for fiscal austerity. The government announced on June 20 that GDP had shrunk at a 2.1 percent annual rate in the first quarter; a few days later came word that in May supermarket sales had fallen 2 percent and shopping center sales 13 percent from the same month a year earlier; soon thereafter tax revenue for June was reported to be 4.9 percent below the previous year's level, another sign that the economy was continuing to contract. At the same time, a nasty dispute erupted over demands by the provincial governors for money they said the federal government owed them to cover their June bills, which included obligations such as school lunches for children. Public workers demanding unpaid wages, and jobless people seeking work, were taking to the streets in growing numbers to intensify pressure on de la Rúa, who was increasingly portrayed in the media as a doddering leader lacking control over the ruling alliance.

A new low came on July 10. At its bond auction that day, the government was forced to offer record yields of 14 percent to attract buyers of three-month bills. Paying such high rates to borrow for such a short period was the death knell of many a debtor nation. Even Argentine banks, which had been pressured by the government in recent months to buy its paper, were now balking at adding to their holdings. At that point, Cavallo said he had come to the realization that "we don't have credit." In a speech that evening he unveiled another surprise—a radical shift in fiscal policy known as the "zero deficit."

Having previously scorned spending cuts on the grounds that they would slow the economy, Cavallo announced plans for draconian budget reductions aimed at completely eliminating any need for government borrowing. "We have to go immediately to a zero deficit on the national as well as the provincial level," he said. The zero-deficit rule entailed cuts of 13 percent in government salaries and pensions, and those pensions and salaries would be raised in future months only if tax revenues rose sufficiently to allow it. If tax revenues fell *below* expected levels in a given month, the government would impose even bigger spending cuts at that time. This initiative was entirely Cavallo's; IMF officials were caught off guard.

The political response was harsh. The Argentine media were full of stories featuring pensioners asking how they could be expected to tighten their belts when they already were barely scraping by on their meager monthly dole. Cavallo's aura as a miracle worker seemed dimmer than ever; the cover of the magazine *Veintitrés* featured his picture with clown paint and a sad frown, and in an act of disrespect even some of his detractors found reprehensible, protesters showed up at his daughter's wedding on July 14 and pelted the guests with eggs. The most discouraging reaction, though, came from the markets. Investors and traders might have been expected to applaud the zero-deficit policy for the priority it placed on ensuring the timely payment of their claims over the political needs of the government to pay pensioners and civil servants. Instead, the markets viewed the policy as an act of desperation and delivered a resounding vote of no confidence in Argentina's ability to continue meeting its obligations, as *riesgo país* soared that week from 1,100 to 1,600.

To some, the implications were obvious: Conventional remedies—international rescue loans, voluntary exchanges, government spending cuts—were failing. The Argentine government would have to be told that its debt was unsustainable, and that a restructuring was required. Indeed, one could draw the conclusion that this sort of message should have been sent months earlier.

That was the view expressed by Nouriel Roubini at a private IMF conference on July 26 attended by many top Fund officials. Roubini, who had returned to his New York University professorship from the Treasury, ventured that with hindsight, Argentina would have been better off with a forced debt restructuring than the *blindaje*. Using the term "concerted PSI" (private-sector involvement) to refer to a forced restructuring, Roubini stated:

> While one could argue that . . . the catalytic approach had to be given a chance . . . one can otherwise argue that failure to provide more meaningful and concerted PSI early on probably made things eventually worse. . . . Faced with a political inability to solve its fiscal and structural problems and facing a large debt burden, the country is now teetering on the verge of a default that may imply massive losses to investors as well as significant disruption of economic activity in the country. . . . The decision to avoid concerted forms of PSI probably ended up being a mistake.

The argument fell on deaf ears. If it had been a mistake to give Argentina the first IMF loan, that mistake was about to be repeated in spades.

[CHAPTER 7]

Doubling a Losing Bet

HEADS OF STATE meeting lower-ranking officials from other countries usually stick to pleasantries and generalities rather than delving into the nitty-gritty of policy disputes or negotiations, and that was the pattern at the Casa Rosada on August 3, 2001, when Fernando de la Rúa welcomed John Taylor, the U.S. undersecretary of the Treasury for international affairs, who was on a hastily arranged visit to Buenos Aires. The Argentine president talked about his country's history and culture and its friendship with the United States. But there was no mistaking the meaning of the soulful appeal he delivered to Taylor: "I am looking at the man who holds the fate of my country in his hands."

Seven months had passed since the agreement for the *blindaje*. Of the $14 billion that Argentina was to borrow under that program, the Fund had disbursed $6 billion, with the rest scheduled for disbursement later in 2001 and in 2002. Now the Argentine government wanted an "augmentation"—a new IMF loan of up to $8 billion, above and beyond the $14 billion—and it wanted the money pronto.

The country's economy was in its deepest hole yet. Throughout July, following the announcement of the zero-deficit law on July 10 and more indicators of falling production and sales, *riesgo país* hovered in the 1,400 to 1,600 range, corresponding to borrowing rates for the government of about 19 to 22 percent. Although the government was not raising money from private investors at that stage, the high yields demanded by the markets were sending a relentlessly pessimistic message about the country's chances for escaping its trap, and they were driving up interest costs for Argentine businesses to new highs. The most urgent problem was in the banking system, where $5 billion in deposits, about 7 percent of the total, flowed out of the banks in July—not a full-blown run but plenty worrisome. Much of this activity, which was conducted by corporations and large investors rather than small retail depositors, involved converting pesos into dollars and moving the money abroad. This meant that the central bank's reserves of dollars were also dwindling fast; at the time of Taylor's August 3 visit, reserves totaled $20.4 billion, down from $28.8 billion at the beginning of July. At that rate of decline, convertibility was facing a serious threat, because the system required an ample cushion of reserves to cover the supply of pesos. Accordingly, the de la Rúa government was seeking aid from the IMF with the aim of halting the withdrawals from the banks and reversing the decline in reserves. The plan was to deposit the money in the central bank, thereby replenishing reserves and delivering a reassuring message that the supply of cash in the banking system was ample to accommodate all comers.

The stage was being set for another IMF rescue that would attempt to preserve convertibility and keep Argentina from violating its obligations to creditors. Once again, the hope was that a large infusion of money from the Fund would restore calm, ease the concerns of investors and depositors, and give the government time to address credibly its long-term debt problem.

The Argentine government was offering a monumental quid pro quo—the zero-deficit law, which Cavallo had launched with plans for $5.6 billion in spending reductions for 2001 and 2002 including the 13 percent cut in pensions and civil service wages. With the zero deficit, Cavallo was finally moving to the logical extreme of the policy he had initiated in 1991. Convertibility was a legal restriction on the government's ability to print money. Now the government—"out of credit," as Cavallo had acknowledged—was putting a legal restriction on its ability to spend money above and beyond what it could collect in revenue.

Admirable though this additional self-restraint might have been, its timing was abysmal. Such an approach might have been desirable in the past, but at a moment when the country was well into its third year of recession, with unemployment above 16 percent, questions abounded about whether the government could implement such a policy for long, or whether it was even advisable economically. The drastic tightening in fiscal policy could send the economy reeling further, which would cause tax revenue to fall, forcing the government to slash spending anew in an endless tail-chasing exercise. Moreover, the intensified austerity seemed likely to generate a popular revolt—if not in the streets, then in congressional and provincial elections that were looming in mid-October. In addition to the cuts in pensions and government salaries Cavallo was promising, he was vowing to bring the provinces to heel as well, by withholding some federal transfers to them, which would severely curtail their ability to pay their employees and deliver services. To be sure, if the markets were to become convinced that the government's policies were putting the country's debt on a long-term sustainable path, interest rates might come down, confidence might return, and the economy might recover. But not one of Cavallo's other initiatives had generated such a response, and the markets were signaling profound doubts about this one too.

The IMF's stance was that it would back the zero-deficit policy, provided this was truly where the Argentine body politic wished to go under such desperate circumstances. That was Köhler's response when Cavallo first called him at the time he was unveiling the plan.

The Fund was deeply skeptical that the zero deficit would attract much endorsement beyond the confines of the Economy Ministry, so the managing director admonished Cavallo that he must demonstrate broad political support for it rather than implement it by executive decree. Cavallo promised that he would secure congressional enactment of the law, along with backing from the provincial governors. By the end of July, despite strikes and protests by Argentines outraged that their living standards again were being crimped, both houses of Congress had indeed approved the policy, "so I was in a position to tell Köhler, 'Look, we have demonstrated what you requested,'" Cavallo recalled.

Distasteful as the zero-deficit rule might be, the Argentine government could not borrow at affordable rates, so it had no other choice, as Cavallo and his top aides repeatedly emphasized. No other choice, that is, except for default and/or devaluation—and concerning those sorts of options, Argentine officials were as militant as ever in refusing to consider them.

"The Fund said, 'What you're doing [the zero deficit] is not politically sustainable,'" recalled Federico Sturzenegger, who was secretary for economic policy at the Economy Ministry. "We told them, 'What is not politically sustainable is the alternative.'"

That argument packed a wallop. But it begged the question: If what the Argentines were doing was indeed unsustainable, and an IMF loan would only delay "the alternative," then did it make sense to delay, since doing so would cause problems, vulnerabilities, and frustrations to fester? Would it not be better to use the aid to make the alternative as painless as possible, rather than trying to avoid it altogether? The metaphor of a cancer patient helps to illuminate the dilemma: Surgery to remove a tumor may be traumatic, but delaying the operation is obviously unwise if other, less radical remedies have proved ineffective and appear almost certain to allow the malignancy to grow and spread.

During Taylor's trip to Buenos Aires, a déjà vu episode provided a reminder of how low the chances were that an additional IMF loan would succeed. In a meeting with a group of Argentine bankers at the U.S. ambassador's residence, the Treasury undersecretary posed the following question: Suppose the IMF agrees to the augmentation of its current program. In six months, would Argentina have to ask for still more money? His aide, a career Treasury economist named Natan Epstein, interjected that the same question had been asked by Taylor's predecessor, Timothy Geithner, on a visit to Buenos Aires in late 2000 during consideration of the *blindaje*. In fact, Epstein said, when Geithner posed the question, he had been sitting in precisely the same chair Taylor occupied at that moment.

The IMF's board traditionally adjourns for two weeks in August, affording an opportunity for the management and staff to take vacations. In August 2001, the hiatus began as usual, but for many in the Fund's top hierarchy, the rapidly deteriorating situation in Argentina brought a premature end to their holidays. Köhler cut short a vacation in Maine to fly back to Washington, and upon his return he began presiding over discussions in a conference room down the hall from his office. For three days in the second week of August, a pitched battle ensued about the proposal for the additional $8 billion loan.

All of the participants in the discussion accepted the premise that a default, a devaluation, or both would have a severe impact on the Argentine economy. Their concerns included not only the short-term effects of bankrupting people and firms who had borrowed in dollars, but also the prospect of inflicting a lasting blow on the nation's collective attitude toward property rights and the rule of law. As Jack Boorman, director of the Policy Development and Review Department, put it later: "Argentina had a terrible history of credit culture, and it had done a terrific job of signaling to the public [in the 1990s] that it was not going to dishonor contracts. One was loath to give that up." On the other hand, even strong supporters of that argument acknowledged that the debt was so burdensome, the interest cost so high, the economy so weak, and the government's ability to achieve the necessary spending restraint so questionable, that the odds were clearly against the prospect that the IMF loan would enable the country to recover. Much discussion centered on the zero-deficit policy and the likelihood that it would unravel because of the difficulties of forcing the provinces into honoring the principle.

The debate, in short, was a well-balanced, nuanced exposition of the pros and cons of giving Argentina $8 billion more. And as the meetings progressed, participants noticed that Köhler seemed to be growing exasperated with what he was hearing from the Ph.D.'s. Finally, the talks culminated in dramatic fashion with a request from the managing director.

I want each staff member present to state his or her opinion forthrightly, Köhler said, by responding to two questions: First, should the program be augmented as proposed? And second, what are the chances that doing so will succeed?

Polling the staff, to be sure, was not a matter of allowing the majority of the economists to decide the matter; the IMF does not operate by democratic rules. Rather, Köhler seemed to want to force the senior staffers out of their bureaucratic shells, because too many of them were hedging their bets in apparent fear of being associated with a decision that would end badly. Though no formal head count was taken, a majority of those in attendance were opposed to augmenting the program.

The most positive assessments, unsurprisingly, came from members of the Western Hemisphere Department, notably department chief Claudio Loser, as well as Tomás Reichmann. Remarkably, though, the highest probability they attached to success was 30 percent, according to the recollections of several participants. Reichmann recalled his main argument thus: "As an institution, we cannot be seen as the ones who pulled the plug on a country where the legislators and executive branch are making such efforts, so long as there is a chance the situation will work out—especially given the horrendous costs of the alternative."

That worry—that the IMF would be blamed for Argentina's fate if it cut the country off—permeated the arguments of many on the "pro" side. One participant who gave it particularly heavy weight was Thomas Dawson, the director of the IMF's External Relations Department, whose concerns about the Fund's image were naturally paramount. Precisely how many others raised this anxiety, and how strongly they pressed it, is impossible to say; memories differ and fade. But in interviews long after the fact with people who favored giving Argentina the loan, it was striking how many cited the "blame" issue as justification for approving the loan. In some cases, their reasoning was that although the chances of the program's failure might be high, it was not 100 percent, and if the program did fail, it would be better for Argentina if its people blamed their own leaders rather than look for scapegoats overseas.

Spearheading the opposition to the proposed increase in Argentina's loan were the new chief economist and head of research, Kenneth Rogoff, a Harvard professor who had replaced Mussa, and his deputy, Carmen Reinhart. The chances of success, Rogoff said, were essentially zero. Rebutting those who were worried that the Fund would be blamed for Argentina's collapse if it refused to provide additional money, Rogoff and Reinhart emphasized that augmenting the program would impose a substantial encumbrance on Argentina's taxpayers. As Reinhart observed later: "These aren't grants; these are *loans*," which, coming from the IMF, are far more costly to default on than private credits. "And increasing them adds to Argentina's repayment burden."

One of Rogoff's Harvard colleagues, Richard Cooper, had authored a paper that Rogoff thought had an obvious bearing on the issue at hand. The paper showed that in nearly two-thirds of the cases in which a government devalues its currency, the resignation or firing of that nation's finance minister follows within a year, and governments often fall as well. The ramification of this finding is that a country's policymakers, recognizing the likely danger to their tenure in office, will do everything possible to stave off a devaluation; their time horizons will be short, and their decisions distorted, by concern for their political futures. In Argentina's case, Rogoff believed, Cavallo and his colleagues fervently wanted to avoid a crash occurring on their watch, and they were evidently willing to take extreme measures in furtherance of that aim. But the Fund was doing the country no favor by lending in support of that policy, in Rogoff's view. Rather than throw money on the embers of a dying regime, he contended it would be better for the IMF to use the resources available for Argentina to aid the country after a default and devaluation had occurred.

Reinhart, an expert on financial contagion, sought to allay fears expressed by IMF colleagues in some departments that an Argentine default would foment financial crises in other emerging markets—Brazil being one particular source of anxiety. She noted the contrast with the situation in 1998 when the Russian default came as a shock to the global financial system. "A 'credit event' in Argentina is widely anticipated and has been (partly) discounted by the markets for some time," Reinhart and other members of the Research Department staff wrote in a memo dated August 15. "The possibility that a default by Argentina triggers a sharp reversal of capital flows to other countries in South America is therefore relatively small."

The voices in opposition to a bigger loan included one senior member of the Western Hemisphere Department, John Thornton—an unusual dissent at the hierarchical Fund, because he was disagreeing with his department head in a debate with people from elsewhere in the institution. Thornton, a Briton, had worked on Ecuador, a country that ended up in default, and he saw the same dynamics leading Argentina inexorably down the same path. Asserting that the rescue had scant chance of fulfilling its aims, Thornton was particularly dismissive of the zero-deficit rule. Although setting a balanced-budget objective for an entire year might be laudable, he said, the rule being implemented by the Argentines smacked too much of desperation to be credible and was unworkable on a month-by-month basis as the Argentines were proposing. How could the government cut pensions and wages one month, increase them a couple of months later, and then cut them again depending on the flow of tax revenue?

One immensely influential participant at the meeting—Stan Fischer—stayed silent during the survey. Fischer had announced his resignation as first deputy managing director in May; his relationship with Köhler, Fund staffers noted, seemed strained at times, and he no longer had the close ties with the U.S. Treasury that he had enjoyed during the Clinton administration. Like other members of management, Fischer did not express an opinion directly while staff members were being polled because the idea was that staffers should feel comfortable expressing their views freely. But it was no secret that Fischer favored giving Argentina an augmented loan. Staffers recall him as saying that when a country was willing to go to such extraordinary lengths to secure IMF support, the Fund had to go the one last mile, since its Ph.D.'s could not possibly know for certain that their rescue efforts would flop.

The proponents' argument that the rescue stood some chance of success was, in a way, irrefutable. No one could rule out entirely the possibility of a market reception so enthusiastic, and the resumption of an economic cycle so virtuous, that Argentina would undergo a miraculous revival. But the thinness of the reeds upon which the proponents' case rested is apparent in a confidential staff report written at the time for presentation to the executive board that laid out the reasoning for approving the new loan.

As in the past, the report contained projections showing that with the IMF program in place, Argentina's debt dynamics would be stable rather than explosive. According to the projections, the government's debt-to-GDP ratio would rise a bit at first—from 57 percent of GDP in 2001 to nearly 58 percent in 2002—and then decline, to 56.6 percent in 2004, 53 percent in 2007, and 48 percent in 2010. This time, however, the adjective "optimistic" was not quite adequate to describe the assumptions underlying those projections. "Credulity-straining" was more like it.

Despite the economy's weakness, the report assumed that the Argentine government could run a far tougher fiscal policy than it had ever done in the past, thereby enabling the government to pay down a substantial amount of debt with surplus funds. On a primary basis (that is, excluding interest), the report projected budget surpluses from 2002 to 2010 in the range of 3.4 percent of GDP to 5.7 percent of GDP. Even during the boom, Argentina had never come close to such a thrifty policy; the best year was 1993, when the primary surplus was 1.5 percent of GDP.

Moreover, despite the tightness of fiscal policy and the forces that were then exerting recessionary pressure on the economy, the report assumed that Argentina would begin recovering almost immediately in the fourth quarter of 2001 so that the downturn that year would be limited to a 1.4 percent decline; it assumed further that the economy, after rebounding to 2.5 percent growth in 2002, would expand at a 4.5 percent annual rate from 2003 to 2010.

Those figures showed what would be required for Argentina to keep its debt from exploding—an implausibly, extraordinarily favorable confluence of economic and political events. "Implausibly" and "extraordinarily favorable" are not my words; they are the words that the IMF staff wrote in its own postmortem issued in 2004, which looked back at how Argentina's prospects should have been assessed in August 2001 on the basis of more true-to-life assumptions: "With GDP falling at an annual rate of 4 percent and spreads reaching 1,000 basis points [in August 2001], preventing a further rise in the debt ratio would have required an implausibly large primary surplus of about 8 percent of GDP. Thus, by this point, barring some extraordinarily favorable shock, the debt dynamics were clearly unsustainable."

Of course, the confidential staff report written in August 2001 used rosy assumptions because it was aimed at bolstering the argument that giving Argentina a bigger loan package could work. That was the case Köhler wanted to make. On the day after surveying senior staffers' opinions, the managing director convened the group to announce his decision: He would back the proposed augmentation. Like others, Köhler was concerned that Argentines would forever blame their problems on the Fund and the international community if support were cut off at that stage.

Whatever Köhler thought, however, was subject to the approval of the IMF's main shareholder, and a few blocks away from the Fund's headquarters, Bush administration officials were about to bollix up matters still more.

The wail of a small child is an unusual occurrence when the president of the United States is on a conference call with his top aides. But the cries of Will Hubbard, age three, interrupted a phone conversation concerning Argentina's travails in which President Bush was participating from Air Force One. Will's father, Glenn Hubbard, the chairman of the Council of Economic Advisers, who was working from home, acknowledged that the child making the ruckus was his, and quipped, "He's crying for Argentina."

Intense as the IMF's internal debate about Argentina had been, the one under way within the Bush administration was even more bruising. It was somewhat disjointed and disorganized at times, with long-distance conference calls one of the main venues for the highest-level discussions, because during much of the period in question, top members of the administration were on their August vacations. Bush was at his ranch in Crawford, Texas, with National Security Adviser Condoleezza Rice, and Treasury Secretary Paul O'Neill was at his family home in Bethany Beach, Delaware. The president rarely weighed in during the debates, preferring to listen to his advisers, and he generally deferred to O'Neill, whose department held the main authority over U.S. policy concerning the IMF.

The administration's "tough love" policy concerning financial crises was already looking less stiff-necked than initially advertised. A few months earlier, the United States had backed a large increase in the size of the IMF's program for Turkey, a move heavily influenced by concerns about the country's strategic importance as a base for U.S. forces in the Middle East. And in early August, Washington had acquiesced in a $15 billion IMF loan to Brazil aimed at sheltering that country's economy from the turmoil in Argentina. The Bush approach seemed to be just as bailout-prone as the Clinton administration's, which at least had pulled the plug in one major crisis—Russia's.

For seasoned observers of the global economy, the discrepancy between the administration's rhetoric and action was predictable. Many economic policymakers had come to office spouting resolve to resist demands for big international bailouts, only to find that when the chips were down, saying "no" was difficult, especially where major countries were concerned. Bush administration officials insisted they were already taking a harder line on the issue, by limiting bailouts solely to IMF money and refusing to follow the Clinton administration's policy of fattening up rescue packages with U.S. taxpayer funds. But that was a minor departure from prior practice. The more telling explanation that administration officials offered was that they could not act precipitously in halting international rescues, for fear of shocking the global financial system too brutally; rather, the policy would have to be implemented gradually.

Hubbard and his colleagues on the Council of Economic Advisers (CEA) were the most hawkish in arguing that it was time to draw the line, by using U.S. influence at the IMF to block Argentina's request for an augmentation of its loan. Representatives of the National Security Council and the State Department were much more favorably inclined toward giving Argentina more IMF money, as foreign-policy-oriented agencies almost always are in these instances because of concerns about the diplomatic repercussions. In Argentina's case, the risk was that a financial meltdown would undermine not only the forces of economic orthodoxy but also the president's cherished goal of creating a free trade zone in the Western Hemisphere. Bolstering the diplomatic case for granting the loan was a well-orchestrated series of phone calls from Latin American leaders pleading Argentina's case personally to Bush. Nevertheless, as some administration officials pointed out during the debate, Argentina's geopolitical significance paled by comparison with Turkey's, so if the Bush team was going to take a stand against bailouts, Argentina would be a good place to do it.

In between the CEA hawks and the foreign policy doves was the Treasury Department. That may seem surprising, given the criticism O'Neill had leveled at the Clinton administration. But the Treasury is the agency with primary responsibility for ensuring financial stability; it cannot be cavalier about such matters, and within the department, some policymakers were worried that an implosion in Argentina would spread financial turbulence worldwide. Instead of flatly rejecting Argentina's request for a bailout, Treasury officials concluded that the IMF ought to give the country a new sort of loan, different from the ones the Clintonites had mobilized.

The upshot of this decision was to make hash of a rescue that was already a very long-shot proposition. Argentina had been done a disservice in the 1990s by being touted as a model for other developing countries to follow; now, it would be done a disservice by being used as a guinea pig for a novel approach to IMF lending that can only be described as muddle-headed. For this, blame belongs to O'Neill and his international point man, undersecretary John Taylor.

In contrast with O'Neill's shoot-from-the-lip style, the fifty-four-year-old Taylor was a cautious policymaker, often painfully indecisive. Easygoing and pleasant, with a stocky build and thick gray hair, he had a sterling academic background—not in international matters but as a monetary economist; he was the author of a much-cited guideline, known as "the Taylor rule," concerning how central banks should set short-term interest rates. But he frustrated administration colleagues with his penchant for agonizing about matters large and small, and he frequently left people scratching their heads about where he stood.

One striking illustration of this trait was how he handled a request from the White House for recommendations on the issue of whether Argentina should dollarize. Taylor insisted that his staff draft a memo in which the pros and cons for each option (pure dollarization, a floating peso, and a devaluation followed by dollarization) would be almost identical in number, so as not to bias the memo's readers in any particular direction. So Delphic was he on the subject, even in internal discussions, that his staff had no idea whether he favored one option or the other until February 2002— well after Argentina's default and devaluation—when he was put on the spot while testifying before a congressional committee and said that he would have favored dollarization.

Taylor explained the episode, and his propensity to keep his policy conclusions close to his chest, thusly: "I'm a real fan of good, objective memos. I work for the Secretary of the Treasury, and my job is to provide the best advice I can to him. I know I made my views clear to people I was advising, but I'm not the secretary; I'm not the decision maker."

This method of operating was a huge change from the way the Treasury's international policymaking had worked during the Clinton years. Under former secretaries Robert Rubin and Larry Summers, financial crises were an occasion for freewheeling discussions in which staffers would thrash out every conceivable option, with junior staffers encouraged to challenge the opinions of their superiors in front of the secretary or deputy secretary if they wished. Taylor, by contrast, guarded his access to O'Neill and made it clear that he was the one primarily responsible for delivering advice to the secretary on international issues. Another important difference concerned the way the department interacted with other countries. The Clinton-era Treasury had been unafraid to tell crisis-stricken countries exactly what to do; in one extreme case during South Korea's crisis, David Lipton, the undersecretary for international affairs, was dispatched to Seoul to stay in a hotel with the IMF mission and convey to both the Fund and Korean officials what the U.S. government wanted in the rescue program. That was not the style when the international portfolio was run by Taylor, who was much more hands-off. During the Argentine crisis, his attitude sometimes drove White House officials to distraction, especially Gary Edson, the deputy national security adviser responsible for international economics, who hounded Taylor at interagency meetings to engage directly with Argentine officials and exercise the leadership the U.S. government can provide at such junctures. Taylor tended to resist such prodding with the explanation that Washington could not, and should not, order countries around. For much of 2001, Treasury economists found him unwilling even to entertain the idea that Argentina should be challenged on the need to forcibly restructure its debt. Department staffers discussed the idea among themselves but dared not put such radical notions in memos, because they knew Taylor, an optimistic man by nature, wanted to consider only "voluntary" solutions to the problem and was fearful of leaks.

His boss, O'Neill, though agreeing in principle with the view that the Clinton Treasury had been too assertive, was less reticent about voicing his opinion to officials of other countries, and when he got an idea in his head that made sense to him, he did not agonize long. In early August, he waded into the debate over giving Argentina additional IMF money. Speaking by phone with Cavallo, O'Neill declared that using the Fund's resources in a conventional way—to replenish reserves—would not help put the country on a sustainable path.

As Cavallo recalled the conversation, the Treasury secretary asked him what interest rate Argentina was paying on its debt, and when Cavallo said 14 percent, O'Neill replied: "Domingo, you have to find a way to tell your creditors, 'Instead of paying 14 percent, we will pay you 7 percent.'" That raised the specter of Argentina defaulting on its obligations, and Cavallo asked if O'Neill intended that result. When O'Neill assured him he did not, Cavallo said, "Paul, I would be the happiest man in the world if I found the mechanism to get a lower interest rate without going into a formal default." O'Neill said he would get Taylor to work with Cavallo's team and devise an approach for how the new IMF loan could be used toward that end.

From that conversation sprang the idea, refined further in a series of meetings with Argentine officials in Taylor's office, that at least some of the IMF money would be used to help Argentina restructure its debt. How this was supposed to work was never spelled out in detail, and even some of the economists who worked on it later pronounced themselves mystified. One principle was clear: The restructuring would have to be voluntary rather than coercive, and it should be "market-based," in accord with the administration's ideological preferences. Bondholders would have to be enticed, rather than bullied, into swapping their high-interest securities for lower-interest ones, and that was where the IMF's money was supposed to come in: It would give the bondholders some assurance that the new securities had a much greater chance of being repaid than the old ones. Under one proposal that the Treasury and Argentine Economy Ministry officials batted around, for example, the IMF would guarantee the first few interest payments on the new lower-interest bonds.

O'Neill's basic instincts could not be faulted. He recognized that Argentina had to lighten its debt load significantly—give its bondholders a haircut—and he wanted to avoid the sort of rescue he had derided, where "the IMF throws money at everybody and the private-sector people get to take their money out." The problem was that he wanted to achieve this goal with none of the muss and fuss that would naturally arise from forcing the bondholders to accept a reduction in their claims. He seemed convinced that with a bit of financial engineering, a voluntary bond exchange combined with a sprinkling of IMF funds could lead to a major restructuring of Argentina's debt.

Treasury staffers protested that the numbers did not add up: The amount Argentina owed its private creditors—about $95 billion—swamped the amounts of money the IMF was putting on the table, and a few billion dollars in IMF money could not be "leveraged" into a much greater amount of debt restructuring as O'Neill seemed to think. In response, O'Neill went into a mode department officials were becoming all too familiar with—the CEO who expects his subordinates to achieve the goal he sets out for them, by hook or by crook, just as he had done at Alcoa. "You're smart people," O'Neill told them. "Why can't you figure this out?"

Others in the administration agreed with the Treasury staff that O'Neill's proposal concerning how to use the IMF money made no sense, and many saw that the plan's main appeal was that it could be touted as a break from Clintonian policies. Hubbard, in particular, was beside himself. He went to the Treasury to meet Taylor, who defended O'Neill's position, and there ensued such a heated conversation that "I was afraid it would lead to a damage in their relationship that would be very hard to repair," recalled Will Melick, the CEA chief of staff. As much as Hubbard preferred to refuse any IMF loan for Argentina, he said that if a loan must be granted, he would favor making it much bigger than the $8 billion being contemplated, so that it could actually do some good. The middle ground favored by O'Neill and Taylor—a moderate-sized loan, to be used for a voluntary restructuring—was the worst of all possible worlds, in the view of Hubbard, who declared during one interagency conference call that the Treasury position "failed introductory finance."

At the IMF, where intense negotiations were under way with the Argentines on the terms of the new loan after Köhler had given the go-ahead, O'Neill's proposal sparked an uproar. From his new perch in the chief economist's office, Rogoff fired off a scathing memo in mid-August concerning the Treasury-backed plan, which envisioned using $6 billion of IMF funds for restructuring. The memo ridiculed the notion that the money could be leveraged into a restructuring of much greater value. "After one strips out all the window dressing, there is no way to make $6 billion in liquidity worth more than $6 billion in liquidity," the memo stated. "But there are many creative ways to make it less."

Other IMF officials worried that the Treasury's approach would undermine any chance that the Fund program had for restoring confidence in the Argentine economy, by signaling bondholders that they were definitely in store for a haircut at some point in the future. Some at the IMF objected that the use of Fund resources in the manner O'Neill suggested was not only pointless but even improper. Boorman, among others, raised an incisive question: If a country is insolvent, with an unsustainable debt burden, and needs to undergo a debt restructuring, why should taxpayer money be used to soften the blow suffered by private creditors? Shouldn't the creditors simply take their losses?

O'Neill's heels were well dug in, however, and Taylor showed no sign of breaking ranks with his volatile boss, telling those who questioned the approach that some way had to be found of making it work. In the end, a compromise was struck—a "Solomonic decision," in the words of Cavallo, who said Stan Fischer helped to broker it, although its origins are murky. Of the $8 billion in new money that the IMF would lend, $5 billion would go immediately for the conventional purpose of bolstering Argentina's reserves, and $3 billion more would be lent to facilitate a voluntary debt-restructuring plan if Argentina and its creditors were able to forge one.

The term "Solomonic" is rich in irony, for in this case the powers-that-be were cutting the baby into a $5 billion piece and a $3 billion piece. Whatever King Solomon might have thought, the plan moved ahead with the backing of Köhler and O'Neill. Within the G-7, the British, Canadians, Japanese, and others voiced strong objections to the program, including O'Neill's plan to use IMF resources for debt restructuring. Once again, however, their protests stopped short of rebellion.

On August 21, weeks of uncertainty about the IMF's intentions ended when the Fund announced that agreement with Argentina had been reached on the $8 billion augmentation, pending approval by the executive board. The press release noted that in addition to the zero-deficit rule, the authorities in Buenos Aires had pledged that in coming months they would introduce "legislation to reform Argentina's revenue-sharing arrangements with the provinces." That passage seemed straightforward enough, but much head-scratching ensued over the portion of the press release concerning the debt-restructuring proposal. "The [Argentine] authorities are . . . considering the possibility of a voluntary and market-based operation to increase the viability of Argentina's debt profile," the release said, adding that $3 billion of the new loan might be used "to support such an operation."

"It was quite embarrassing for us," recalled Alberto Ramos, who was working on Argentina in the Western Hemisphere Department. "People were calling and asking, 'What is this [the $3 billion] for?' And I had to say, 'I don't know.'" That admission encapsulated the degree to which the United States was making policy for the IMF, even to the bafflement of Fund staffers.

On the day the IMF announced the agreement, Barry Eichengreen of the University of California at Berkeley, one of the world's foremost academic experts on financial crises, happened to be in Argentina. An essay he wrote on August 27, six days after the announcement, was noteworthy for its prescience:

> The local stock market, the Merval, jumped by eight percent on the announcement, as jubilant traders shed their pessimism. The streets were bustling that evening and the tango palaces were packed with dancers. But by the next morning the familiar mood of melancholy resignation had returned. The realization had dawned that the IMF package offered no magic formula for getting growth going again. And without growth, it is hard to see how political support for paying the foreign debt can be sustained.

The nation's fundamental problem, Eichengreen observed, was a matter of "simple arithmetic," because with interest rates so much higher than growth rates, "even a relatively modest debt burden can rise explosively." Although de la Rúa and Cavallo were trying to break out of this bind with the zero-deficit rule, the rule "only makes the problem worse" by requiring spending cuts that cause the economy to contract further, Eichengreen wrote, adding that popular fury over the level of austerity was already high: "When I was in Buenos Aires, it was the university teachers and the employees of the national television network who were marching in the streets. On other days it is other groups." Perhaps growth will "miraculously resume," Eichengreen concluded, but the far more likely outcome was this one: "More spending cuts will lead to more unemployment. Unemployment will fan political discontent. And political discontent will presage the abandonment of the zero-deficit rule. As investors see the writing on the wall, they will abandon the country, whose financial difficulties will return with a vengeance."

The IMF executive board met September 7 to approve formally the augmentation of Argentina's program. With its action that day, the board cleared the way for the immediate disbursement of $6.3 billion to Buenos Aires, the second-largest disbursement in Fund history (the bulk of which was the $5 billion earmarked in the new program for the central bank's reserves, and the remainder consisting of money due under the *blindaje*). This roughly doubled the amount that Argentina owed the IMF, and it raised the size of Argentina's program to 800 percent of its quota (its contribution to the Fund), well above the normal 300 percent limit.

All of that information was conveyed in a subsequent press release, which also included details about the fiscal and other commitments that Argentina had undertaken. Not revealed to the public was the fact that two of the twenty-four directors, one from the Netherlands and the other from Switzerland, had abstained from the vote rather than join the traditional consensus, an unusually strong sign of dissent in the board. (These directors represent groups of nations, not just their own.)

"I said I considered most of the assumptions underlying the revamped Argentinian program unrealistic," Onno Wijnholds, the Dutch director, later disclosed, explaining that he viewed as a "leap of faith" the projections of the government's fiscal surplus and debt.

"I concluded by saying that I did not believe that a virtuous circle would be achievable for Argentina, as matters had been allowed to deteriorate for so long. And I expressed concern that under the program the Argentine people were going to be condemned to years of stagnation, if not negative growth, with no real prospect of a medium-term solution."

Also not revealed to the public was a secret agreement between Cavallo and IMF management—so secret, in fact, that only a few Fund staffers knew of it.

The agreement was called the "stop loss," because it would be activated if Argentina lost too much of its reserves. Should reserves fall to $16 billion, Cavallo would be required to consider all alternatives, including the end of the convertibility system.* This time, the IMF was insisting on the sort of fallback provision that had been missing from the *blindaje*—a recognition that Argentina must be prepared to change its economic regime radically if the program were to go completely off track. The Fund wanted to be clear, at least to Cavallo, that this was the last chance for him to establish that Argentina could avert default and maintain convertibility, because no further rescue packages would be forthcoming to preserve the policy structure then in place.

Behind the pact was the sensible idea that Argentina should not cling too long to convertibility once the evidence clearly showed that the system stood no chance of surviving. Although a change in currency regime would be disruptive no matter what, the cost was sure to increase the longer Argentina waited; as a memo written in July by the Argentina task force put it: "It would be advisable to adopt alternative measures before the reserves were depleted and major

---

* A letter outlining the accord was drafted by IMF staffers but apparently never signed by Cavallo, though he readily acknowledged the existence of the pact when I asked him about it. His recollection of the terms was that the stop loss would be triggered if reserves fell to 70 percent of Argentina's monetary base, which would have meant about $10 billion. Other evidence, however, suggests that the stop-loss figure was $16 billion.

damage is done to the banking system." So if a major new outflow of money were to materialize, negotiations should commence for a regime change, because Argentina would be much better off taking such a step in a well-coordinated and planned manner, rather than having the markets force regime change on it. Simply allowing events to unfold, and letting the system be overwhelmed by a financial or political tsunami, would mean the government would be making major decisions on the fly—and possibly in the midst of anarchy.

For similar reasons, plans were afoot around this time for a secret meeting with top Argentine policymakers to discuss various options for replacing convertibility. The idea was that Fund staffers would huddle with a handful of Economy Ministry officials—Daniel Marx and a couple of others—somewhere away from the prying eyes of the news media. (Brazil and Uruguay were mentioned as possible venues.) There, the IMF would share some of the many papers the staff had written on the advantages and disadvantages of dollarization, a float of the peso, and in-between approaches. Reichmann broached the idea for such a meeting with Marx, who was amenable to the idea of prudent contingency planning.

But these hush-hush initiatives, laudable as they were in principle, ultimately produced nothing in practice.

The secret pact with Cavallo gave Argentina so much leeway that the program had to go *very* far off track to trigger the stop-loss provision. Once replenished by the new IMF loan, reserves would total $24 billion; thus a massive amount of money would have to leave the country before the $16 billion stop loss would kick in. The secret meeting with Marx and his colleagues never was held, and the Fund analyses remained unseen by the Argentines. The reasons offered in retrospect for this missed opportunity are manifold—though not satisfying. First, the chances to gather everyone together evaporated during the hectic months of autumn 2001, which included the September 11 terrorist attacks on the World Trade Center and the Pentagon. Second, Cavallo was adamantly opposed to considering alternative currency regimes, and although IMF officials understood that he would permit underlings to attend the secret meetings, they thought he seemed unlikely to make use of the information. Third, the press might have gotten wind of the meetings, and if word had leaked out, the crash would have been a self-fulfilling prophecy.

The long and the short of the matter is that another sorry chapter was about to unfold in Argentina's relations with the international community, compounding the errors that had already been committed. Despite all the thought given to challenging the Argentines aggressively on the need to consider an entirely new economic policy framework, the IMF would essentially adopt a passive stance during the last few months of 2001 as the country hurtled toward regime change—literal regime change, that is, involving not just a shift in economic policy but the ouster of the government as well. The Fund would remain engaged with the Argentine authorities; individual staffers would make efforts to move policy in the right direction, and the Fund would hold Buenos Aires responsible for complying with the conditions of the new program, refusing in the end to make further disbursements. But as an institution, the IMF would not muster sufficient gumption to proactively impel the Argentines to change course in a fundamental way before disaster struck. Nor would the U.S. Treasury, which could have intervened directly (as the Clintonites had in previous crises) but would instead defer to the Fund. This stance would continue even after the hopelessness of the situation had become incontrovertible. The phrase Mussa has used to assess the IMF's performance during this period is "a failure of intellectual courage." Analysis of the events in question leaves that assessment hard to dispute.

[CHAPTER 8]

Regime Change, Ready or Not

FOR CONSPIRACY BUFFS who suspect that the IMF works in cahoots with a cabal of private-sector financiers, fodder can be found in the list of participants at a five-hour meeting that Horst Köhler attended on October 18, 2001, at the Palace Hotel in New York City. The IMF managing director was seated at the center of a long rectangular table, around which sat a couple dozen titans of global finance who had been invited to meet with him for a private discussion. They included CEOs and other senior executives from Citigroup, J.P. Morgan, Merrill Lynch, Credit Suisse First Boston, American International Group, Putman Investments, PIMCO, and a number of financial giants from Europe and Asia as well.

The meeting was the semiannual gathering of the "Capital Markets Consultative Group," which Köhler established shortly after becoming IMF managing director. The idea behind the group was that the Fund's top management ought to have candid, off-the-record exchanges on a periodic basis with leading financial industry players, because the IMF, Köhler sensed, had become too distant from the global markets whose behavior the Fund was supposed to understand, anticipate, and influence. The agenda for the meeting, held five weeks after the September 11 terrorist attacks, was supposed to be dominated by general topics such as the world economic outlook, prospects for international capital flows, and new initiatives to strengthen the prevention of crises. IMF officials are uncomfortable discussing much about individual countries with the group, since they could be accused of leaking inside information. But the financiers had their own agenda. They wanted to devote a substantial amount of time to Argentina, a subject about which they had something important to say.

It was clear by then that the IMF's second rescue was faring dismally. The announcement of the deal on August 21, 2001, had failed to bring *riesgo país* down from the stratosphere; the figure dipped as low as 1,380 on September 4, then started climbing into the 1,500s and 1,600s by month's end, amid more grim indicators about the state of the Argentine economy. The bad economic news was attributable in part to the September 11 attacks, which threw a new damper on the spirits of consumers, businesses, and investors, but even before the attacks the data were continuing to flash recessionary signals. Most discouraging were figures showing that tax revenue was falling—an 8.7 percent drop in July from the same month a year earlier, followed by a 3.4 percent decline in August—which provided fresh evidence that fiscal austerity was deepening the recession rather than closing the budget gap. (Besides the recession, another reason for the revenue decline was that the crisis atmosphere was prompting a growing number of individuals and businesses to stop paying taxes in full or on time.) A particularly stark manifestation of the cycle's unending viciousness came on October 2, when the government announced that revenue had fallen by 14 percent in September and that in accord with the zero-deficit rule, spending would be cut by an additional $900 million to compensate. Instead of rallying in appreciation of this display of fiscal rectitude, the markets plunged even further, with investors complaining that the spending cuts were only creating a worse predicament. In the first half of October, *riesgo país* ranged between 1,700 and 1,900.

On the streets of cities in Buenos Aires province, the crisis now had a visible symbol—the patacón, a new type of currency denominated in bills of 1 to 100, with one patacón officially equal to the dollar and the peso. The patacón was issued by the provincial government, which began using them in late August to pay suppliers, pensioners, and employees. The issuance of currency at the provincial level was a disturbing symptom of economic anarchy, and a number of other provinces were issuing similar forms of scrip, because under the zero-deficit rule, Cavallo had cut federal payments to them, which left them bereft of pesos to meet their obligations. Technically a bond redeemable at 7 percent interest in 2002, the patacón was trading at about a 15 percent discount from the peso shortly after its debut, and was in only spotty use. Some businesses accepted them—McDonald's, for example, offered a "Patacombo," consisting of two cheeseburgers, fries, and a soft drink, for five patacónes, provided the customer had exact change. But other firms would accept only partial payment in patacónes, and some not at all, which upset people who received them in their pay packets. "Give me pesos, give me pesos," chanted thousands of teachers and other municipal workers who massed outside of the provincial governor's palace in late August. Unsurprisingly, this state of affairs translated into a continued decimation of the de la Rúa government's tattered political base. The president's approval ratings, which were hovering at around 20 percent in July, fell to single digits by October, and a survey of Buenos Aires residents showed that half favored Cavallo's resignation. The governing coalition suffered a crowning blow in national legislative and provincial elections on October 14, in which the opposition Peronists gained control of both houses of Congress as well as many governorships. The results heaped fresh doubt, if any more were needed, on Cavallo's ability to deliver the measures needed to achieve the zero-deficit target.

Small wonder, then, that the financiers meeting with Köhler were extremely downbeat concerning Argentina's outlook. Taking the lead in the discussion was William Rhodes, a Citigroup senior vice chairman. Age sixty-six, with slicked-back hair and wire-rimmed glasses, Rhodes was a veteran of countless debt crises. He had chaired the committees of bankers in negotiations with many financially strapped countries, including Argentina, during the 1980s and 1990s.

On its present course, Argentina was not going to make it, Rhodes contended. The country had to undergo a debt restructuring, and by this he meant a substantial reduction in the value of the claims held by creditors, not a voluntary exchange like the megaswap. The window of opportunity for voluntary deals had closed, he said. A chorus of others agreed. Continuing to give the country IMF funds would not save the economy in the long run, they argued. Political support for the government was clearly evaporating, with the recent election undermining the government's ability to implement its policies. The bankers wanted to end the suspense about the country's bind, which was likened to a "Sword of Damocles" hanging over international financial markets, making it more difficult for institutions like theirs to mobilize financing to other emerging markets.

This was a remarkable moment. The major creditors of a country were effectively saying that the government should pay them less than they were owed, on involuntary terms. Up to that point, the IMF and the U.S. Treasury had resisted sending that message to Argentina. Partly this was a matter of legal scrupulousness: Public servants must be extremely careful in addressing such a subject, because if they say anything that can be construed as encouraging a country to default, they can be held liable for the ensuing losses under a legal principle known as "tortious interference." To convey the message, therefore, they must use indirect wording. For example, they can tell a country's finance minister that his country's debt does not appear sustainable, and that international aid will not be provided under such circumstances; such language would presumably force the country's authorities to recognize that an involuntary debt restructuring was the only option. But in Argentina's case, the IMF and the Treasury had refrained even from going that far, preferring to support Cavallo's insistence that the country's obligations must be honored.

The official community had waited so long that now the message was being sent by the very people who would suffer the financial loss. As one financial industry official who attended the meeting observed:

> Think about it. This was the first time I can recall that the private sector took the initiative, to go to the IMF and to the debtor and say, "The game is up, you need a broad-based restructuring that involves a reduction in the value of our claim." This isn't the debtor running up the white flag. This isn't the IMF. This is the investment banking community. We came to this conclusion very reluctantly. Hell, the last thing I should be doing is tell a country we should give up our claims. But there comes a time where you have to face reality.

There was one dissenter among the bankers. David Mulford of Credit Suisse First Boston, the chief architect of the megaswap, breezed into the meeting late, apologizing that he had been unavoidably delayed. Addressing Köhler, he said that the other financiers might believe Argentina's situation was hopeless, but he did not agree. He argued that the opportunity still existed for some sort of voluntary bond exchange that would ease Argentina's debt burden and save the country from a forced restructuring, which he warned would be very damaging. But others, including Rhodes, strongly disputed that a voluntary deal made any sense at that point.

"Before Mulford's arrival, there was almost unanimity in terms of how bad the situation was," recalled another participant. "The corridor gossip was that his view must have been affected by the fact that he had done the megaswap. He couldn't turn around and admit things had gone so wrong."

The IMF officials present at the meeting kept their counsel. But that evening, Rhodes called Cavallo to convey the consensus of the private-sector participants. At long last, Cavallo was getting the message; the ship's captain now understood not merely that his vessel's hold was filling with water but that he needed to prepare the lifeboats. Several days later, he flew to New York to meet with two other officials who had also met the bankers—Treasury's Taylor and New York Federal Reserve Bank president William McDonough. Over dinner at the Regency Hotel on October 23, Cavallo agreed that instead of a "voluntary" restructuring, Argentina would soon announce plans for an "orderly" restructuring. The distinction may sound like hair-splitting, but "orderly" is a euphemistic way of saying "forced." Whereas a government conducting a voluntary debt restructuring is promising to continue paying its creditors what they are owed regardless of whether they accept the new terms being offered, an orderly restructuring suggests, implicitly at least, that a creditor who refuses to go along risks getting nothing, or will be coerced one way or another into accepting reduced payment. The government cannot overtly threaten to stop paying, because such a threat would legally trigger an "event of default." But to members of the financial community, the implications of an "orderly restructuring" are clear.

Sadly, all this movement was coming at a time when the opportunity for "orderly" action initiated by the government of Argentina had already passed. At that juncture, of course, no one could foresee what would happen, but within two months the government's debt restructuring would turn into an outright cessation of payment to private creditors, and it would come amid mob rule, with the banks closed and individuals and businesses unable to obtain access to their money. The end of convertibility, likewise, would be a chaotic process, with the peso dropping vertiginously, to less than one-third of its $1 parity. These factors would cause the country to fall into paralysis and depression in 2002.

* * *

Matthew Fisher was dubbed "the undertaker" by emerging-market investors, a name he good-humoredly accepted. The term referred to his role as the IMF's chief specialist in countries that are belly-up, or nearly so. A former official of the British Treasury, with degrees from the London School of Economics, the forty-five-year-old Fisher headed the Capital Markets Division in the Policy Development and Review Department. That job thrust him in the middle of most emerging-market crises, and it positioned him as the Fund's point man in cases where countries restructured their bonds or defaulted, such as Pakistan, Ukraine, and Ecuador. He had become heavily involved in analyzing Argentina's prospects once the country's fortunes turned rocky; he was the head of the group that produced the Plan Gamma memo.

Fisher was expecting to attend a surprise sixtieth birthday party for his boss, PDR chief Jack Boorman, on Saturday, October 27, 2001. But his plans abruptly changed when, a couple of days before the weekend, he was told to fly promptly to Buenos Aires—on the orders of Boorman, who did not realize he was disinviting a guest from his own party.

The urgency behind Fisher's trip was that the whole dynamic of the crisis was changing now that Cavallo had recognized the need for an orderly restructuring of Argentina's debt. The game was no longer about ensuring that the country could continue paying its creditors in full, or enabling the government to lure the creditors into a voluntary swap. Now it was about helping the country through the process of compelling those creditors to accept less than full payment, in a way that would inflict the least amount of collateral damage. Fisher's superiors wanted him to talk directly with top officials at the Economy Ministry and guide them toward the best approach to an inherently risky undertaking. The challenge was diplomatic as well as economic, because "it was very hard for the Argentine officials to come to grips with the reality of the restructuring and its possible implications," said one foreign banker who was advising them. "For many of them, it was viewed as a personal defeat. These people were working very hard, and shared the view with Mr. Cavallo that the country should not and did not need to restructure its external debt. So it was very hard for them to accept that the country might have to do it."

Matthew Fisher's mission was clandestine—or at least that was the intent. The Argentines' willingness to launch an orderly restructuring was not yet public, and Fisher was afraid that if his presence in Buenos Aires were revealed, some of the more savvy players in the markets who were familiar with his area of expertise would deduce that Argentina was contemplating a move akin to default, causing all hell to break loose. To his distress, he feared that his cover had been blown when, upon leaving a meeting in the Economy Ministry to go to the men's room, he found himself surrounded in the corridor by camera-wielding journalists snapping his picture. He was greatly relieved the next day when the only photos of IMF officials in the local newspapers were of the Western Hemisphere Department's John Thornton, who had accompanied him to Buenos Aires. The markets would remain unaware that Argentina was getting a visit from the undertaker.

Among Fund economists who were working on it, the task of Fisher's mission was known as "threading the eye of the needle." This phrase referred to the extraordinary delicacy of how to restructure the debt without causing the collapse of the banking system. Therein lay the crux of the problem: Just as Calomiris had predicted a year earlier in his visit to the Argentine embassy in Washington, Argentine banks had accumulated major new holdings of government bonds, much more than before, because the cash-starved government had pressured them to lend to it. Loans to the public sector now constituted about 27 percent of the banks' assets, compared with 17.9 percent at the start of the year. A deep reduction in the value of those bonds would leave many of those banks insolvent—and the mere announcement of such a move might panic depositors into a mass withdrawal of funds. Once a bank run starts, it often becomes a self-fulfilling process, as each depositor fears that if other depositors withdraw their money first, no cash will be left in the vaults. And if the banking system fell apart, the economy would quickly follow for lack of credit and a breakdown in the payments system that is vital for the wheels of commerce to turn.

Fisher came with an idea—albeit a highly tentative one—for how to thread the eye of the needle. Argentina should inform its creditors that it needed to reduce its debt by about 30 percent to 40 percent, which the Fund reckoned would be a substantial enough cut to make the debt sustainable without unduly ravaging the balance sheets of Argentine banks. For its part, the IMF or other elements of the official community would take action aimed at shoring up the banking system and calming depositors who would be tempted to run, at least during the three to four months required for a fully legal debt exchange. For example, Argentina might get a fresh supply of dollars for its central bank reserves, one purpose being to assure the nation's public that there was no shortage of cash in the banking system. Fisher did not claim that this plan constituted an official offer; the idea had been discussed with members of the IMF's top management, who did not commit to it but agreed to consider it if the Argentines were interested.

The plan Fisher was bringing to the table in October 2001 was precisely the sort that many Fund officials now wish had been pushed earlier. If the IMF had refused to provide Argentina with conventional, catalytic loans, or had called a halt to its conventional lending much earlier in 2001, that might have forced Argentina into an orderly restructuring, with the country receiving a substantial aid package aimed at helping it survive such a step.

Nobody can say for sure how Argentina's economy would have fared compared with the actual result. But if done earlier, such an approach could have been tried at a time when the country's banks were less vulnerable, its recession less drawn out, its supply of reserves less depleted, its political atmosphere less sulfurous, and the IMF less tapped out in the credit it had already extended. Perhaps the economy would have undergone a substantially less wrenching downturn. Perhaps fewer Argentines would have fallen into poverty, and fewer children would have succumbed to malnutrition.

Reality did not afford such a benign outcome. The proposal was tabled late in the game. In any event, the proposal went nowhere because IMF and Argentine officials could not agree on how a debt restructuring should proceed.

Cavallo and his aides were nervous about a number of problems associated with the restructuring. One was litigation: Foreign bondholders might well sue to demand full repayment of their claims, creating legal complications that would gum up the restructuring. More worrisome than litigation, though, was the concern about the banking system. "You have to bear in mind, the population was very much aware of the exposure the banks had to government securities," said Guillermo Mondino, the Economy Ministry's chief economic adviser. Accordingly, the team at the Economy Ministry wanted to restructure in two stages—first the domestic creditors, then the foreigners, the idea being to offer maximum protection to the local banks. Under their plan, a relatively modest haircut would be administered to the domestic creditors, who would be given new securities paying about 7 percent in annual interest instead of the higher rates they were currently getting. This would be followed by the lengthier and legally more complicated operation of organizing an international bond exchange in which the foreign creditors would get their haircut—presumably a much deeper one, though that was unclear.

Matthew Fisher and his IMF colleagues wholeheartedly agreed that it was necessary to protect the banks in some manner. But the Fund's economists, along with investment bankers that the Argentines hired to advise them, warned that the two-step approach would surely backfire because it was even more likely to generate litigation. The foreign creditors would react with outrage to the prospect of getting a worse deal than domestic creditors, and their threats of legal action would arouse worries that the domestic banks were going to be forced to take even deeper losses after all—and that, in turn, would trigger a run on the banks. It would be much better, though hardly a guarantee of success, to offer all creditors the same deal at once, and use other measures to protect the banking system, the Fund contended.

"The whole situation was extraordinarily precarious, and it was quite clear that things could collapse at any moment," Fisher said. "Within that framework, the question was what was the least awful way to proceed. There seemed to be no point to choose something that had disaster as a certain outcome. Our prediction was that the two-step approach might buy a couple of weeks' extra time, but at some point, confidence would collapse and the game would be over."

The Argentines could not be dissuaded. The undertaker returned to Washington October 30. In a speech to the nation November 1, de la Rúa announced the government's plans for an "orderly" debt exchange (although confusing matters somewhat, he and other Argentine officials were quoted as using the word "voluntary" as well), and Cavallo explained that the operation would be carried out in two steps as the government had envisioned, with the first stage involving the $55 billion in debt held by Argentine banks, pension funds, and other domestic investors. By cutting the interest rate on that debt to approximately 7 percent, the government would save $4 billion a year.

This was not a default, Cavallo maintained, and in an important sense, he was right: Argentina was not explicitly refusing to pay, so it was technically upholding the sanctity of contracts. "The public debt paper resulting from this operation will be the debt of a fiscally responsible and solvent nation that does not fail to honor its commitments," Cavallo declared, noting that certain tax receipts would be earmarked to guarantee payment on the new paper.

But the markets understood that bondholders' claims were being forcibly reduced, with worse terms likely in the offing for those who balked at accepting the government's proposed exchange. "It's like having a gun against your head," Christopher Eccelstone, an analyst at Buenos Aires Trust Company, was quoted in one wire-service story as saying. On the day of the announcement, the price of the benchmark government bond fell 14 percent, to about forty-two cents on the dollar, and *riesgo país* hit 2,300. Five days later, Standard & Poor's, which had repeatedly lowered the government's bond ratings in the second half of 2001, knocked the rating down to "SD," or "selective default." Foreign bondholders, though not directly targeted by the first stage of the swap, were particularly upset over signs that they would be treated in a "discriminatory" fashion, and as the IMF had feared, they threatened lawsuits. Many foreign portfolio managers publicly endorsed the idea that Argentina needed to give them and other bondholders a haircut; the problem was that they could not abide being treated unfavorably compared with other creditors. To press their case, more than two dozen large investors formed the Argentine Bondholders Committee, which hired counsel and was reported to be readying litigation in late November.

At the IMF, a staff memo delivered to the board on November 2 derided the government's plan as "not consistent with fiscal reality" and raising a major risk of causing a bank run. Fund economists were wondering among themselves when the run would start, since the situation was so tenuous. "The real mystery to me was why anybody left deposits there," said Carmen Reinhart, the deputy to chief economist Ken Rogoff. "I remember kidding Ken, who has this paper titled 'Seven Mysteries of International Finance,' that I've got one puzzle that beats all the others."

The wait for full-fledged panic would not be long.

The annual meeting of the IMF and World Bank has traditionally been a grand affair, with thousands of policymakers, bankers, investors, academic economists, and representatives of civil society from around the world converging on Washington (or, every third year, another city outside the United States) during the usually pleasant days of late September or early October. In 2001, however, the September 11 attacks, together with the threat of antiglobaliza-tion protests, forced the two institutions to postpone the annual meeting and convert it into a bare-bones gathering in Ottawa on a chilly weekend in mid-November. The IMF's effort to rescue Argentina was one of the major topics the assembled policymakers had to deal with, and by coincidence, on the very day the meetings got under way—Friday, November 16—the Fund's bailout reached a milepost underscoring how wretchedly it had flopped.

That day, the last of the dollars that the IMF had lent Argentina in the August "augmentation" in effect vanished from the nation's public coffers. This is not to say that anyone in a position of respon-sibility was hiving off with the money; there is no evidence whatso-ever to suggest that. But depressing news could be detected by closely scrutinizing the data showing the daily rise and fall in the reserves held by the Argentine central bank. On November 16, fol-lowing a steady decline that gained momentum in late October, the reserves dropped to $19.44 billion, almost exactly the same level as immediately before the IMF replenished the central bank's reserves with a disbursement of nearly $5 billion in early September. In other words, the money lent by the Fund to replenish the reserves, and restore confidence in the banking system, was no longer there. Pre-cisely where it had gone is impossible to say. A portion of it (about $850 million) had been used to make interest and principal pay-ments to the IMF and World Bank, but the inescapable conclusion is that most of the depletion could be attributed to the steadily increas-ing demand for dollars in October and November by people and firms exchanging pesos for greenbacks, many of whom were ship-ping their money abroad. In essence, the Fund's largesse had once again enabled a lucky few to pull their money out of the country ahead of a crash. Even though the IMF money was gone, Argentina was still obligated to repay its loan to the Fund.

Notwithstanding the sorry fate of the recent loan to Argentina, a small drama was unfolding at the Ottawa meeting concerning whether the IMF should disburse more. Most of the media attention at the meeting was devoted to how the terrorist attacks would affect the global economy, but on the sidelines Cavallo was furiously trying to mobilize support for his effort to keep Argentina from default and devaluation. The economy minister was under tremendous strain, and it showed. At a breakfast meeting with Köhler and other top IMF officials, Cavallo spoke virtually uninterrupted for forty-two minutes (one person present at the breakfast, knowing the minister's penchant for loquacity, timed him) in a harangue that covered a variety of topics ranging from Argentina's development in the 1990s to the merits of convertibility, as well as rationalizations for many of the policy measures he had taken. Scheduling problems allowed only an hour for the breakfast, and to the irritation of Köhler in particular, "there was almost no time left for an exchange" by the time Cavallo finished, recalled one participant.

Cavallo's most urgent need, quite simply, was money. Tax revenue was continuing to plummet in November, and Economy Ministry officials had been scrambling to find funding for the government's operations anywhere they could, by delaying outlays and raiding pension funds and the like. Sizable debt payments were coming due late in the year and in 2002, and without the cash to cover them, Argentina would default. Accordingly, Cavallo wanted to obtain further disbursements of the $9 billion left in Argentina's IMF program as quickly as possible, at the very least the $1.24 billion that was scheduled for disbursement in December.

But before disbursing the $1.24 billion, the IMF would have to approve Argentina's performance under the program, which required sending a mission to Buenos Aires to conduct a review. And despite Cavallo's persistent entreaties during the autumn months, Köhler had balked at even sending a mission because too many uncertainties remained about Argentina's ability to fulfill the program's conditions. First the managing director had wanted to wait until after the October 14 elections, then until after congressional passage of the 2002 budget; now he wanted to wait until after the New Year—a time frame that Cavallo objected was far too long.

On bureaucratic grounds, the IMF had reasonable justification to withhold further disbursements. The conditions of the August program included a commitment by the government to meet the $6.5 billion deficit target for 2001 originally set under the *blindaje*, and with tax revenue continuing to fall, that goal looked well out of reach. (Indeed, on the day after the IMF–World Bank meeting ended, the government acknowledged that the deficit for 2001 was likely to be $7.8 billion.) As for Argentina's promise to reform its revenue-sharing arrangement with the provinces, IMF economists were skeptical that a deal the government had struck with the governors measured up to the standards the Fund had been expecting. Those transgressions might have been overlooked if Argentina's prospects for the coming year had shown signs of sustainability, but to the contrary, the outlook contained no basis for hope. The economy was still contracting sharply, and total failure was already a certainty for the objective, spelled out in the August program, of securing "a major improvement in market confidence, allowing the government to re-enter international bond markets in 2002." That meant Argentina would have no way to raise the cash it needed to pay off substantial debt obligations coming due soon after the New Year.

There was the rub. "What was causing everything to fall apart was that the reaction from the markets was just not what we expected," said Tomás Reichmann. "The whole positive effect we wanted to see just did not occur. There was no major slippage from Argentina's side [in its implementation of the conditions]. But there was nothing very encouraging either." Moreover, having given Argentina not just one but two "last chances" in the form of large rescue loans, IMF officials felt they could hardly be faulted for failing to try again when doing so would obviously serve little purpose. The "blame" issue, in other words, was no longer much of a concern. As Claudio Loser put it to reporters at the Ottawa meeting: "We already gave them a large amount of aid . . . if that is not major support, I frankly don't know what is."

To compound all the other problems, relations between Cavallo and Köhler had reached the poisonous stage. The IMF chief was fed up with Cavallo's practice of unveiling surprise initiatives, and he had come to view the economy minister as a man disconnected from the political reality in his country. Cavallo, for his part, let it be known to intimates that he had little respect for Köhler's intellect, and he thought Köhler was allowing his judgment to be clouded by his resentment over the pressure he had gotten from O'Neill, especially on the August restructuring proposal.

Despite all the odds working against him, Cavallo was able to squeeze out one last victory at the Ottawa meetings. In a whirlwind of bilateral meetings with his counterparts in the G-7, he distributed a one-page sheet with numbers purporting to show that the government would meet the zero-deficit target in 2002—and although even some of his own aides thought the projections were little more than fantasy, they apparently had the desired effect. The G-7 ministers concluded that refusing to send an IMF mission would only arouse antagonism in Argentina, and they backed Cavallo's request for the prompt dispatch of a Fund team. So Köhler agreed, but with extremely grudging assent that underscored the ill will between him and Cavallo.

"Köhler did not want to give me the satisfaction of telling me in Canada" that a mission would be sent, Cavallo recalled. "He wanted to talk directly to de la Rúa, not me." Throwing up his hands in disgust, Cavallo said his reaction was "Fine! Tell de la Rúa!"

These were the inauspicious circumstances under which Reichmann was dispatched to Buenos Aires with his team—the mission that would end with Reichmann's being ordered to return to Washington and leaving the Olivos presidential compound in a helicopter. Considering all that had transpired, it is not surprising that the economists on this mission strongly doubted they would complete the review necessary for Argentina to receive the $1.24 billion disbursement. A close look at Argentina's deteriorating finances would bear out their gloomy presupposition that the country had no realistic chance of meeting the zero-deficit goal in 2002, given the acute additional pain that the necessary spending cuts would entail. And the unexpectedly dramatic events of late November and early December would hammer the final nails in convertibility's coffin. This was the period during which a major run would start on Argentine banks in the last three days of November, and the government would impose the *corralito* measures on December 1 restricting savers from withdrawing their deposits, which finally inspired the IMF's top leadership to summon Reichmann to Washington and cut off further support for the country.

For its part, the U.S. Treasury was by this point comfortable in its conviction that pulling the plug on Argentina would not result in serious financial consequences internationally. A young Massachusetts Institute of Technology economist who was an expert in emerging-market crises, Kristin Forbes, had joined the department's international staff in late August as a deputy assistant secretary, and in the fall she conducted an analysis predicting that the contagion from an Argentine collapse would be mild. Financial turmoil can spread through several channels, and Forbes's conclusion (like that of the IMF's Carmen Reinhart) was that none of these was likely to create major problems in Argentina's case. Argentina's exports and imports constituted a relatively low share of its GDP, so a sharp decline in Argentine demand for foreign goods would not likely affect important neighbors such as Brazil—certainly not to the extent that Brazil's slump had affected Argentina. And although a couple of Spanish banks that had lent heavily in Argentina would suffer, the financial impact of a crash on most other countries would be limited, Forbes believed. That was because, by contrast with the Russian case in 1998, a default in Argentina would come as no shock to the markets.

In sum, no one with major influence in the international community was making the case for extending Argentina's financial lifeline any further. Indeed, at the IMF, attention was shifting to the question of how better to handle similar cases in the future.

*   *   *

Now it was the IMF's turn to surprise Cavallo—and a good many other people as well.

The occasion was a speech by Anne Krueger, the IMF's new first deputy managing director, at the National Economists Club in Washington on the evening of November 26, 2001. Krueger, who was sixty-seven, was the Bush administration's choice to replace Stan Fischer in the Fund's number-two post, and she came to the job with impeccable conservative credentials. As a professor at Stanford, she had been a senior fellow at the Hoover Institution, a think tank teeming with former Reagan administration officials and leading intellects of free-market economics. During a stint as chief economist of the World Bank in the early 1980s, Krueger had played a key role in shifting the institution's ideology sharply to the right, toward a much greater emphasis than before on open trade, privatization, and deregulation.

Given her background, Krueger would hardly have been expected to spearhead a radical plan calling for greater government intervention in markets. But in her speech she did just that, by proposing that the IMF should create a sort of international bankruptcy procedure for overly indebted countries stricken by financial crises. The plan would fill what she called a "gaping hole" in the international financial system by giving countries an orderly process for working out debts, including the means to block panicky investors and lenders from withdrawing their money. For the Fund, which had historically frowned on measures restricting the flow of capital across international borders, this marked a major departure from past policy.

The shift in approach owed much to the sense of frustration at the IMF over its failings in Argentina, in particular its inability to find some middle course that would protect the country from some of the consequences of default without resorting to giant, high-risk bailouts. As it happened, a similar sense of frustration was afflicting Treasury Secretary O'Neill, who was struck by the differences he saw in the way overly indebted companies and countries were treated.

"In corporate America, we have Chapter 11 [the section of federal bankruptcy law that pertains to debt workouts], and here we have Argentina where no one has come up with an equivalent process that could take care of the situation," he fumed privately to a senior U.S. banker. To be sure, O'Neill understood that Chapter 11 could not be applied directly in Argentina's case; for one thing, the law contains provisions for removing a debtor's management—inappropriate measures for a sovereign government. But he raised the subject over breakfast with Köhler and Krueger on September 17, and in a typically feisty moment three days later at a Senate hearing, he publicly recounted the conversation, saying he had told the IMF officials, "Now is the time that we need to take action that's been talked about for years, that's never been done. We need an agreement on an international bankruptcy law, so that we can work with governments that, in effect, need to go through a Chapter 11 reorganization."

The IMF staff had been studying and drafting proposals of that nature for years without ever getting it past the executive board. Taking her cue from the Treasury chief's words, Krueger started dusting off those plans and crafting one of her own. The result was a far-reaching scheme with a name and acronym only the wonkiest of IMF-ers could love: the Sovereign Debt Restructuring Mechanism, or SDRM. Creating the mechanism, Krueger declared in her speech, would be "an investment in a more stable—and therefore more prosperous—global economy." The model, she explained, "is one of a domestic bankruptcy court," although "it could not operate exactly like that."

This was music to the ears of many experts who had been arguing for years that nations sometimes need protection from their creditors just as companies and people do. After all, a bankruptcy court can grant multiple protective measures to a financially troubled firm whose bankers and bondholders are snatching every dollar available and refusing new credit. Filing for protection with the court brings the "grab race" to a halt, thereby giving the firm breathing space while it negotiates new and more realistic terms for repaying its debts. A court decree can enable the firm to obtain the cash it needs to continue operating, by guaranteeing that new loans will be repaid ahead of old ones. Once the firm reaches a settlement with most of its creditors on the amount of debt it will pay in the future, the court can force all creditors to accept those terms, subject to a vote. The purpose of the last provision is to thwart "vultures" and "rogue creditors," who sometimes buy bonds of bankrupt firms at pennies on the dollar, and then file lawsuits in the hopes of getting a better deal than other creditors.

All these procedures are aimed at balancing the rights of creditors and debtors, increasing the chances that both will emerge better off than they would otherwise. However, no such court exists at the international level to aid countries on the brink of default. Countries that suspend payments on their obligations risk becoming embroiled in destructive wrangles with their creditors. Krueger cited the case of Peru, where the vulture fund Elliott Associates, having bought Peruvian bonds at a deep discount, had used its legal leverage to block a debt restructuring until the government finally forked over a lucrative settlement in 2000.

Under Krueger's plan, the IMF could call a halt to a run on a country whose government had become so burdened with debt as to cause the markets to stampede. In effect, the Fund would be sanctioning the country's decision to suspend payments to foreigners and impose controls on the outflow of capital. The country would have to show that it was prepared to correct problems in its economic fundamentals and negotiate in good faith with its creditors. During this cooling-off period, or "standstill," creditors could gather their wits, the country's authorities could devise a sensible plan of action, and all parties could begin an orderly process for deciding how claims will be repaid. The procedure could also induce new financing for the country by providing assurance that any loans made after the commencement of the standstill would be treated as senior to all preexisting private claims. Once an agreement was struck concerning debt repayment, all creditors would be bound to honor the terms negotiated, provided they agreed by supermajority vote representing, say, three-quarters of the principal amount of the claims.

To make the whole scheme work, the world's nations would have to agree collectively to make legal changes that would run roughshod over the claims of some creditors. That was the move needed, Krueger indicated, to deal with the rogues, because many emerging-market bonds, especially those issued in the United States under New York state law, contain clauses requiring the unanimous approval of all bondholders for any changes in payment terms. The laws protecting those rights would have to be superseded by new laws ensuring that a supermajority of creditors could impose its will on a litigious minority if necessary.

Krueger's proposals arrived too late for Argentina. Two or three years would be required to enact the necessary legislation in countries around the world, she said in her speech, so "none of what I have to say tonight has implications for our current negotiations with member countries—Argentina and Turkey, for example."

But Cavallo saw it otherwise. In his view, Krueger's speech had implications aplenty for Argentina—negative ones. The issue was not so much the content; in fact, Cavallo told me that had the proposed mechanism been available in 2001, he would have taken advantage of it. The problem was timing. According to Cavallo, the speech spooked the country's citizens to such an extent that it was a major factor behind the accelerated run on the banks in the final three days of November. "One of the things the speech said was that temporary exchange controls may be necessary while a country is conducting debt restructuring," Cavallo said. "For everyone reading that, it reinforced their views that Argentina will introduce exchange controls. I am not saying that the very drastic run [on the banks] was generated only by Anne Krueger. But I am sure it added to it."

That interpretation of events is more than a little self-serving. True, the greatest outflow of bank deposits came in the days immediately following Krueger's November 26 speech. But Argentines had ample reasons for panicking about their savings as the November days ticked down. Eleven years earlier, the government had frozen deposits to quell a crisis. "Bankers from my own institution, based in Buenos Aires, were calling and asking, 'Should I pull my money out of the bank on Friday before I go out of town?'" recalled a foreign banker who was advising the Economy Ministry. "People were actively talking about the parallel to the 1989 freeze." And although the economic team "was working extremely hard," he added, "at the same time some senior staff members would resign, and then tell friends in the financial community, 'You can't believe the chaos inside the ministry.'" With tension wound so tight, it was just a matter of time before ordinary middle-class Argentines became alarmed enough to run for their deposits.

Cavallo also cited Krueger's speech as one of his justifications for imposing the *corralito* on December 1. In discussions with IMF officials, he argued that by limiting deposit withdrawals and barring the transfer of money abroad, he was employing the same kind of measures—exchange controls—that Krueger had depicted as necessary for many countries in crisis. Meritorious though this reasoning may have been, however, it did not change the opinion of the IMF's hierarchy that with the *corralito* in effect, the convertibility of the peso and dollar was now meaningless.

"After the *corralito*, it was clear to everybody at the Fund, from management on down, that the convertibility system had reached a point of no return," said Loser, who explained the logic thus:

> The one-to-one relationship was based on the notion that there would be free exchange between pesos and dollars, and the central bank would back with the dollars it held all the pesos that people owned. With the *corralito*, people did not have access to the markets to get dollars when they wanted. At that point the demand for dollars far exceeded the availability, so the *corralito*

was imposed because if the run on the banks had continued, the central bank would have lost all its reserves and eventually it would have had to devalue. There was no way out.

Many Argentines grasped the point: Convertibility was no longer convertible. By the end of that week, long lines were forming outside currency exchange houses, and black-market money changers were multiplying on the streets, where the going rate was up to 1.25 pesos per dollar.

"Subdued," "chastened," "a different man"—all these are recollections of Cavallo's demeanor when he arrived at the IMF's headquarters on December 7, 2001, in his last visit to Washington as economy minister. No longer the haughty savior of the nation, poised to launch bold policy measures on his own initiative, Cavallo was now listening attentively to what his international benefactors had to say and promising to meet their conditions for a continued relationship.

Four days had passed since Tomás Reichmann had departed Olivos by helicopter, and two days had passed since the IMF had announced that it was "unable at this stage" to complete the review of its program. Despite this rebuff, Cavallo was not prepared to take "no" as the Fund's final answer, so he had flown to Washington with a couple of aides to make one more pitch for the assistance that he hoped would pull his country back from the abyss. As for the Fund, it seemed incapable, notwithstanding all the negative signals it had sent, of telling Cavallo in a forthright manner that his approach needed a radical readjustment.

At lunch in an executive dining room with Köhler, Krueger, and a handful of other top Fund officials, Cavallo was handed a one-page document titled "Steps to Reaching a Sustainable Program." The steps, numbered one through six, provided this crisply worded list for what the two sides needed to do to get the Fund program back on track along the lines envisioned in August, including the zero-deficit rule:

Step 1. Reach agreement on numbers on present policies for 2002, 2003, 2004, and 2005.

Step 2. Agree on magnitude of required adjustment to achieve zero financing gap in 2002 and over the medium term, while safeguarding social priorities:
  (a) Needed fiscal adjustment.
  (b) Magnitude of debt restructuring.

Step 3. Determine:
  (a) Tax measures and magnitude, including removal of tax concessions.
  (b) Primary expenditure measures and magnitude.

Step 4.
  (a) Do a debt restructuring that assures inter-creditor equity so as to produce a deal acceptable to a large majority of creditors.
  (b) Take measures to restore adequate liquidity conditions in the banking system.

Step 5. Then examine whether this combination can lead to growth.

Step 6. If yes:
  (a) Sustainable—complete review, etc.
  (b) Remove exchange controls, etc.

The list was remarkable for what it omitted. Nowhere did it say that Argentina should scrap convertibility and replace it with a different regime—the obvious choices being a floating peso or a devaluation followed by dollarization. Such a recommendation would have been a logical extension of the position the IMF had taken by summoning Tomás Reichmann back to Washington and refusing to complete its review. It also would have been a logical extension of the conclusion Fund officials had reached in the aftermath of the *corralito*.

This was a last chance to hand Cavallo some of the internal memos the staff had prepared on options for new monetary and foreign exchange systems, and to confront him with the need to begin preparations for implementing one of them. Conceivably, the IMF might even have offered an entirely revamped program, designed to help Argentina through this arduous adjustment. About $9 billion remained in the existing program, and this money—perhaps supplemented with funds from the G-7 or other sources—might have been used on an emergency basis to instill confidence in the banking system or keep the peso from plummeting below its fundamental value. Again, there is no way to know whether this approach, or simply insisting that Cavallo begin considering the Fund's options papers, would have saved businesses, banks, wealth, jobs, and lives. But even at such a late stage, the IMF's top management declined to make it crystal clear to Cavallo that clinging to convertibility was no longer tenable.

In no small measure, the problem was the disposition of Cavallo himself. For all of his newfound humbleness, he declared at the outset of the meeting that the one subject he would not discuss was the abandonment of convertibility. He knew that Krueger, in particular, viewed the peso's exchange rate as seriously out of line; she had told him so during her career as an academic. As far as Fund officials could surmise, he was not willing to engage on the subject, and under those circumstances, they adhered to the principle that the choice of currency regime is fundamentally a decision belonging to each member nation. A related concern was the issue of blame. If IMF officials explicitly urged a devaluation, Cavallo could hold them accountable for the outcome. "That was never the main concern, but it was definitely present," Reichmann said. "We were no saints. That idea had crossed our minds, and it had some influence on the decision."

The secret strategy that some IMF officials hoped to execute at the meeting was to guide Cavallo in an elliptical way to the realization that convertibility was dead. By tackling the six steps on the one-page list, he would come face to face with the extraordinary fiscal pain required to achieve the zero deficit in 2002, which because of the economy's poor state would include additional cuts in pensions and wages well beyond the ones already imposed. Once he came to grips with reality of that sort, Fund officials hoped, he would understand the impossibility of keeping the game going as it was.

The scheme backfired. "The big surprise," said Carmen Reinhart, "was that he said, 'OK, we'll do it.'" Indeed, after lunch, Cavallo went to work with staff members of the Western Hemisphere Department, and spent much of the weekend poring over spreadsheets with budget details. He quickly promised to get rid of some tax breaks for business that the IMF had never liked, and began contemplating the spending cuts he would have to push through Congress. Fund officials regarded this talk as a fanciful exercise, because by this point Cavallo was so politically weakened that he stood no chance of securing backing for such measures. Even so, Cavallo headed back to Buenos Aires on Sunday, December 9, telling reporters, "We completely agreed with the staff of the Fund on the numbers, so now we have to adopt decisions in Argentina." Having encouraged Cavallo in this charade, the IMF was in no position to contradict him.

But Cavallo was returning to a country whose low spirits had fermented into seething fury. To millions of Argentines, the *corralito* breached their limits of tolerance; their inability to obtain access to their own money, far more than the other belt-tightening moves the country had been put through, offended their sense of justice and fueled their suspicions that they were being robbed. Amid the summer heat, each day brought some new reason for blood to boil, nerves to fray, and despair to spread. Forced to hoard their money for essentials, middle-class Argentines were cutting their spending to the bone. As one vendor at a news kiosk told *La Nación,* lamenting the sharp decline in his sales: "If you didn't have cash and you had to choose between a newspaper and a sandwich, which would it be?"

To pay its December bills and foreign debts, the government seized more billions of dollars in pension-fund assets and converted them into treasury bonds. Labor unions responded with mass protests. Cavallo's efforts to introduce a budget with massive new spending cuts stalled, as leading opposition politicians controlling Congress insisted that he resign. On December 14, Daniel Marx, the finance secretary, became the third high Economy Ministry official to quit in two months; he had resolved to do so when the *corralito* was imposed over his objections. Reports circulated that the government was preparing more drastic curbs on bank withdrawals. Sullen groups of jobless and poor people started milling outside of supermarkets, demanding food and occasionally engaging in acts of vandalism and looting.

Cavallo could see now that the endgame was in play for convertibility. He induced Marx's predecessor, Miguel Kiguel, to come back to the Economy Ministry on December 14, and assigned him to start considering dollarization as part of a secret, three-man committee. But the government's time was up. "We had one meeting," Kiguel recalled, before popular frustration finally detonated, pitching the country into the maelstrom that many had dreaded—though few could have imagined its nightmarish dimensions.

Thousands of demonstrators poured into the streets on the scorching day of December 19. In Buenos Aires, they marched on the Casa Rosada; in Córdoba, they destroyed the municipal government building. A televised speech that evening by de la Rúa, vowing to "assure order throughout the republic" and declaring martial law, only evoked more antigovernment fervor among middle-class

Argentines incensed at his lack of sensitivity to their plight. Residents of the capital went to their windows, banged pots and pans, and defied the martial-law order by swarming into the Plaza de Mayo, while in other cities and towns supermarkets and banks were pillaged.

The next day, with the media reporting the shocking news that sixteen people had been killed, the government announced Cavallo's resignation. But that failed to appease the demonstrators, and de la Rúa quit next, handing the presidency to Ramón Puerta, who as president of the Senate was the constitutionally designated successor. Word of the government's complete surrender sparked joyous celebrations followed by another evening of violence and looting. The Peronists, who as the largest single party in Congress now held control over the government, quickly elected a provincial governor, Adolfo Rodríguez Saá, to the presidency, with the understanding that he would hold the post for just a few months until elections could be called. On December 23, Rodríguez Saá was sworn in and, to thunderous cries of "Argentina! Argentina!" in the halls of Congress, declared a suspension of payment on the government's debt, stating that "the gravest thing that has happened here is that priority has been given to foreign debt while the state has an internal obligation with its own people."

Even then, the tumult was far from over. More demonstrations erupted after Christmas, as middle-class savers vented their fury over the continued imposition of the *corralito*; they refused to accept government officials' insistence that the banks simply did not have sufficient cash on hand to meet all depositors' demands. The protests blocked the main streets of Buenos Aires for hours during the day, and in a nighttime confrontation on December 28 that left several police officers injured, demonstrators besieged the downtown area and broke into the Congress building, where they set fire to furniture before being driven off. The presidency of Rodríguez Saá ended with his resignation after just one week as Peronist politicians withdrew their backing from him, in part because he showed signs of wanting to run for a full term rather than serve merely as a care-taker. Once again the presidential sash reverted to Senate president Puerta, but this time he refused to accept it and quit, so power went nominally to Eduardo Camaño, the majority leader of the lower house, who called a special session of Congress for January 1 to choose a new leader under the terms of the Constitution. (Amid all this chaos, there was one saving grace: The military was staying in its barracks, aware that despite popular revulsion over politicians' behavior, the Argentine people would not stand for a return to the juntas of the past.) The hot-potato game over the presidency finally ended with the selection by Congress of Senator Eduardo Duhalde, the Peronists' candidate in the 1999 presidential election.

Then came the long-expected but nonetheless seismic shift: At Duhalde's behest, Congress approved legislation on January 6, 2002, ending the convertibility system and fixing the peso at a rate of 1.4 per dollar with a view to letting it float in a matter of months. There was no choice, for as the new head of the Economy Ministry, Jorge Remes Lenicov, aptly put it that day, "We are in a collapse. We are broke."

[CHAPTER 9]

A Pit Too Deep

THE RIOTS had subsided, and the presidential sash had stopped changing hands, but the political atmosphere was still volatile when I traveled to Buenos Aires in February 2002 on assignment for the *Washington Post*. Fears of a new social explosion were running high, and the scars of a wounded capital were plainly visible. Heavy metal shutters protected the facades of banks, which were pockmarked and spray-painted—*ladrones* (thieves) being the most popular epithet. Enormous crowds were massing frequently in the Plaza de Mayo, banging pots and pans, roaring chants, and waving banners.

As I wandered amid the mostly middle-class protesters, their faces etched in loss and embitterment, I was consumed by the question of how this country, which had previously shown so much promise, had come to such a pass. In the preceding chapters I have furnished some answers to that question. But they raise other lines of inquiry, which I address in these two final chapters: Could Argentina's collapse have been avoided, or at least mitigated? Are other nations at risk of suffering similar fates? If so, what changes should be made in the international financial system? What can be done to minimize the chances that nations clawing their way into the First World are plunged into pits of despair so deep as to threaten their progress for decades?

These questions entail looking at ways to revamp the architecture of the global financial system so that fewer crises arise, and that when they do, they are managed with the least possible cost in both the short and long term. Abstract and complex though these issues may be, addressing them is a matter of vital importance, because the way the system works now, globalization all too often seems to play malicious tricks on countries. The points in question affect the lives of real people, numbering in the untold millions, a fact I came to appreciate more deeply during my stay in Buenos Aires in early 2002. First, however, a brief review of the conditions that were taking hold in Argentina at that time is informative, for under its existing architecture, the system could hardly have achieved more abysmal results.

The nation's banking system was ceasing to perform its vital role as a provider of credit and dispenser of payments, the result being an accelerated contraction in all sorts of economic activity. At the dawn of the new year, the *corralito* had become the *corralón*, meaning that in addition to the limitation on withdrawals from checking and savings accounts, time deposits were frozen as well, because that was the only way to keep savers from pulling all of the ready cash out of the banks. With people able to obtain money only for the most necessary transactions, the shortage of funds spread through the economy like a debilitating virus. Consumers were husbanding cash for groceries, medicine, rent, and the like; although Argentines lucky enough to have credit or debit cards could use them to purchase some goods and services, merchants sometimes refused to accept the cards for fear that the banks issuing the cards would collapse. To conserve precious currency, families with maids were cutting back on housecleaning; taxi riders were switching to buses; people with broken appliances were postponing repairs. Realtors could not generate home sales, because prospective buyers lacked sufficient funds for down payments. The incomes of millions of people shriveled as a consequence of these sorts of problems, generating a multiplier effect as the affected individuals, in turn, curtailed their purchases.

El gran debut of the floating peso came on February 11. The lines stretched for a half block or more that day at the foreign exchange houses downtown, and people who came at midday to swap their pesos and dollars faced waits of as long as three hours, causing at least one woman to pass out from the heat. By the time it was over, the peso was selling at about 2.03 per dollar. That plunge was not as deep as some had feared, and Argentine television stations reported that evening that the majority of people thronging the exchange houses were selling dollars rather than dumping pesos. But many of those selling dollars were doing so not out of any sense of confidence in Argentina's economic future but because they badly needed cash to pay bills, for which pesos were now required. That was the case for Ana, a forty-year-old teacher who confided to one of my *Post* colleagues that, like many Argentines, she kept her savings in dollars in her house and was swapping some of them for pesos so she could pay her gas, electricity, and Internet access bills. "You just can't put your money in banks here," she said. "We have had the same type of problems in the past, but this is a much different situation."

The exchange rate of the peso swung wildly in the weeks and months that followed, to as low as 3.90 per dollar in June, leaving businesses scrambling to figure out what to charge for their products, with many forced to trim operations and idle workers. The Argentine affiliate of Deere & Co., the farm-equipment maker, was selling tractors and combines only to farmers who could pay in dollar bills (and that was plenty of greenbacks, since the machines could cost tens of thousands of dollars). Many businesses that depended on imported parts and supplies were unable to obtain them, because suppliers abroad, instead of shipping as they normally did on credit, were insisting that Argentine customers pay up front, and foreign banks were refusing to issue letters of credit that would normally guarantee such payments. Auto-industry component manufacturers could not get imported parts for door locks and armrests, for example, which forced Ford Motor Co.'s Argentine factory to shut down temporarily. Foreign medicines went missing from store shelves, as did other imported items such as printer cartridges.

The country was now paying the price for the failure to deal with the crisis preemptively, and that price was even higher for the lack of contingency planning between the IMF and the Argentines about how to dismantle convertibility in the least damaging way. The new, inexperienced government was announcing, on its own, plans to help the economy adjust to collapse; the IMF was essentially reduced to the role of horrified bystander. The Fund's reluctance even to try rescuing Argentina at this point was understandable, because the new government's hold on power was tenuous, and its ability to implement a coherent policy questionable. But the costs of the Fund's passivity during late 2001 were becoming clear. The Argentines had not been forced to face reality and use the Fund's analyses to prepare a game plan that might have helped ameliorate the impact; instead, amid a dysfunctional political atmosphere, the government was haphazardly taking measures that worsened the crisis still more.

To head off mass bankruptcy, the government decreed that most people who had borrowed in dollars could repay their loans in depreciated pesos, at a rate of one peso per dollar. At the same time, to appease savers, the authorities announced deposits would be converted at a different rate—1.4 pesos per dollar. As a result, the banking sector, which was already on its knees, was rendered prostrate. The disparity between what banks could collect from their borrowers, and what they owed their depositors, added up to billions of dollars in new losses. So for people and businesses in need of credit, obtaining bank loans became all but unthinkable. As for depositors, they felt cheated, notwithstanding the concession the government had given them: Since their deposits were denominated mostly in dollars, they felt entitled to get dollars back or, as an alternative, pesos at the market rate of 2 to 1 or 3 to 1 instead of just 1.4 to 1. Their angry reaction led to a deepening of the banking system's woes, as thousands of them obtained court orders requiring the return of their deposits in full, and money began draining anew from the banking system. The outflow of funds from the system reached 200 million pesos a day by April, and the economy headed into another downward spiral when the government, having encountered a rebellion in Congress against a proposal to straighten out the banking mess, closed the banks and exchange houses on April 19 while policymakers sought to devise a new plan.

With people scraping by on whatever cash they had hoarded, the result, as the newspaper *Página/12* described it, was "empty businesses, movie theaters without audiences, bars that wait in vain for the regulars to arrive ... taxis without passengers and traffic in downtown Buenos Aires as light as during the summer holidays." When the banks reopened a week after the closure, they still were not lending; how could they, bankers asked, when they had no idea how many of their depositors would win court orders, and could not even prepare meaningful statements of their financial condition?

Even for a nation already in prolonged recession, the rate of economic decline was shocking. "We thought we were in bad shape before. Now we're almost nostalgic for October [2001], when unemployment was only 18 percent," Federico Thomsen, a Buenos Aires economist, told me during my visit in February. (At that time, joblessness was about 22 percent and rising fast.) "Then your main concern was job uncertainty. Now you also have uncertainty about your savings, and the value of the peso. This is why there is so much protest in the streets. It's really the floor moving under people's feet. You don't have anything that's solid or predictable."

Among those for whom the bottom was falling out was Oscar Quinteros, the railroad and subway worker whose memories of the 1990s as a "golden age" were recounted in Chapter 2. His economic situation had been steadily deteriorating in 2000 and 2001 because the subway-services company for which he was doing electrical work as a contractor was failing to pay him on the grounds of its own financial difficulties, and the firm filed for bankruptcy protection from creditors in early 2002, offering Quinteros only a vague promise to send him some portion of what it owed at some point in the future. Quinteros found a few odd jobs, as he had in previous years—mowing lawns, gardening, and bricklaying—but, he explained, "people who had hired me back in the past had their money [trapped] in the *corralito*," so they could not pay him either. In contrast to the days when he could afford to buy modern appliances, "now I counted every penny when I was taking a bus or buying milk or bread for the kids," and the strain on his marriage became overwhelming. "I was morally broken, with no job and no possibility to get one," he said, adding that his wife, a primary school teacher, had to work two shifts—both morning and afternoon classes—and as she became the family breadwinner, "I lost her respect, and we split." He moved to a little shed in the yard, while his wife and daughters stayed in the house, a state of affairs about which he said: "I was such a mess. Everything was wrong."

The fortunes of Silvia D., the psychotherapist, were likewise undergoing a major adjustment. Together with another psychologist, she had launched a new family therapy operation, borrowing $30,000 to rent a huge flat downtown, hire a receptionist, and install telephones, computers, and fancy furniture. But the venture, which opened in May 2001, quickly began to bleed cash, with few clients willing to pay the steep hourly charges amid the darkening economic climate. By November 2001, Silvia's partner, having lost her other job at a private institution, could not pay her half of the loan installments—a worrisome development, because Silvia's house served as collateral for the loan. The following March, after the *corralito*, Silvia's practice was down to about eight hours a week, and with her house in danger of being taken over by the bank, she canceled the lease on her new office and fired the receptionist. "I cut the maid, the gardener, the yoga instructor, French lessons, cable TV, tennis lessons, and there were no more fancy clothes or fancy restaurants," she said. When she fell behind on payments on her Peugeot, she had to sell that too, and she could no longer afford to support her parents, who fortunately were able to rely on payments from one of Silvia's brothers living abroad. Visiting her son in Europe became out of the question. She thought of selling her house, which a real estate firm had once appraised at $250,000, but the same firm told her it was now worth only $80,000.

As for Miguel Machado, the onetime sugarcane cutter who landed a job in a flour mill, he became unemployed when the mill closed in late 2001, and after searching several months in vain for another job—"there was nothing to be had, anywhere," he said—he and his children joined the swelling ranks of the *cartoneros*, the army of people who pick through the trash in Buenos Aires. Six nights a week, five hours each night, rain or shine, the family rode a train into the capital to hunt for bottles, cardboard, newspapers—anything that could be sold for recycling. On a good night, the haul could be sold for perhaps $10 or $12, but the family had to make sure to arrive early, because competition for the rubbish was fierce. The number of *cartoneros* had multiplied more than tenfold, to an estimated 40,000, since the crash, and the provincial government had even set aside special trains, with the seats removed, for their use. One of the major occupational hazards was broken glass inside of garbage bags; Machado's nine-year-old son Lucas said he had cut his hands twice. The kids related how their lives had changed since their father lost his job. Breakfast used to consist of yogurt and cereal; now, if they were lucky, they could have dry cereal—no milk—and for dinner, his parents sometimes had only maté, the traditional Argentine herb tea. Their father fretted that street life would turn his boys into criminals. "I constantly remind them that we are honest people," he said, lamenting how different their existence had been in the 1990s when "they didn't have to be here in the streets with me until all hours of the night." Romina, fifteen, first said she didn't mind the work, even though she sometimes had to push a dolly laden with as much as 400 pounds, because she enjoyed the people she met. But then some of her bitterness spilled out: "Let me tell you what's hard," she said. "What's hard is waking up in the morning, fixing my father's maté and doing all the stuff that needs to be done around the house, going to school, coming home to study, then coming out here to work, getting home at midnight, then waking up six hours later and doing the same thing over again. . . . Sometimes I do miss my old life where I could just stay home and study."

Hard-luck stories abound in all economies, even rich and growing ones, as jobs disappear, industries' fortunes wane, technologies change, and adjustments in government policies inflict pain. What makes the stories of Argentines like the Machado family, Oscar Quinteros, and Silvia D. so depressing is that the forces that ravaged their livelihoods could have been forestalled or at least attenuated. Argentina should not have fallen to such a shattered state.

Years after Argentina's collapse, debate about its causes continues to rage among economists and other policy experts. The extraordinarily wide range of conflicting explanations stems partly from the desire of the intellectual combatants to validate their ideological predispositions. But it also reflects the monumental dimensions and speed of the country's descent from the state of grace it had achieved in the late 1990s.

One conclusion, drawn by critics of free-market policies, is that Argentina's crisis offers an indictment of the entire Washington Consensus, or the "neoliberal model" as it is sometimes called. This view is based on a cartoonish sort of logic that paints cause-and-effect correlations with an absurdly broad brush, not unlike blaming juvenile delinquency on rock and roll. Policies such as open trade, privatization, and deregulation were not responsible for the events that brought Argentina to such a pitiful state. If the effects of those policies were as deleterious as critics sometimes suggest, the Argentine economy would have fared much more poorly from 1991 to 1998, and market-oriented countries such as Chile would have performed worse than other nations in the region with heavily interventionist policies, such as Venezuela and Cuba, instead of the reverse. The manner in which the Argentine government implemented some free-market reforms, especially privatization, is worthy of much criticism. But that does not mean that the reforms had a negative overall impact, or that they somehow rendered the country prone to collapse.

Policies that were otherwise sensible, as many of Argentina's free-market measures were, ended in tears because of particular errors, not because the policies were fundamentally ill-conceived or contributed directly to the country's downfall. But what were those particular errors?

Some economists blame the convertibility system, arguing that it was doomed to fall apart sooner or later because of its inflexibility and the unnaturalness of the linkage between the Argentine and U.S. economies. Others vociferously argue exactly the opposite—that Argentina's problem was its failure to adhere faithfully to the monetary rules of a rigid currency peg, and that the loss of market confidence in its policies can be traced to episodes that stirred doubt about the government's commitment, such as Cavallo's efforts to incorporate the euro into the valuation of the peso. Yet another theory, dubbed the "sudden-stop" hypothesis, attributes the country's woes in large part to the reversal of capital flows that emerging markets in general suffered following the Russian default in 1998.

Other analysts point the finger at fiscal policy—here again, from divergent perspectives. Some accuse Argentine policymakers of having been profligate; others contend that, to the contrary, the country's problem was an overly restrictive policy that reflected a foolish desire to satisfy the IMF. The clash between these two schools of thought is not as contradictory as might be assumed, because each aims most of its criticism at different time periods. The advocates of the "too-loose" theory tend to focus on the 1990s, arguing that the deficits the government ran, though not excessive by normal standards, were too large for a country that depended on market confidence to sustain the convertibility system. The advocates of the "too-tight" theory tend to focus on 2000 and 2001, contending that once the economy had fallen into recession, contractionary tax and budget measures were counterproductive.

Since all of these arguments have some merit, they have influenced the interpretation of events offered in this book to at least some extent. But some correspond more closely than others with the evidence that I have unearthed and reviewed. To sum up the conclusions from the material presented in previous chapters, the main cause of Argentina's crisis was the disjunction between convertibility and the policies required to nurture and ensure its viability—in particular fiscal policy. As difficult as it may be to prove how events might have played out differently, Argentina almost surely would have spared itself much grief if it had run substantially more stringent budget and tax policies in the 1990s, and an excellent chance for doing so was missed during the 1996–1998 boom. One can easily imagine how much better positioned the country would have been to withstand the post-1998 environment had it been running fat surpluses in the years before; worries about its debt would have been minimized, and the government would have had much greater room to ignite growth when it desperately needed to do so.

Argentines in the mid-1990s—leaders and citizens alike—wanted to hold fast to convertibility for a good while longer, with considerable justification. To that end, they should have squarely faced the fact that their fiscal policy was not sufficiently prudent. The excuse often offered for failing to tackle these issues is that nobody could have foreseen the events of 1998–1999 such as the Russian default and the Brazilian devaluation. But some observers perceived the need for much greater discipline, notably the private economist Mario Teijeiro; why didn't (or couldn't) others see it as well?

The responsibility for this immensely consequential lapse, and for other missteps as well, belongs first and foremost with Argentina itself. IMF officials are fond of pointing out that Argentines owned their policies lock, stock, and barrel, and that is undeniably true. Indeed, it is time to explode once and for all the popular myth that the IMF was dictating policy to Buenos Aires throughout the 1990s. If anything, as countless episodes have shown, the remarkable characteristic of relations between the IMF and Argentina during much of this period is the extent to which Argentine officials were leading the Fund around by the nose, in everything from the initiation of convertibility in 1991 to the announcement of the zero-deficit policy in 2001.

At the same time, however, Argentina's errors were indulged by the policy elites of Washington and the financial elites of Wall Street. The IMF may be fairly accused of what might be called "poster-child syndrome" in the enthusiasm it manifested for the country's adoptions of reforms that the Fund had favored. The invitation for Menem to speak at the 1998 IMF–World Bank meeting was but one illustration of the syndrome. More serious were the Fund's projections of the economy's growth in the mid-to-late 1990s—growth forecasts that "were based on what was, in hindsight, an overly favorable reading of the structural reforms that had taken place and prospects that further reforms would be implemented," as the IMF staff's postmortem on the crisis acknowledged. The consequences were grave: By assuming high growth rates for an extended period, Fund officials were dulled to the country's fiscal shortcomings and debt buildup. Instead of confronting the Argentine government with a choice—exit from the convertibility system or adopt much tighter fiscal limitations—the IMF let matters slide.

But global financial markets were even more grievously at fault in this regard. Private international financiers and bond investors were willing to supply the country with all the capital it required; accordingly, it is far from clear that a more confrontational IMF stance could have changed Argentine policy much in the mid-1990s, when the Fund's program was merely precautionary. Some market participants blame the IMF for fueling their optimism, but in one instance when the Fund blew the whistle loudly and publicly—the Ter-Minassian visit of April 1998 when her "Molotov cocktail" comment and other warnings were widely circulated—the markets paid little heed. That episode undercuts any complaint financiers may advance about being misled by the Fund. If they really pay such close attention to the Fund's assessments, they showed no such sign in that case.

Some wise observations on the role that the markets played were offered by Roberto Lavagna, Argentina's economy minister, during a visit to Washington in early 2003. At a meeting with a group of reporters in Lavagna's hotel suite, a colleague of mine asked him what ought to be learned from the Argentine experience.

"The lesson is, we must pay attention to bubbles," the minister replied. "With stocks, or companies, or countries, all are part of the same phenomenon. Probably Argentina is the best example of a country." For developing nations, he added, "the worst period is when financial markets have the most liquidity. This is when countries make the worst mistakes. That is certainly the case in Argentina."

Provided in this book has been damning evidence reinforcing that insight about the propensity of international capital flows to accentuate the danger of crises. The information shows how, in Argentina's case, large injections of foreign funds became the economic equivalent of steroids and undermined policy discipline. Also shown is how the markets' decisions were distorted by factors such as the conflicts of interest among sell-side investment banking firms and the perverse incentives created by emerging-market bond indexes. Even if these pressures did not distort global markets, flows of capital from abroad still would pose steroid-like risks for emerging-market countries. But the markets are distorted in those ways, and that makes the problems posed by these capital flows all the worse.

Although that may be the most important lesson to be grasped, it is far from the only one. Countries can also commit serious mistakes when financial markets are pulling money out—for example, by trying to sustain the unsustainable, as Argentina did in 2000 and 2001. At that point, a crash of some sort was almost surely inevitable; it definitely became more so as time passed and the economy slipped deeper into its vicious cycle. But at nearly every step of the way, the crisis could have been mitigated even if it could not have been prevented.

Sitting at a polished mahogany table in his U.S. Treasury office, John Taylor pulled out his wallet and handed me a card with two small charts on it. "I carry this with me all the time," said the undersecretary with an earnest smile.

One chart on the card showed what had happened to global markets following Argentina's default. The other showed what had happened following Russia's default in 1998. The contrast was stark; the contagion effects on other countries of the Argentine default were much more muted than had occurred in the Russian default.

Carrying around such a card may seem unusual, but Taylor was trying to make the case that the Argentine crisis was handled better than is commonly understood. This is the theory: Although IMF rescues failed to keep Argentina from defaulting and devaluing, they still had important benefits, and this applies to the second rescue in August 2001 as well as the *blindaje* in December 2000. Markets worldwide would have reacted with much greater shock had Argentina been forced into restructuring its debt as early as mid-2001. Giving the country a second chance to turn things around also gave the markets time to adjust psychologically to the possibility of an Argentine default, and as a result, contagion was minimal when the crash did come.

Taylor is one of quite a few policymakers and former policymakers who cling to the belief that lending Argentina large sums was the right thing to do, even as late as August 2001. Of all the arguments advanced for augmenting the Argentine program, Taylor's may be the hardest to refute, because contagion is notoriously unpredictable: Who knows whether contagion might have spread in worse fashion if the IMF had abandoned Buenos Aires a few months earlier than it did?

The what-ifs are endless, and the major decisions the international community took with regard to the rescue of Argentina were agonizing. That should be apparent from the material presented in this book about the debate, including the evidence confronting policymakers at the time. But that material, in my opinion, strongly bolsters the conclusion that Argentina was badly served by the global institutions on which it had come to depend. Nations experiencing reversals of the sort Argentina was undergoing in 2000–2001 should be able to count on the international community for well-designed support to break their falls; at the very least, rescue attempts are supposed to alleviate damage, not exacerbate it. The Fund's second loan package for Argentina, in particular, failed to meet this minimum standard. As the Fund staff, to its credit, later acknowledged in its postmortem report, the second loan "only postponed the inevitable and, by raising the debt burden, also meant that the costs of the eventual collapse were all the greater." When default and devaluation finally came, Argentina had already entered its fourth year of recession, the nation's once-healthy banking system was badly weakened, and billions of dollars in foreign exchange reserves had drained from the central bank's coffers. Moreover, the government was deeply indebted to the IMF, which thus had a much-diminished capacity to provide assistance that might have cushioned the blow.

As for Taylor's argument concerning contagion, the limited fallout that the Argentine default ultimately had in other countries' markets suggests, if anything, that earlier fears about the contagion problem were inflated. Moreover, the Argentine people would presumably take cold comfort from the knowledge that the August 2001 rescue attempt may have saved the world from contagion. In the process, they were saddled with more than $6 billion in additional debt to the IMF—no trivial sum for a country whose GDP the following year would be just slightly over $100 billion.

In the final analysis, therefore, the approach that was taken almost surely made the outcome much worse than it had to be. Conventional, catalytic IMF lending ought to have halted, certainly by August 2001 and arguably as early as the *blindaje*. The international community should have provided assistance only on condition that Argentina's debt be restructured to sustainable levels, with the aid aimed at limiting the extent of the resulting economic shocks. Such a package could have given the Argentine government the resources needed to quell the run on the banking system before it became so ruinous; emergency loans to the banks could have assured citizens that their banks had plenty of cash and that there was no reason for panic withdrawals. Moreover, a large international loan could have given the Argentine government financial ammunition to buy pesos and limit the downward "overshooting" of the currency that aggravated the damage to the economy in 2002.

Again, Argentina's government—by refusing, until it was much too late, to restructure the debt in a meaningful way or to contemplate changes in convertibility—must bear its fair share of the blame for the outcome. But the IMF and its leading shareholders, particularly the United States, have the power in such situations to force countries into changing tack by rejecting requests for support. In Argentina's case, top international policymakers succumbed instead to the tendency to keep playing for time when disaster looms, hoping against hope for a shift to better luck despite the serious misgivings among many that the strategy will work. Although playing for time can be an important objective of crisis management, and the eagerness to stave off a default-devaluation scenario in Argentina was understandable, the country's would-be saviors engaged in time-buying exercises in 2001 that were based on far-fetched odds of success. This is not mere hindsight; as we have seen, plenty of well-founded argumentation was presented at the time that the approaches taken were futile and, by piling more debt on top of an already unsustainable debt load, would work against Argentina's long-term interests.

These conclusions are not novel. But the depth of the folly that was perpetrated should be manifest in light of the account provided in this book concerning the internal debate among international policymakers and the process by which they stumbled so belatedly toward the right alternatives in the final months of 2001. Most disheartening of all is the evidence that the decision to make the August 2001 loan, and other measures that went sour, were driven by outsiders' agendas that did not dovetail with the interests of the Argentine people. The IMF's desire to skirt blame for the collapse consistently tilted its policymaking in the wrong direction, toward delaying the day of reckoning. The same holds for the Bush administration's wish to differentiate itself from the Clinton administration, which in the case of the August 2001 rescue led to an attempt at financial engineering so half-baked and perplexing that it made an already-rickety program even more certain to fail. Finally, there was Wall Street's voracious appetite for fee income, which helped inspire the megaswap, the ultimate exercise in costly time-buying.

Lamentation about the aftermath of the crisis may seem misplaced to some readers who have a passing familiarity with news from Argentina, because the overall outcome was not as bad as many economists had feared. The economy bottomed out in the second half of 2002, and in 2003 it grew by more than 8 percent. Contrary to the worries of many who had expected that the country would revert to its hyperinflationary ways, consumer prices rose less than 4 percent in 2003, compared with a 40 percent increase the previous year, thanks to a firm hand on the monetary tiller at the central bank. And in fall 2004, Argentina was well on the way to posting another year of high growth with low inflation.

As welcome as the revival was, however, it had many of the hallmarks of a dead-cat bounce. (This macabre metaphor, popular on Wall Street, refers to the fact that anything will rebound if it falls from a great enough height.) Per capita GDP in 2004, adjusted for inflation, was still about 13 percent below the 1998 level; the shortfall in dollar terms was about 55 percent. Nearly one-fifth of the Argentine labor force was still unemployed, based on figures that count as jobless those being paid by government workfare programs, and about 45 percent of the population was living below the poverty line. The economy was growing mainly by using the massive amounts of spare capacity that had been idled during the deep downturn, with another major source of stimulus coming from sky-high world prices for soybeans and grains. Whether Argentina could sustain growth at a decent pace, much less at the sizzling rates of 2003, would depend on the economy's ability to generate new investment in expanded production capacity—a highly uncertain matter, since capital from foreigners was not likely to be forthcoming for some time.

Furthermore, the governments of President Eduardo Duhalde, and of his successor Néstor Kirchner, had deferred tackling some tough problems that the country would have to reckon with eventually. Most important, the government became embroiled in confrontations with holders of the nation's defaulted bonds concerning what fractional amount of their value the government would pay. After a long delay, government officials offered in September 2003 to pay twenty-five cents on the dollar, a proposal that investor groups rejected as "not serious" and really worth only about ten cents on the dollar once unpaid interest was factored in. A second offer in May 2004 was greeted with only slightly less bondholder hostility, even though it improved the terms sufficiently to raise the true payback rate closer to twenty-five cents on the dollar. The government justified its position on the grounds that the drastic shrinkage of the Argentine economy in dollar terms left it unable to pay any more without severely impinging on the welfare of its own people. This argument had merit, and the government's "take it or leave it" stance was hugely popular with the Argentine public. But it was setting up an Argentina-versus-the-world dynamic that boded ill for the country's long-term future. Bondholders were filing lawsuits in courts around the globe in hopes of seizing any assets that might be deemed to belong to the Argentine government, and although their success was minimal, the legal wrangles were casting a dark cloud over the ability of Argentine firms to raise money and operate internationally. Adding to the noxious economic environment was a game of chicken between Buenos Aires and the IMF, in which Argentina would periodically threaten to default on its loans to the Fund unless it received enough fresh loans to pay off the amounts coming due. Argentine officials knew the Fund was anxious to avert a default, which would have damaged its financial condition, but they also knew that defaulting to an official lender would put their country even deeper into international pariah status than it already was.

Perhaps most worrisome was the mind-set that was gripping the Argentine body politic. Well into 2004, much of the country and its leadership were still wallowing in self-pity about the injustice they felt they had suffered, and they were venting their anger on the private sector in all its forms. A particularly destructive example of this phenomenon was the government's tolerant attitude toward the increasing number and boldness of *piqueteros*—well-organized groups of demonstrators, often wielding clubs, who disrupted traffic, business, and ordinary life by blocking major roads, occupying office buildings, and sometimes engaging in acts of vandalism and violence against corporate targets such as McDonald's restaurant outlets and the Sheraton Hotel. Claiming to represent the disenfranchised poor, the groups were shutting down key bridges and highways in the Buenos Aires area several times a week in late 2004, sometimes making general demands for increases in welfare payments and jobs for the unemployed, sometimes making specific demands for handouts of food and cash for charities. The "no repression" policy of President Kirchner concerning this lawlessness was clearly having a negative impact on the willingness by businesses of all sorts—foreign and domestic—to invest in the country. It was symptomatic of a general hostility toward commercial interests, especially foreign commercial interests, that threatened to snuff the entrepreneurial spirit needed for a lasting and solidly based rebound. Having erred by opening its arms too widely to overseas investors in the 1990s, Argentina was erring excessively in the opposite direction.

In sum, notwithstanding the recovery, Argentina's bust still ranks as globalization's biggest. Although not as directly threatening to international stability as the tensions that have erupted in the Middle East, its implications for America's ability to exercise global leadership are disquieting, as indicated by the political turn the country has taken. More important, and ominous, are its ramifications for the wider developing world in signaling the susceptibility of their economies to meltdowns.

These concerns would be less pressing, of course, if Argentina were *sui generis,* its crash a unique "perfect storm" reflecting a confluence of events unlikely to occur anywhere else in the world for decades. Was it?

[CHAPTER 10]

Don't Cry for Them, Argentina

REST EASY, because Argentine-type bubbles are not about to materialize elsewhere. Markets have a marvelous capacity to self-correct, and Argentina's default chastened international investors and lenders so severely that they have demonstrated a new level of sobriety in their approach to emerging-market countries. This caution on the part of global-market players should reassure the world that there is no longer much reason to worry about global markets pumping up the economies of developing nations to the point of intemperance.

Unfortunately, the preceding paragraph is a laughable fantasy. By late 2003, investors' eagerness to roll the dice in emerging markets was reaching levels not seen since the Asian crises of 1997, causing much unease among policymakers and expert observers. "Is this another bubble?" the *Financial Times* fretted in an editorial January 16, 2004. The newspaper's use of the B-word was justified, and was being echoed elsewhere.

The clearest indicator of the optimism infecting the markets was the overall level of country risk on emerging-market bonds. This figure, which shows the spread between the yield on U.S. Treasuries and the average yield on all the bonds in the EMBI-Plus index, narrowed in 2003 by 347 points, to under 400 in mid-January 2004. This meant that instead of demanding more than 7 extra percentage points of yield above Treasuries on their emerging-market bonds, investors were willing to accept less than 4 percentage points of extra yield. Readers may recall that Argentine bonds were offering a similarly modest degree of extra yield during the frothiest days of the mid-1990s. Unsurprisingly, borrowers in developing countries were rushing to take advantage of the bargain-basement deals. More emerging-market debt was issued in January 2004 than in any month since just before the devaluation of the Thai baht.

What accounted for the markets' renewed appetite for risky investments in far-flung lands? Simple: During 2003, professional investors, especially bond investors, were growing increasingly desperate to earn higher returns on their portfolios, because interest rates in the United States were at forty-five-year lows, and rates in other rich nations were at rock-bottom levels as well. So money was pouring into emerging-market-bond mutual funds, and portfolio managers were scouring the globe for securities offering more lucrative yields, bidding up their prices. Global financial markets, in other words, had a lot of liquidity—precisely the conditions noted by Economy Minister Lavagna as the ones that lead developing countries astray.

From his think-tank perch, the Cassandra of the Argentine crisis, Desmond Lachman, sounded the alarm in an article titled "Chasing Yield," published in the spring 2004 issue of *International Economy* magazine. Expressing astonishment that Brazilian, Polish, and Turkish bonds were yielding so little more than Treasuries at a time when the debts of those nations were burdensome and rising, Lachman wrote: "One must wonder whether there is not something fundamentally flawed in the market for emerging market debt" that causes money managers to "pay all too little attention to the longer-run individual country economic fundamentals." As for finance ministers in emerging-market countries, he fretted, "all too many" of them "tend to view rising emerging market debt prices as market validation of improved domestic economic fundamentals," the result being that they "all too frequently allow complacency to creep into their policy thinking."

Even the Institute of International Finance, the Washington-based organization that represents financial firms that invest in emerging markets, issued a warning that some of its members might be making foolish bets. "We are not sitting here and predicting a crisis in emerging markets," said Charles Dallara, the institute's managing director, at a January 15 news conference in which the group issued a forecast of continued strong flows into emerging markets in 2004. "But because spreads have moved so far, so fast, they are vulnerable."

Apologists for the trend argued that fundamentals had improved enough to warrant a major reduction in emerging-market country risk. The global economy was expanding in 2004, and far fewer emerging markets had currency pegs than in the 1990s, which diminished the danger that their currencies would come under speculative attack. But quite the opposite conclusion about emerging-market fundamentals could be drawn from the IMF's semiannual *World Economic Outlook* published in autumn 2003. Its third chapter was titled "Public Debt in Emerging Markets: Is It Too High?"—and its answer to the question posed was unsettling. The average debt of emerging-market governments stood at about 70 percent of GDP at the end of 2002, 15 percentage points higher than the level five years earlier, and it had recently surpassed the average level for advanced countries. For nations like Colombia, Poland, and Lebanon, the prudent debt-to-GDP ratio is much lower than it is for the likes of the United States, France, or Norway, the report contended, adding that although "there is no simple rule" for determining the point at which a country's debt is excessive, "[t]he increase in public debt to high levels in many emerging market economies in recent years has once again raised concerns about debt sustainability and whether there could be a repeat of the 1980s debt crisis."

Perhaps caution about emerging-market debt will return to the financial markets. At the end of 2004, however, the bulls were continuing to run wild; spreads fell back to record lows after having risen at midyear, and borrowing by emerging-market governments and companies was headed for a new annual high. Whatever happens, global investors have once again demonstrated their capacity for funneling excessive sums into countries with high and rising levels of vulnerability.

Since many innocent people may be hurt as a result, the need is urgent for changes in the system that will reduce the incidence of emerging-market bubbles and give the international community better tools to contain the damage when the bubbles burst. In the past, many bold proposals have encountered objections that they would diminish private flows of capital to emerging markets. But those objections, which were never very compelling, should be accorded even less weight in light of what is now understood about Argentina, and especially in light of the bubbly conditions that were taking hold in emerging markets in 2004. The following discussion concerning the policy implications of the Argentine crisis indicates the scale of ambition that is warranted.

It will be no easy task to rid the IMF of the poster-child syndrome that prompted the Fund to give its imprimatur to Argentina's economic policies during the period when the country was setting itself up for a fall. Human nature and political realities being what they are, IMF officials will always have difficulty resisting the temptation to lavish praise on countries that are implementing orthodox economic policies and enjoying rapid growth. But the Fund would be well advised to remain as coolly detached as possible in such instances. The Argentine story underlines the limitations of the free-market approach promoted by Washington, and much other experience from the developing world has shown that these sorts of policies are not growth elixirs. They may spur supercharged expansions for a period of time, but in many cases performance tends to flag after a while, for reasons that vary from country to country.

The IMF has taken a couple of steps toward better decisionmaking in this regard. At an institution where high-ranking officials are rarely dismissed, someone was actually fired for responsibility in the Argentine fiasco—Claudio Loser, the longtime head of the Western Hemisphere Department. A warm, funny, and intelligent man, Loser was the scapegoat for decisions that were mainly the responsibility of people who ranked both above and below him, in the opinion of many of his former colleagues (an opinion that, as far as I can tell, is correct). Since Loser is Argentine, the fact that he was singled out for the Fund's failings may seem emblematic of his country's mistreatment. But prominent heads should roll in a case like this, and a department director is probably the proper level to choose for purposes of sending the signal to staff members that they will be held accountable for erroneous policy judgments.

In another initiative aimed at promoting accountability, the IMF established the Independent Evaluation Office in 2001 with a broad mandate to scrutinize the Fund's operations and issue reports, especially concerning matters where controversies have arisen. To imbue the office with as much independence as possible, its director, who is chosen by the executive board, is prohibited from going to work on the IMF staff after concluding his term (four years, with a possibility of an additional three years) and has full control over his own staff. Critics of the IMF eagerly awaited the evaluation office's assessment of the Fund's performance in Argentina, and the report that the office published in July 2004 did not pull punches. In exhaustive detail, its critique exposed the flaws in the Fund's approach; although the report blamed "the failure of Argentine policy makers to take necessary corrective measures at a sufficiently early stage," it said that in the mid-1990s the IMF "repeatedly overlooked weaknesses" in areas ranging from fiscal policy to labor market reforms to tax compliance. The authors were especially scathing concerning the Fund's rescue attempts in the latter half of 2001, blasting the institution at one point for causing Argentina to "engage in desperate attempts to save what was by then clearly unsustainable." Appropriately, the report's blistering language seemed likely to cause the public servants involved to cringe in embarrassment and reflect at length on their mistakes, thereby minimizing the chances that those mistakes would be repeated.

It remains to be seen whether the threat of major censure by the evaluation office, and the firing of a department head, produce meaningful change in the IMF's culture and operations. There are ample grounds for skepticism. But in making the global system less prone to emerging-market crises, it is even more important to alter financial market behavior, especially in light of the conflicts of interest and other factors distorting the movement of international capital. As noted previously, the ability of portfolio investors to move money unfettered across national borders is a matter of controversy among economists, much more so than is the freedom of trade in goods. With regard to this aspect of global capitalism, the Argentine crisis underlines the need for major repair. It points inexorably to the conclusion that government efforts to tame and modulate international capital flows should be substantially greater than they are today.

The prevailing orthodoxy in the early and mid-1990s was that notwithstanding the risks, developing countries should open up to foreign capital. The IMF and the U.S. Treasury were fairly dogmatic in pressing countries to do so, believing that the explosion in the volume of international flows would prove largely beneficial. Fund and Treasury officials looked askance at moves to regulate the movement of money. One of the policies they discouraged other countries from emulating, for example, was the approach adopted by Chile, which effectively taxed "hot" inflows of short-term money by requiring foreign investors and lenders to deposit amounts equal to 30 percent of their investments in non-interest-bearing accounts for one year.

Even after the crises in Asia and other regions, many among the high priesthood of economic policymaking maintained the position that although international capital is prone to boom and bust cycles, the expansions that it helps to foster are arguably worth a certain measure of instability. In this view, crises are like "growing pains" for developing countries: Suppose, for example, that a country can grow at 7 or 8 percent annual rates in most years by opening its doors to foreign capital—versus, say, 5 or 6 percent without it? And suppose the price of an open-door policy is a crisis every decade or so; isn't that an acceptable tradeoff?

With good reason, however, many economists who previously favored greater freedom of capital movements have become less enthusiastic, and the Fund itself came around to a more neutral position. In a survey of the evidence published in May 2003, four Fund economists, including chief economist Ken Rogoff, wrote that "there is as yet no clear and robust empirical proof" that countries grow faster by linking their financial systems more deeply to the outside world. In the long run, countries should aim to be as open to foreign capital as the United States or Britain are, but for now, "financial integration should be approached cautiously," the Fund economists said. "The process of [opening up capital markets] appears to have been accompanied in some cases by increased vulnerability to crises."

This analysis does not mean that cross-border flows of capital should be severely stifled, much less eliminated entirely. But within the category of foreign capital, some types pose greater risks than others, much as certain kinds of cholesterol are beneficial for the heart while others clog the arteries. In the "good cholesterol" capital-flow category, the best is foreign direct investment—spending on plants and equipment by multinational industrial firms such as Nike or Ford or Motorola. Direct investment creates jobs and in some cases transfers technology to developing countries. Moreover, it is not prone to panicky exodus the way portfolio capital is; whereas owners of stocks or bonds may wish to withdraw their money from a country simply because they fear others are doing so, and can sell their securities with a tap of a computer key, owners of factories are much more likely to be patient and stable investors.

As for "bad cholesterol" flows, gradations of risk exist even within this category. Equity (stock market investing) is a less problematic form of foreign capital than debt, because when economies weaken, firms with shrinking profits can cut or halt their dividend payments without facing financial ruin. By contrast, in the case of bonds, bank loans, and the like, debtors must pay interest and principal on their obligations regardless of economic conditions; the penalty for nonpayment is the enormously disruptive consequences of default. Since markets are aware of these facts, they are more likely to be stampeded from countries that have high foreign debt than from countries that have high foreign equity.

The implications are clear: Public policy should shift incentives away from the bad-cholesterol types of foreign capital and toward the good kind; and it should seek to minimize the distortions caused by conflicts of interest and other such problems.

Fortunately, a model exists for dealing with the conflict-of-interest issue. In April 2003 federal and state regulators reached a settlement with Wall Street concerning the scandalous behavior that had been uncovered in the stock market businesses of many brokerage houses. Under that settlement, ten of the largest firms agreed to a number of measures to raise barriers between research and investment banking, including a prohibition on investment bankers becoming involved "directly or indirectly" in evaluating analysts' job performance. The big investment houses also agreed to create a $432 million fund to pay for research by independent firms (firms with no investment banking businesses) that would be distributed to investors along with sell-side reports.

These reforms should be implemented in Wall Street's emerging-markets business as well as in stocks. Requiring sell-side firms to fund independent analyses of emerging markets would be especially desirable, because it is unclear whether conflicts of interest will truly disappear from sell-side research as long as analysts know that their firms' profitability depends heavily on winning investment banking fees. Far too little independent research is available for emerging-market investors, and subsidizing it with money from sell-side interests would help generate an increase in objective analysis.

Much harder to fix is the pernicious influence of the EMBI-Plus index in inducing large portfolio managers to lend heavily to countries with burdensome debt. Other benchmarks offer some improvement over the EMBI-Plus but not much. Almost no matter how they are constructed, emerging-market bond indexes prompt money managers to lend excessively to some country or another by dint of the country's index weighting. It would be preferable if portfolio managers could ignore indices altogether, but their clients—ultimately, the people whose money is being invested—generally want some objective way of measuring the managers' performance. That consideration evidently takes priority over the potential harm caused to countries by the distortional effects of indices on the global allocation of capital.

The downside of indices is all the more reason rich-country governments should be taking steps to dampen the eagerness of financial institutions and wealthy investors to lend to emerging markets. One effective measure might be a tax, imposed by the world's governments, on international lending—not a punitive one that would discourage such activity completely but one that would be steep enough to make lenders circumspect. The inspiration for this idea comes from James Tobin, the late Nobel-prize–winning economist, who favored using such taxes to throw "sand in the gears" of international speculation. More recently, Ted Truman of the Institute for International Economics, a former top Treasury and Federal Reserve official, proposed an annual fee of 0.1 percent on all forms of cross-border investment. (The fee would be imposed by all IMF member governments on the average annual gross value of all outstanding cross-border investment, so it would be a tax on the stock of investment rather than flows of investment as Tobin envisioned.) Truman's motive was not to throw sand; in fact, he deliberately proposed a rate low enough that decisions by investors and lenders would barely be affected, but he wanted to raise revenue—about $25 billion to $30 billion a year, he reckoned—for a new type of IMF rescue facility, and he thought of the tax as a form of insurance premium that international investors should pay. Truman's proposal could be modified to apply only to debt capital, with the tax rate set a bit higher, and the revenue could be used for all sorts of international public purposes—one possibility being to beef up the IMF's war chest. (If the war chest grew too large, excess funds could be returned to member-country taxpayers.)

Another worthy proposal came from Ken Rogoff, before he joined the IMF as chief economist, in a paper he coauthored with his colleague Jeremy Bulow. The international financial system is biased in a number of ways in favor of extending debt capital rather than equity to emerging markets, Rogoff and Bulow observed. Among other things, international equity investors must depend on local courts in emerging markets to remedy any grievances they have; international bond investors enjoy the jurisdiction of courts in places like New York and London, because bond contracts are usually written to ensure that they do. One way to change that bias would be to scrap laws in the United States, Britain, and other countries that allow governments issuing bonds to waive the "sovereign immunity" they would otherwise have for their commercial property, such as state oil company revenues. The legal details are complicated, but the bottom line of the Rogoff-Bulow proposal is this: An investor wanting to put money in, say, Mexican bonds would have to rely on Mexican courts, the same as an investor in Mexican stocks. The legal incentives, in other words, would at least be neutral in tilting capital less toward lending and more toward equity investing.

Beyond those ideas, emerging-market countries should be aggressively prodded—by the IMF, the U.S. government, and any other institution that might have clout—to consider imposing controls of the sort Chile imposed to limit capital inflows. The IMF has cautiously accepted the proposition that Chilean-style controls may be useful for some countries. Regrettably, though, the Bush administration Treasury maintained a hostile attitude toward such controls and toward any emergency restrictions that countries might impose in a crisis to prevent capital flight. The Treasury even went to the extent of holding up U.S. free-trade agreements with Chile and Singapore until those two nations accepted provisions that could penalize them for losses suffered by investors stemming from restrictions on capital movements. Bush administration officials declared their intention to extract similar concessions from all Latin American countries signing on to a Western Hemisphere–wide trade deal, should such a pact come into being. This sort of market fundamentalism gives capitalism a bad name in the developing world; the U.S. Treasury should rethink its knee-jerk opposition to capital controls.

The best proposal might be the development of a market for new types of bonds that work more like equity than debt. These securities, called growth-linked bonds, would pay interest that rises or falls depending on a country's GDP. Instead of being forced to shell out interest payments based on a prefixed schedule, a government would be allowed to pay less when the economy weakens and required to pay more during boom times. That way, the economy would be less likely to get caught in a vicious cycle of sluggish growth, rising deficits, and market anxiety. Argentina proposed issuing these types of bonds in 2003 as part of the restructuring of its defaulted debt, and the Bush administration liked the idea. Growth-linked bonds pose a classic catch-22, however: Wall Street is unenthusiastic about them because investors often balk at new types of investments, and until many bonds are being bought and sold, investors cannot have confidence markets will function smoothly. In short, without a market, there is no demand; without demand, there can be no market. Moreover, in the market for fixed-income securities, investors strongly prefer to be assured of predictable payment streams. That is natural; "fixed" is supposed to mean exactly that. But for the sake of limiting future crises—a goal bondholders surely share no less so than policymakers—Washington, the G-7, the IMF, and financial market leaders should be encouraging the use of growth-linked bonds by as many emerging markets as possible.

Whatever action may be taken to tame international capital flows, it surely cannot suffice to end crises altogether. The next time one erupts, maybe the international community will be able to muster a better response than it did in Argentina—but to that end, it must start focusing promptly on what it did wrong and how its approach to crisis management might be altered.

Sometimes a principle is stated with such simplicity and elegance that beholding it causes related concepts to fall into place, bringing clarity to an otherwise confusing welter of ideas. One such principle leaped at me from the page when I read this reminder in the context of how to guide international policy in future financial crises: "A better approach would recognize that default is a natural feature of the market mechanism, not something to be avoided at all costs. But it would seek to limit the costs of sovereign defaults when they do occur."

That passage comes from a paper by Andy Haldane of the Bank of England and Mark Kruger of the Bank of Canada. The two economists argue for what they call a "middle way" between two extreme positions in the debate over how to manage crises. On one end of the spectrum are proposals for the IMF to provide emergency assistance in almost unlimited amounts. The problem with such approaches is that they would engender too much moral hazard, because investors and lenders, confident in being bailed out, would pour money into emerging markets without regard to risk. At the other end of the spectrum are proposals to abolish the IMF, or severely truncate its activities, leaving countries to fend for themselves. Such laissez-faire approaches would have the virtue of eliminating the moral-hazard problem. But when crises hit, millions of innocent people would suffer unduly for the sins of their leaders.

The middle way proposed by Haldane and Kruger takes as its starting point the principle that IMF rescue loans must be strictly limited in size, to "normal" amounts (300 percent of quota, as per IMF rules). In many cases, the combination of a limited-size loan, together with economic reforms and perhaps a voluntary debt restructuring, would presumably suffice to quell a crisis. Only in truly exceptional situations that "threaten the stability of the international monetary system" would larger loans be allowed; those would require a special report by the IMF staff, which would be made public, plus an audit by the Independent Evaluation Office to hold Fund officials accountable.

Here is the controversial part of the Haldane-Kruger scheme: It would make standstills—suspensions of debt payments—much more acceptable than they are today as a "backstop" measure in dealing with crises. In cases where limited IMF loans were not working, or appeared unlikely to work, the country in question would be encouraged to declare a standstill, including controls on the outflow of capital if necessary. That would bring a halt to the panicky withdrawal of funds, giving the country breathing space while it took remedial actions such as a comprehensive debt restructuring and the design of a new economic program. The IMF and the official international community could take a "supporting role" in the standstill, perhaps by offering modest additional loans up to the allowed limits, provided the country was meeting certain conditions.

This set of procedures would undoubtedly accomplish Haldane and Kruger's first goal of recognizing that default is a natural feature of the market mechanism rather than a scourge that must be avoided in any way possible. But what about their second goal—limiting the costs of sovereign defaults when they do occur? Argentina's case strongly suggests that Haldane and Kruger's proposal, by itself, would not be adequate.

Remember that Argentine and IMF officials all along were fearful—and understandably so—that if Argentina halted payments on its debt, the gates of hell would open in the form of bank runs and mass peso-dumping. Something was needed to minimize the impact, and as previously suggested, the most useful step would have been a major international loan package, probably in the $15 billion to $20 billion range.

For clarity, this kind of loan needs a special name, because it must be distinguished from the conventional, catalytic loans of the sort the IMF gave Argentina to prevent it from defaulting and devaluing. The IMF has multiple boring names for its loans—"standby arrangements," "supplemental reserve facility," and the like—and since I cannot hope to match international bureaucrats' skill at creating dull nomenclature, I'll propose an irreverent name for the kind of loan I wish Argentina had gotten: a "take-the-plunge" loan, which would be tailored strictly for countries that restructure their debts to sustainable levels, or abandon an unsustainable currency peg. An alternative name could be a "Roubini-Setser" loan, because the argument for it is eloquently stated in a book published in 2004 by Nouriel Roubini and Brad Setser. They make the case that the IMF should be *simultaneously tougher and more generous* in many of the crises that it encounters (my emphasis):

> Tough because the IMF should be willing to make an upfront judgment that a country won't be able to avoid a restructuring and thus be willing to refuse the country's request for help unless the country is willing to develop a credible plan to restructure its debts (and to change its exchange rate regime, if needed). More generous because the IMF should also be more willing to provide meaningful financial support to a country undergoing a restructuring. This is particularly true if the country, encouraged by the IMF, decides to restructure early on, before digging itself into a deeper hole.

Lamentably, the opposite approach was taken in a number of the IMF loans that were dispensed during the Bush administration. As Roubini and Setser point out, "the IMF has drifted into a world where it makes very large loans to try to help very indebted countries avoid any debt restructurings"—this, despite proclamations by administration officials and the G-7 that the time has come to limit the size of IMF loans, especially in cases where debt sustainability is questionable. Citing Brazil and Turkey as prime examples, Roubini and Setser observe that in the 2001–2004 period the Fund gave some of its largest loans ever in relation to the recipient countries' GDP, and the indebtedness of these countries also was higher than that of previous borrowers.

I propose a marriage—it would have to be a shotgun marriage, with both parties harboring deep misgivings—between the Haldane-Kruger standstill approach and the Roubini-Setser toughness-generosity combo. Although the two teams of economists disagree with each other on a number of important issues, the strong points of each proposal could be combined to forge a marked improvement in the current architecture. The hybrid would work this way:

1. IMF loans would be held strictly to normal limits in cases of conventional rescues, and standstills would become a standard part of the crisis-resolution toolkit.

2. But for countries that needed to restructure their debts or change their currency regimes, take-the-plunge loans would be available from the IMF in copious amounts, with much lighter restrictions. Of course, such countries would have to agree with the Fund on a sensible set of economic policies, and show good faith in dealing with creditors on the terms of any debt restructuring.

3. The only exceptions to rule 1—the only cases in which the IMF could make above-normal conventional loans to a country—would be if the stability of the international monetary system were threatened, or if the country in question were clearly suffering from a liquidity crisis rather than a solvency crisis.

4. The Fund would adopt safeguards to assure that it adhered to rule 3:

    a. In cases where Fund officials believed it was necessary to make a conventional loan above normal limits, the staff would have to prepare a special report justifying the move, which would be made public, as suggested by Haldane and Kruger. In fact, the Fund has already adopted a similar rule.

    b. To stiffen the Fund's backbone, an independent body of outside experts would also prepare, and make public, a report assessing the case for making a conventional loan above normal limits—if possible, before the managing director submitted the loan to the IMF board. This group, which would ideally number around five people, would be drawn mainly from academia, and it would have the power to scrutinize proposed loans to see whether the requirements for large conventional loans truly were being met.

This set of rules would give both the IMF and debtor countries a much greater incentive than they have now to pull the plug on unsustainable policies. The IMF could still offer above-normal loans when it should, and if it came under pressure to lend when it should not—for example, to prop up a country with unsustainable debts or a doomed currency regime—the panel of outside experts would serve as a powerful counterforce.

This approach could allow the IMF to position itself quite differently from its usual role in cases where it was offering a take-the-plunge loan to a country that was restructuring its debts. Instead of appearing to be an enforcer of austerity aiming to ensure that a country makes full payment to bondholders, the Fund could be perceived as the deliverer of a safety net at a time when a country was undertaking a program of shared sacrifice. Bondholders and other foreign creditors, after all, would be suffering losses at the Fund's insistence.

That would make it easier for the Fund to demand that the government adopt meaningful economic reforms as part of the deal.*

No crisis-management approach is perfect, and the Haldane-Kruger-Roubini-Setser combination is subject to a number of objections. Severely curtailing large, conventional rescue loans would deprive the international community of a tool that may be useful in some instances. Brazil offers perhaps the best case in point. Predictions of a Brazilian default were widespread in 2002, when country risk on the nation's bonds peaked at about 2,400 during presidential elections. Instead of succumbing, Brazil secured large catalytic loans from the IMF, and the new government of President Luiz Inacio Lula da Silva stuck to disciplined macroeconomic policies. In the process, the country-risk level plummeted to about 550, and Brazil was spared the horrors that were visited upon Argentina. Had the IMF insisted on a restructuring, the Brazilian economy would surely have undergone much tougher times.

Brazil thus would appear to vindicate the value of large, conventional IMF rescues. But as this book was being completed, the jury

---

* Credit must be given where credit is due. In Uruguay, the IMF—backed by the Bush administration—employed an approach similar to the one outlined here, complete with a take-the-plunge loan.

Uruguay was the only country to suffer serious contagion effects from the Argentine crisis. In mid-2002 the Uruguayan government and the Fund agreed on a plan for a rescue loan that would be contingent on a debt restructuring. The government induced creditors in 2003 to accept a stretched-out payment schedule on their bonds; although technically voluntary, the deal essentially forced them to take a haircut, because it was clearly done under the threat of default. Meanwhile, the IMF's loans, totaling about $3 billion, gave the nation's central bank enough reserves to calm the jitters of depositors and prevented a disastrous bank run. The investment bankers and officials involved in the operation touted it as precisely the sort of rescue that should have been done in Argentina.

Serious doubts remain, however, over whether Uruguay's plunge was sufficient, because in the effort to keep the debt restructuring voluntary, the government administered only a modest haircut to bondholders. Many experts fear that the country remains burdened with too much debt, so if another crisis erupts, and another haircut is required, the Fund will no longer be in a position to help because it will have already lent so much.

was still very much out on whether Brazil's IMF program had succeeded or merely postponed disaster. The Brazilian economy remained stagnant in 2003, and although growth was finally picking up in 2004, the government's debt remained alarmingly high, raising concerns about whether the da Silva administration could stay on course. The dramatic improvement in the country risk level, though partly a result of investor appreciation for the government's strong policies, was also attributable to the 2003–2004 bubble in emerging-market bonds. Thus a serious danger remained that Brazil's virtuous cycle—lower interest rates, stronger growth, a declining debt-to-GDP ratio—would turn vicious.

A second, more important objection can also be lodged against an approach that seeks to limit the costs of default—namely, that default will become too easy and too painless. If that were to happen (so the argument goes), countries would have an incentive to abrogate their debt obligations willy-nilly, which in turn would severely diminish the willingness of global financial markets to provide capital to developing nations. This objection is based on the logical concern that if creditors' rights are inordinately weakened, credit will cease to flow or become prohibitively expensive. To cite a simple example, homeowners would not benefit if the law were changed to prevent banks from foreclosing on people defaulting on their mortgages; banks merely would stop lending on homes.

But if the Haldane-Kruger-Roubini-Setser approach is implemented skillfully, the incentive for countries to default should increase only marginally. As Argentina's tale shows, top economic officials strenuously seek to avoid defaults, devaluations, and any number of other such departures from previously stated promises, because they know the political costs are likely to be high. Standstills and defaults will inevitably be painful even if accompanied by loans to soften the impact. If cases arise in which a country's top officials are itching for an excuse to renege on their national obligations, or are refusing to show any sort of good faith in their dealings with creditors, the IMF can—and should—withhold support.

As for the prospect that financiers would become less inclined to provide capital to emerging markets, if this book has shown anything, it is that such a scenario ought not to keep anyone awake at night. Indeed, a good case can be made for yet another measure, beyond Haldane-Kruger-Roubini-Setser, that would help limit the costs of sovereign default.

As a caricature of an avaricious coupon-clipper, Kenneth Dart was in a class by himself. A member of a reclusive, strife-ridden Michigan family that had made billions of dollars from manufacturing Styrofoam cups, Dart was a resident of the Cayman Islands, where he lived on a guarded compound. According to one of his brothers, from whom he was estranged, he once considered making his home on his 220-foot yacht, which was armored to withstand torpedo fire. He had escaped federal tax liability by renouncing his U.S. citizenship and becoming a citizen of Belize, and he gained notoriety in the mid-1990s when the Belizean government sought to open a diplomatic post for him in Sarasota, Florida, where his parents, wife, and children lived. In investing his fortune, he demonstrated a keen eye for squeezing money out of emerging markets, especially those of countries in financial distress. Argentina was a logical candidate for his attention.

Dart owned $595 million in face value of Argentine bonds, which he had bought at bargain prices in November and December 2001, just prior to the default, when the bonds were trading at a deep discount, about 38 cents per dollar of face value. As far as he was concerned, he had a legitimate claim to the full amount of principal and interest due; the bonds, after all, contained guarantees that the Argentine government would pay those sums, on time, with no changes in payment terms unless bondholders unanimously agreed—the provision typically contained in sovereign bond issues under New York state law. In September 2003 a federal district court in Manhattan awarded a summary judgment in his favor, declaring him entitled to the immediate payment of $700 million in principal and unpaid interest. To be sure, winning such a judgment against a sovereign government is far from the same thing as being able to seize its valuable assets; the Argentine government had taken care to put its financial holdings safely out of the reach of foreign courts. Other bondholders who were pursuing litigation were seeking to attach government assets such as a naval vessel, or Argentine corporate funds that they claimed belonged to the government—to no avail. But Dart had established himself as a tenacious pursuer of his contractual rights, with high-powered attorneys who knew how to exercise leverage to the fullest.

People who know Dart say privately that in contrast with the image he has acquired in the media, he is a surprisingly mild-mannered fellow and devoted family man who does not seek out legal confrontations. But during the 1990s, he had engaged in a considerable amount of litigation over his international holdings. He was a lone holdout from Brazil's debt restructuring, filing a lawsuit claiming the right to full payment on bonds he had bought for $375 million, about a quarter of their face value. Although he eventually lost the lawsuit, he reaped an enormous profit by selling the bonds for more than $900 million. In Argentina's case, after winning an appeal of the judgment against the government, Dart's lawyer was quoted as saying: "There are some assets that are ripe for enforcement, and we are working on the most effective way of enforcing the award."

Dart was hardly typical of Argentina's bondholders, whose ranks included hundreds of thousands of unsophisticated, middle-class investors from Italy and elsewhere. So as undeserving a claimant as he may seem, that should not undermine the legitimacy of the grievances held by other bondholders. They were understandably upset at the losses they had suffered and the Argentine government's willingness to pay only a fraction of what they were owed.

But Dart's lawsuit raised anew the need for changes in the international legal environment to make sovereign defaults less costly and ensure that they can proceed smoothly. Dart was showing all the signs of being a rogue creditor—one who is prepared to litigate to get a better deal than other creditors are willing to settle for.* Such holdouts pose little problem as long as their numbers are kept to a minimum; a restructuring can proceed anyway, and if the rogues eventually get extra money, the total amount involved will not be significant. But here again is a collective-action problem: Once other creditors see rogues filing lawsuits, they are likely to start wondering why they should accept the terms of a restructuring when they might get a more generous settlement by joining the holdouts. And for rogue creditors with patience, the payoff can be huge; according to one IMF study, investors who file lawsuits to block sovereign debt restructurings have earned annual returns of 50 percent to 300 percent. The more creditors find rogue status attractive, the more difficult it becomes to persuade creditors in general to accept a reasonable reduction in their claims.

That, as noted in Chapter 8, was one of the main reasons for Anne Krueger's proposal in November 2001 to establish an international bankruptcy system for countries. One of her major aims was to curb the power of rogue creditors to use litigation to block a country from restructuring its debts. Krueger's plan would effectively create new international law that would allow a supermajority of bondholders to approve a restructuring regardless of the guarantees in existing bond contracts requiring bondholders' unanimous approval.

By the time Dart's lawsuit was filed, Krueger's Sovereign Debt Restructuring Mechanism (SDRM) had been shelved, the victim of an alliance among some elements of the Bush administration, Wall Street, and emerging-market governments. Even though Krueger

---

* Dart bought a sufficiently large position in one particular bond issue for him single-handedly to block any changes that other holders of that issue might accept. As his lawsuit pointedly noted, "Because [his investment firm] holds more than 33 1/3 % of the aggregate principal in the series, it has the power to veto any proposed amendment . . . that could substantially affect its right with respect to the Bond."

had diluted the plan to accommodate some objections, the critics were still vehement in their opposition. The scheme made default too easy, some complained, and this would lead to a drying up in flows to emerging markets, or at least significantly raise the cost of borrowing. It would give the IMF too much power, according to others, making The Fund something like a bankruptcy judge in cases where it was also a creditor. The rogue-creditor problem, still others said, is mostly a figment of bureaucratic imaginations.

The SDRM lost out in early 2003 to a less potent bankruptcy scheme. This plan involved no centralized official action to override the rights of individual creditors. Instead, international lenders and the countries they financed would voluntarily agree to insert provisions called "collective-action clauses" (CACs) into the contracts of sovereign bonds when those bonds came to market. The CACs would specify procedures for what would happen in the event of a crisis, allowing a supermajority of bondholders, rather than 100 percent, to approve a standstill or debt restructuring if such actions proved necessary.

The triumph of CACs over the SDRM offered some depressing insights into the difficulty of making headway on international financial reforms. The idea of introducing the clauses had been proposed years earlier and had stalled amid opposition from Wall Street; only when the more radical SDRM reared its head did private financiers come around to backing CACs as the lesser evil. And despite the apparent enthusiasm of Treasury Secretary O'Neill for the SDRM, the man who quashed it was Undersecretary John Taylor, who in an April 2002 speech declared that the "decentralized approach ... makes much more sense and is much more workable" than Krueger's plan—a striking example of the lack of coordination between the Bush Treasury and the IMF (not to mention the lack of coordination within the Treasury itself). Eventually, with U.S. clout working its usual magic, CACs won endorsement from the G-7 and the IMF's policy-setting committee of member-country finance ministers, and several emerging-market countries began issuing bonds with the clauses in 2003.

CACs are fine as far as they go, but they have some major drawbacks and loopholes. Many lawyers question whether inserting the clauses into one bond issue will mean that the rules apply across all issues from the same sovereign borrower, especially if the other bonds have been issued in a different legal jurisdiction. A related problem is what might be called the "overhang" issue: Many old-style bonds—those with clauses requiring unanimous approval for changes in payment terms—remain outstanding and do not mature for a number of years. (Among these, for example, are the Argentine bonds held by Kenneth Dart.) Thus, even if all newly issued bonds contained CACs, using them to provide the option of orderly debt restructuring for countries would still be a distant dream.

That is why I hope a new Treasury team, when one comes to office, will resurrect the SDRM. Whatever happens in Argentina's restructuring and the Dart case, Dart has offered a timely reminder that rogues still have the potential for behavior inimical to the public interest. Yes, the establishment of an SDRM might mean that investors become more skittish about emerging markets. If that occurs, then again, so be it. I realize that a few Wall Streeters might suffer some diminution in their bonuses as a result. Don't cry for them, Argentina.

One additional point is in order concerning the implications of Argentina's downfall—and that point is what it means for the U.S. economy.

In magnitudes that Argentines could only dream of, the U.S. government has been spending more than it raises in taxes, and American consumers and businesses have been importing more goods than they have been exporting, with borrowing from foreigners covering much of the gaps. The record budget deficit of about $413 billion for 2004, and the record trade deficit of even greater magnitude, may be explained away by short-term factors—lingering effects of the U.S. recession, costs of the wars in Iraq and Afghanistan, weakness in demand overseas for U.S. exports. But the worrisome issue is not the red ink recorded in 2004; it is the prospect that these gaps will remain extraordinarily wide in the future.

The risks of continuing this arrangement were spelled out in a paper by former Treasury Secretary Robert Rubin and two coauthors, Peter Orszag of the Brookings Institution and Allen Sinai of the advisory firm Decision Economics, which they presented to the American Economic Association in January 2004. The authors noted that based on reasonable economic and political assumptions, federal government deficits would total about $5 trillion over the coming decade, in the absence of drastic changes in the policies in effect in 2004. In turn, the national debt would rise from 35 percent of GDP in 2003 to 50 percent of GDP in 2013—the highest since the mid-1950s, when the United States was still paying down the debt it incurred to fight World War II. The projected red ink and increased debt would be even greater in the years thereafter, when the baby-boom generation reaches retirement age and starts to collect Social Security and Medicare benefits, the authors observed.

This debt buildup usually has been viewed as a long-term problem that would crimp the living standards of future generations, rather than as a potential source of financial instability, because as noted in Chapter 1, rich countries are significantly less susceptible to panics by foreign investors than emerging markets are. According to the authors, however, a substantial danger lurks in the near term—a warning laden with credibility from Rubin's decades of experience on Wall Street. No problems had yet arisen, the authors acknowledged, because foreigners had obligingly lent the United States about one-third of the $4 trillion in government debt held by the public, accepting low interest rates in the bargain. The same was true for the trade deficit. Using money that Americans paid for imported cars, electronic gizmos, T-shirts, and all manner of other items from abroad, foreigners plowed those funds into U.S. Treasury bonds, and other securities. But the prospective debt was reaching such excessive levels that global markets could undergo a sudden, negative change in sentiment toward U.S. investments, the authors admonished. That could happen if, for example, a political impasse between Republicans and Democrats led markets to conclude that a budget compromise was impossible and that inflation would likely rekindle as dollars were printed to cover the deficit. The result would be a major sell-off of U.S. bonds and stocks, with investors demanding significantly higher yields on their U.S. holdings, which "in turn can generate a self-reinforcing negative cycle" as rising interest rates, a weakening economy, and widening deficits feed on each other. The authors concluded that "it is impossible to know at what point market expectations about the nation's large projected fiscal imbalance could trigger those types of dynamics," but the financial disarray could inflict "costs far larger than those presented in conventional economic analyses."

Scenarios like the one conjured up by Rubin and his coauthors have seemed implausible in recent years because similar alarms proved false during the previous era of giant U.S. deficits, the 1980s. But only a decade earlier, in the 1970s, there were periods when the United States was losing the confidence of international markets, which included major attacks on the dollar and unloading of Treasury bonds. The origin of those episodes can be traced to the guns-and-butter deficit spending of the Johnson and Nixon administrations.

Bush administration officials have airily dismissed concerns that global markets might stop shoveling money into U.S. securities. "The United States remains the best place to invest," Treasury Secretary John Snow told a congressional hearing in March 2004 in response to a question about the possibility that foreigners might dump their U.S. assets. "On a risk-adjusted basis, we have the highest return . . . because of this extraordinary economy, and this extraordinary system of laws. We protect capital." In an op-ed article in the April 2004 *Financial Times,* Snow argued that the trade deficit "reflects foremost the strengths of the U.S. economy—high productivity, strong U.S. growth relative to growth abroad, and the relative attraction of investing in our robust, dynamic economy." Such soothing rhetoric may prove well founded; the United States may dodge the financial-crisis bullet indefinitely. But does the talk about deficits reflecting economic strength sound familiar?

It *could* happen here. Americans who give Argentina's story fair consideration and conclude otherwise are deluding themselves. The risks are much lower for the United States than they were for Argentina, but they are unacceptably high. The words of Miguel Kiguel, Argentina's former finance undersecretary, are apropos: "Once you know the markets are there, and there is financing, you behave as if financing will be there forever." The United States has shown every sign of having adopted that same cavalier, incautious attitude in the first few years of the twenty-first century.

The economic upswing that gathered momentum in Argentina in 2003 and 2004—be it a dead-cat bounce or something more lasting—has given the Argentine government and its people a precious opportunity to fix an array of long-standing weaknesses in the nation's economy. Let us hope the Argentines will use this period fruitfully, more so than they did the last time the economy boomed in the late 1990s. Specifically helpful would be for the government to put its fiscal policy on a responsible course once and for all, with the provinces weaned from dependence on the central authorities and ordinary citizens obliged to pay their taxes in full. Above all, it would be desirable for the government to create an investment atmosphere sufficiently attractive that Argentines bring home the billions of dollars they have stashed overseas. Argentina's fate, after all, is primarily in the hands of Argentines. That has been true all along, a point that bears repeating one final time.

The upswing in the global economy has likewise created unusually ideal circumstances for making changes in the international financial system so that the ladder of economic advancement becomes sturdier for the countries seeking to scale its rungs. Reforms of this type are always easier to promote and implement when expansions are under way, employment is rising, and capital is bountiful; they are hard, if not impossible, when the economic pie is shrinking, capital is jumpy, and policymakers need to worry that rule changes will cause financial turbulence to turn contagious.

If the lessons of Argentina's crisis lead to substantial revisions in the rules of global finance, the suffering of the Argentine people will not have been entirely in vain. Timidity and inaction by the international community, on the other hand, would add insult to the Argentines' injury. That, of course, is the least important of many good reasons for bold measures in this regard. For the powers that run the global economy, it is a matter of both simple justice and enlightened self-interest to ensure that the rewards of free markets are spread more widely, more steadfastly, and with far fewer capricious reversals.

Chronology: Road to Ruin

BOOM YEARS:1991–1998

1991

APRIL 1 At the instigation of Economy Minister Domingo Cavallo, Argentina adopts the convertibility system, which rigidly fixes the exchange rate at 1 peso = $1.

1991–94

Inflation subsides, reaching negligible levels by mid-decade. Economic growth soars as the government embarks on a program of deregulating the economy, lowering trade barriers, and privatizing state owned enterprises.

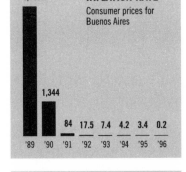

1995

Argentine financial markets are battered by the Mexican peso crisis and the economy falls into a brief recession.

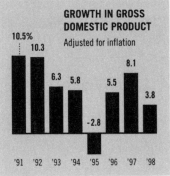

1996–98

The economy rebounds, and money pours in from abroad.

1996

JULY Roque Fernández replaces Cavallo as Economy Minister.

1997

The IMF negotiates a "precautionary" program with Argentina promising to provide emergency loans if needed. Although financial crises begin to devastate some Asian economies, Argentina is relatively unscathed. Meanwhile, however, Argentina's debt burden is growing.

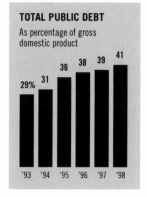

TOTAL PUBLIC DEBT
As percentage of gross domestic product

1998

APRIL IMF officials warn that Argentina could suffer a meltdown, but financial markets pay little heed.

JULY An IMF mission informs the Argentine authorities that the Fund will effectively suspend its programs unless the government enacts tough legislation to reform the nation's labor laws.

AUGUST–SEPTEMBER Financial markets tumble worldwide in the wake of Russia's default on its government debt. The IMF, backing off from its threat, maintains its program with Argentina.

OCTOBER President Carlos Menem is given the honor of addressing the IMF–World Bank annual meeting.

RECESSION YEARS: 1999–Late 2001

1999

JANUARY Stricken by crisis, Brazil devalues its currency and Argentina's exports to Brazil fall sharply.

DECLINE IN GROSS DOMESTIC PRODUCT
In recession years

Argentina's economy slumps as other shocks hit as well. World prices decline for wheat and other Argentine exports. Capital flows to emerging markets dry up. The economy falls into a vicious cycle: recession causes the budget deficit to widen, which sparks nervousness among investors, which causes interest rates to rise, which deepens the recession—and so on.

With the mood among foreign investors having changed,

Argentina's "country risk" (*riesgo país*) remains much higher than it did in the markets' heady days prior to the Russian default.

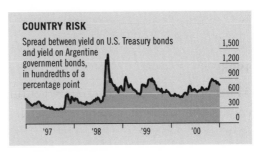

COUNTRY RISK

Spread between yield on U.S. Treasury bonds and yield on Argentine government bonds, in hundredths of a percentage point

1,500
1,200
900
600
300
0

'97   '98   '99   '00

OCTOBER Fernando de la Rúa is elected president, replacing Menem.

NOVEMBER José Luis Machinea is named Economy Minister.

2000

JANUARY With IMF approval, the new government tries to improve the nation's fiscal health by cutting the budget deficit, but this only sucks more oxygen out of the economy. The debt-to-GDP ratio continues to mount.

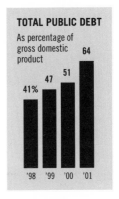

TOTAL PUBLIC DEBT

As percentage of gross domestic product

41%   47   51   64

'98   '99   '00   '01

OCTOBER Vice President Carlos Álvarez resigns. The weakening of de la Rúa's ruling coalition arouses new market jitters about the government's ability to keep the debt at manageable levels. As markets drive country risk to new heights, the government seeks help from the IMF.

DECEMBER The Argentine government and the IMF reach agreement on a program for the Fund to lend $14 billion, to be disbursed over the next three years.

2001

JANUARY 12 The IMF board approves the program. Market sentiment initially improves, but the situation worsens amid mounting evidence that the recession-plagued country cannot muster consensus for fiscal discipline either in the short or long term.

MARCH 2 Machinea, under fire for trying to keep too tight a lid on the budget, resigns as Economy Minister.

MARCH 19 Machinea's successor, Ricardo López Murphy, quits after less than three weeks on the job.

MARCH 20 Domingo Cavallo returns as Economy Minister, in a dramatic move by President de la Rúa aimed at pulling the economy back from the abyss.

APRIL–JUNE The markets, seriously alarmed about Argentina's ability to sustain its debt burden, fail to respond to Cavallo's efforts to restore confidence and growth. The government tries again, with the

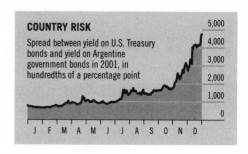

COUNTRY RISK
Spread between yield on U.S. Treasury bonds and yield on Argentine government bonds in 2001, in hundredths of a percentage point

5,000
4,000
3,000
2,000
1,000
0

J F M A M J J A S O N D

"megaswap"—a deal with bondholders in which they voluntarily exchange new bonds for old ones, stretching out interest and principal payments. But the swap, completed on June 3, fails to change market psychology and investors continue to drive country risk levels higher.

JULY With the government unable to borrow at affordable rates, Cavallo announces the "zero deficit" policy, including cuts of up to 13 percent in government salaries and pensions.

AUGUST 21 The IMF agrees to a second rescue, this time an $8 billion package. At the insistence of the U.S. Treasury, $3 billion of the IMF money is earmarked for a vaguely-defined plan to help Argentina restructure its debt.

SEPTEMBER 7 The IMF board approves the second rescue.

OCTOBER 18 Amid continuing signs that the Argentine economy is weakening rather than strengthening, a group of foreign financiers meeting privately with IMF Managing Director Horst Köhler urges that Argentina should restructure its debt.

NOVEMBER 1 The government announces a plan for a debt restructuring, aimed at saving the government $4 billion in interest payments per year.

NOVEMBER 6 In response to the restructuring, Standard & Poor's lowers Argentina's bond rating to SD, or "selective default."

NOVEMBER 16 Argentina's foreign exchange reserves, which were replenished by IMF funds in early September following the IMF's approval of its second rescue, fall back to the prior level. This shows that the IMF's assistance has in effect allowed massive sums of money to flee the country.

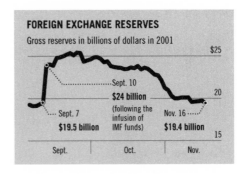

FOREIGN EXCHANGE RESERVES
Gross reserves in billions of dollars in 2001

$25

Sept. 10
$24 billion

Sept. 7
$19.5 billion
(following the infusion of IMF funds)

Nov. 16
$19.4 billion

20

15

Sept.   Oct.   Nov.

NOVEMBER 17–18 Cavallo persuades fellow finance ministers at a meeting in Ottawa that the Fund should at least send a mission to Buenos Aires, keeping alive the hope that Argentina will receive a $1.24 billion disbursal.

NOVEMBER 26 Anne Krueger, the IMF's first deputy managing director, proposes a new international "bankruptcy" system for countries.

NOVEMBER 28–30 Argentine savers, who have been pulling deposits from their banks all year, step up their withdrawals and a full-blown bank run materializes.

DECEMBER 1 The government announces restrictions on bank withdrawals and the transfer of money abroad, in a series of measures that come to be known as the *corralito*.

DECEMBER 3 The IMF recalls its mission chief from Buenos Aires.

DECEMBER 5 The IMF announces that it is "unable at this time" to consider making the $1.24 billion disbursal.

COLLAPSE: Late 2001–2002

DECEMBER 19–20 Mass protests erupt against the government, and the violence forces the resignations of Cavallo and de la Rúa. The presidency goes on an interim basis to Ramón Puerta, the president of the Senate.

DECEMBER 23 Adolfo Rodríguez Saá is named president and announces default on the government's debt to private foreign creditors.

DECEMBER 30 Rodríguez Saá resigns amid continued protests. The presidency reverts again to Puerta, but he refuses to accept it and resigns, so Eduardo Camaño, president of the lower house, becomes interim president.

2002

JANUARY 1 Congress elects Eduardo Duhalde president.

JANUARY 6 The Duhalde government terminates the peso convertibility system.

The peso plunges, hitting a low in June.

Economic output falls 11 percent as the banking system ceases to function properly. Poverty soars.

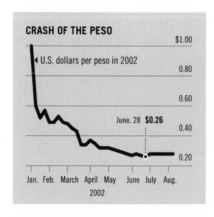

CRASH OF THE PESO

U.S. dollars per peso in 2002

June 28 **$0.26**

$1.00
0.80
0.60
0.40
0.20

Jan. Feb. March April May June July Aug.
2002

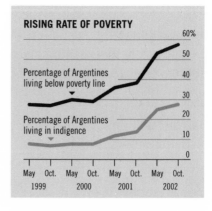

RISING RATE OF POVERTY

Percentage of Argentines living below poverty line

Percentage of Argentines living in indigence

60%
50
40
30
20
10
0

May Oct. May Oct. May Oct. May Oct.
1999   2000   2001   2002

Notes

Except where noted here, the information in this book was derived from interviews. Some of the people interviewed imposed no conditions on being quoted, whereas others felt comfortable speaking candidly only if assured a cloak of anonymity—indeed, many were promised, in accord with "deep background" rules, that they would not be quoted even anonymously unless they granted me permission to do so.

A list of interviewees follows. People interviewed on deep background were included on this list only if they gave permission or if they gave selective permission to be quoted. The list does not include a number of people who wished to remain entirely anonymous. Titles are those held during the period covered by the interview.

International Monetary Fund

Management

Horst Kohler, Managing Director
Stanley Fischer, First Deputy Managing Director
Anne Krueger, First Deputy Managing Director

Executive Board

Thomas Bernes, Canada (and eleven other countries)
Onno Wijnholds, the Netherlands (and eleven other countries)

Staff: Policy Development and Review Department

Jack Boorman, Director
Joaquin Ferran, Deputy Director
Matthew Fisher, Director, Capital Markets Division

Staff: Fiscal Affairs Department

Vito Tanzi, Director

Staff: Research Department

Michael Mussa, Director (and Economic Counselor)
Kenneth Rogoff, Director (and Economic Counselor)
Carmen Reinhart, Deputy Director
Paul Masson, Senior Advisor

Staff: Western Hemisphere Department

Sterie ("Ted") Beza, Director
Claudio Loser, Director
Teresa Ter-Minassian, Deputy Director
Tomás Reichmann, Senior Advisor
John Thornton, Chief, River Plate Division
Alberto Ramos, Senior Economist

Staff: Independent Evaluation Office

Shinki Takagi, Advisor
Isabelle Mateos y Lago, Senior Economist
Ben Cohen, Economist

Staff: External Relations Department

Thomas Dawson, Director

Argentine Government

Menem Administration

Domingo Cavallo, Minister of Economy (also during de la Rúa administration)
Roque Fernández, Minister of Economy
Miguel Kiguel, Undersecretary of Finance
Pablo Guidotti, Treasury Secretary
Rogelio Frigerio, Secretary of Economic Policy
Juan José Llach, Secretary of Economic Policy

De la Rúa Administration

José Luis Machinea, Minister of Economy
Chrystian Colombo, Cabinet Secretary

Daniel Marx, Finance Secretary
Mario Vicens, Treasury Secretary
Guillermo Mondino, Chief Economic Adviser, Ministry of Economy
Federico Sturzenegger, Secretary of Economic Policy
Nicolas Gadano, Treasury Undersecretary
Guillermo Gonzalez, Ambassador to the United States
Mario Blejer, Vice President, Central Bank of Argentina
Andrew Powell, Chief Economist, Central Bank of Argentina
Horacio Liendo, Advisor to Cavallo

U.S. Treasury

Clinton Administration

Timothy Geithner, Undersecretary for International Affairs
Edwin Truman, Assistant Secretary for International Affairs
Andrew Berg, Deputy Assistant Secretary for East Asia and Latin America
Nouriel Roubini, Advisor

Bush Administration

Kenneth Dam, Deputy Secretary
John Taylor, Undersecretary for International Affairs
Randall Quarles, Assistant Secretary for International Affairs
Kristin Forbes, Deputy Assistant Secretary of Quantitative Policy Analysis, Latin America and Caribbean Nations
Steven Backes, Director, Latin America Office
Brad Setser, Acting Director, Office of International Monetary and Financial Policy
Natan Epstein, Desk Economist for Argentina

White House

Clinton Administration

Lael Brainard, Deputy Assistant to the President for International Economics

Bush Administration

Randall Kroszner, Member, Council of Economic Advisors
Will Melick, Chief of Staff, Council of Economic Advisers

Federal Reserve

William McDonough, President, Federal Reserve Bank of New York
Terrence Checki, Executive Vice President, Federal Reserve Bank of New York

Other G-7 Governments

Ian Bennett, Associate Deputy Minister of Finance, Canada (also IMF Executive Director for Canada)

Academics

Charles Calomiris, Columbia University
Nancy Birdsall, President, Center for Global Development
Michael Pettis, Columbia University
Mario Teijeiro, President, Centro de Estudios Publicos

Private Sector: Analysts, Investment Bankers, Portfolio Managers, Traders, Salespeople, Securities Firm Administrators

William Rhodes, Citigroup
Joyce Chang, Merrill Lynch and J.P. Morgan-Chase
Federico Thomsen, ING Barings
Peter Petas, Deutsche Bank and CreditSights
Christian Stracke, Deutsche Bank and CreditSights
Siobhan Manning, Caboto USA
Eric Hermann, FH International Financial Services
Jonathan Binder, Standard Asset Management
George Estes, Grantham, Mayo, Van Otterloo & Co.
Mohamed El-Erian, Pacific Investment Management Company (PIMCO)
Paul McCulley, Pacific Investment Management Company (PIMCO)
Peter Marber, Atlantic Funds
Tom White, Metropolitan Life
Desmond Lachman, Salomon Smith Barney
Walter Molano, BCP Securities
Alberto Ades, Goldman Sachs
Dan McGovern, Merrill Lynch
Ben Heller, HBK Investments
Ben Miller, HBK Investments
Mark Siegel, Mass Mutual Insurance
Lawrence Krohn, UBS Securities and Donalson, Lufkin & Jenrette Securities
Abe Gulkowitz, Deutsche Bank
Robert Kowit, Federated Investors

Trade Associations

Nicola Stock, Association of Italian Bankers

Headhunters

Paul Heller, Cromwell Partners
Deborah Rivera, The Succession Group
Saul Wajcberg, Marc Nichols Associates
Rita Kohn, Dawn Taylor Associates
Stuart Hopard, independent

Individual Investors and Their Representatives

Adam Lerrick (U.S. professor representing bondholders)
Elio Lannutti, Director, Adusbef (Italian consumer/investor group)
Stefan Engelsberger (German investor heading bondholder group)
Felicia Migliorini (individual Italian investor)

Journalists

Isabella Bufacchi, Il Sole 24 Ore (Italy)

Some of the basic statistics and facts cited in this book—such as the annual growth of Argentina's gross domestic product, the amount the IMF lent to Argentina, and the government's annual budget deficit figures—can be found in three IMF reports on the crisis, all of which can be found on the IMF website, www.imf.org. The first is a speech delivered by Anne Krueger, the first deputy managing director, "Crisis Prevention and Resolution: Lessons from Argentina," July 17, 2002. The second is a report by the Fund staff, "Lessons from the Crisis in Argentina," released in March 2004 (hereafter called "the staff postmortem"). The third is the Independent Evaluation Office's "Report on the Evaluation of the Role of the IMF in Argentina, 1991–2001" (hereafter referred to as "the IEO report").

Data on Argentina's unemployment and poverty rates come from the website of Argentina's Instituto Nacional de Estadistica y Censos (National Institute of Statistics and Censuses), http://www.indec.gov.ar.

Prologue

xx   The $3.6 billion withdrawn from bank accounts in the last three days of November was reported in the IMF staff's postmortem on the crisis, p. 61.

xx   The quotation from the woman screaming at presidential spokesman Baylac on television comes from John Lyons, David Plumb, and Helen Murphy, "Argentina to Limit Withdrawals, Overseas Transfers," Bloomberg News, December 1, 2001.

xxi   The announcement that the IMF was "unable at this stage" to complete the review necessary to disburse the $1.24 billion was contained in a statement by spokesman David Hawley, reported in a number of news stories including Emily Schwartz, "Argentina Won't Get $1.24 Billion Loan Now, IMF Says," *Bloomberg News*, December 5, 2001.

Chapter 1

2   Information about the woman who was forced to auction off paintings, and about the March 2002 incident in Rosario, can be found in Anthony Faiola, "Despair in Once-Proud Argentina; After Economic Collapse, Deep Poverty Makes Dignity a Casualty," *Washington Post*, August 6, 2002. An account of the woman who set herself ablaze can be found in Hector Tobar, "The Good Life Is No More for Argentina," *Los Angeles Times*, February 18, 2003. Information about malnutrition among children can be found in Larry Rohter, "Once Secure, Argentines Now Lack Food and Hope," *New York Times*, March 2, 2003. Information about the invasion of *cartoneros* in fashionable neighborhoods can be found in Santiago O'Donnell, "Argentina May Be Down But I Don't Plan to Get Out," *Washington Post*, August 25, 2002.

3   Data showing Argentina's education levels to be the highest in Latin America can be found in *World Development Indicators* (Washington, D.C.: World Bank, 2004), pp. 76, 84.

4   Information about Argentina's score in the Heritage Foundation's "Index of Economic Freedom" can be found on one of the Heritage web pages, http://cf.heritage.org/index/pastScores.cfm.

5   The comment describing Argentina as the "spoiled child of the Washington Consensus" is contained in Nancy Birdsall, "What Went Wrong in Argentina?" remarks at a Center for Strategic and International Studies conference, January 29, 2002.

6   The lines about the "Electronic Herd" come from Thomas Friedman, *The Lexus and the Olive Tree* (New York: Farrar, Straus and Giroux, 1999), 115, 145.

6   I am indebted to Professor Kenneth Rogoff for the metaphor likening foreign capital inflows to steroids. He used it in a column, "This Time It's Not Different," *Newsweek* (Atlantic ed.), February 16, 2004.

7   Data about the amount of business that big securities firms generated by bringing Argentine bonds to market were kindly furnished by Thomson Financial.

7   The report, "Argentina's debt dynamics: Much ado about not so much," was published by the Emerging Markets Research Department of J.P. Morgan Securities Inc., but is no longer readily available and was furnished to me by a confidential source.

9   Data concerning the total assets under management by institutional investors in advanced economies, and the size of those assets compared to secu-

rities outstanding in emerging markets, can be found in the IMF's *Global Financial Stability Report,* April 2004, pp. 115–116, available on the IMF's website.

Chapter 2

13   Information about Cavallo can be found on his web page, www.cavallo.com.ar, and from Matt Moffett, "Seeds of Reform: Key Finance Ministers in Latin America Are Old Harvard-MIT Pals," *Wall Street Journal,* August 1, 1994. The quotation from Broda comes from Nathaniel Nash, "Plan by New Argentine Economy Chief Raises Cautious Hope for Recovery," *New York Times,* April 28, 1991.

15   Detailed accounts of Argentina's failed economic initiatives of the 1980s, and its battles with the IMF, can be found in the IMF's official history by James M. Boughton, *Silent Revolution: The International Monetary Fund 1979–1989* (Washington, D.C.: IMF, 2001).

16   The quotation from Cavallo comes from Anne M. Harrison, "Argentina to Stabilize Currency with Dollar, Gold Standard," United Press International, March 20, 1991.

16–19   Information about Argentina's history in the late nineteenth and twentieth centuries comes from Gerardo della Paolera and Alan Taylor, *Straining at the Anchor: The Argentine Currency Board and the Search for Macroeconomic Stability, 1880–1935* (Chicago: University of Chicago Press, 2001); Mauricio Rojas, *The Sorrows of Carmencita: Argentina's Crisis in a Historical Perspective* (Stockholm: Timbro, 2002); Gabriela Nouzeilles and Graciela Montaldo, eds., *The Argentina Reader: History, Culture, Politics* (Durham, N.C.: Duke University Press, 2002); Boughton, *Silent Revolution;* and Javier Corrales, "The Politics of Argentina's Meltdown," *World Policy Journal,* October 1, 2002.

17   The quotation from Rubén Darío comes from "Argentina as Latin American Avant-Garde," originally from "Argentina" in *Prosa política* by Rubén Darío (Madrid: Mundo Latino, 1911), excerpted in Nouzeilles and Montaldo, *The Argentina Reader.*

18–19   The quotations from the essay by Osvaldo Soriano come from "Vivir con la inflación," originally published in *Nueva Sociedad,* no. 100 (1989): 38–42, reprinted in Nouzeilles and Montaldo, *The Argentina Reader.*

19   The breakdown of machines at the national mint was reported in James Brooke, "Fodder for a Ravenous Inflation," *New York Times,* June 12, 1989. The halt of business among wholesalers and retailers was reported in Eugene Robinson, "Argentina's Long Lines of Inflation," *Washington Post,* January 16, 1990.

19   Data showing the relative decline in Argentina's real GDP per capita compared with developed countries comes from Della Paolera and Taylor, *Straining at the Anchor.* The "developed countries" consist of the nations belonging to the Organization for Economic Cooperation and Development.

19   The extent of soup kitchens in Buenos Aires was reported in James Brooke, "Big Latin Debtors Find That Lacking Austerity, Relief Is Not Coming Soon," *New York Times,* July 26, 1989.

19–20   The rules of convertibility were refined to include some further complexities. The law required that the central bank maintain adequate reserves to cover two-thirds of the monetary base, and these reserves could include not only dollars and gold but other foreign assets denominated in foreign currencies (bonds denominated in Japanese yen, for example). The reserves covering the other one-third of the base could consist of Argentine government bonds denominated in foreign exchange.

21–22   The episode involving Cavallo witnessed by Yair Mundlak was reported in Moffett, "Seeds of Reform."

22–23   Information about Menem's expansion of the public payroll in La Rioja province comes from "Argentina: Letter from Menemland," *The Economist,* October 6, 1990.

23–24   Information about the steps Argentina took to deregulate its economy and liberalize its trade can be found in an IMF report, "Argentina: Recent Economic Developments," April 1998, on the IMF website. Information about the privatization of the state oil company can be found in Robert deVeer, "Something for Everyone; As Latin or Oil Play, YPF Offered the Best of Both Worlds," *LatinFinance,* January 1994.

24–25   Information about Argentina's privatizations comes from both academic papers and journalistic accounts. The academic works include David McKenzie and Dilip Mookherjee, "The Distributive Impact of Privatization in Latin America: Evidence from Four Countries," *Economia* 3, 2 (Spring 2003): 161–218; Huberto Ennis and Santiago Pinto, "Privatization and Income Distribution in Argentina," West Virginia University, 2002, mimeo, part of a project titled "The Effects of Privatization on Income Distribution in Latin America," supported by the Inter-American Development Bank; Sebastian Galiani, Paul Gertler, and Ernesto Schargrodsky, "Water for Life: The Impact of the Privatization of Water Services on Child Mortality," 2002, publication forthcoming in *Journal of Political Economy,* February 2005; and John Nellis, "Privatization in Latin America," 2003, paper prepared as background material for forthcoming edition of a book titled *Washington Contentious.*

Journalistic accounts include Ed McCullough, "Argentina's Antiquated Phone System to Get Revamped," Associated Press, October 22, 1990; McCullough, "Public Ultimate Losers as Privatized Argentina Is Anything but an Eden," Associated Press, February 14, 1993; Thomas Kamm, "Bungled Buyout: Argentine Airline Sale Shows Privatization Is Hardly a Cure-All," *Wall Street Journal,* May 20, 1993; "Privatization, It's Fairly Wonderful," *The Economist,* January 8, 1994; Chris Kraul, "Rail Privatization in Argentina Helps Fuel Economic Recovery," *Los Angeles Times,* October 6, 1994; Jonathan Friedland, "Economy

Minister Rocks Argentine Boat—Cavallo Unnerves Markets, Congress, with Charges of Strong 'Mafia' Hand," *Wall Street Journal*, August 28, 1995; Michael S. Serrill, "Cavallo's Risky Crusade: The Sacked Argentine Inflation Fighter Is Now Accusing Former Cabinet Colleagues of Corruption," *Time*, December 16, 1996; Victoria Godfrey, "Stuck at the Gate: Privatization of Argentina's Airports," *LatinFinance*, October 1997; Ken Warn, "Argentina Seeks Suitors for Its 'Uglies,'" *Financial Times*, May 27, 1997; Gabriel Escobar, "Argentina Examines Seamy Side of Progress," *Washington Post*, April 13, 1997; Tim Padgett, "Mafia Daddy: Afredo Yabrán, a Rich and Powerful Businessman, Has Become a Steady Political Cause Celebre," *Time*, July 14, 1997; Warn, "Criticized Argentine Businessman 'Bows Out,'" *Financial Times*, December 20, 1997; Andrea Mandel-Campbell, "A Noisy Flap over a Silent Partner," *Business Week*, December 29, 1997; Warn, "The Rise and Fall of Yabrán," *Latin Trade*, August 1998; "Argentina, Death, and Corruption," *The Economist*, May 30, 1998; Anthony Faiola, "Latin Nations Pay Price of Reform; Argentina Targets a Decade of Graft," *Washington Post*, March 13, 2000; Oscar Martinez, "Ex-Minister Alsogaray Prepares to Testify on Corruption Charges," Agence France-Presse, June 13, 2001; and Clifford Krauss, "Spain and Argentina Find Themselves in Tangle over Airline," *New York Times*, June 17, 2001.

25–26   The figures on the rise in per capita GDP from 1991 to 1994, and the distribution of gains among different classes of workers, come from a World Bank report titled "Poor People in a Rich Country: A Poverty Report for Argentina," 2000, pp. 3–7, available on the World Bank website, www.worldbank.org.

27–28   Miguel Machado was the subject of a story by my colleague Jon Jeter, "Scrap by Scrap, Argentines Scratch Out a Meager Living; Laid-Off Workers Survive as Trash Pickers," *Washington Post*, June 7, 2003. Machado was reinterviewed more extensively for this book by my colleague Brian Byrnes.

28–29   The quotation from the March 1995 IMF staff report comes from the IEO report, p. 30.

29   The first quotation from Camdessus comes from a speech he delivered May 27, 1996, "Argentina and the Challenge of Globalization," and the second from a speech delivered May 21, 1997, "Toward a Second Generation of Structural Reform in Latin America." Both are on the IMF website.

29   The January 1996 Goldman Sachs report, "A Bravo New World," like most of the other Wall Street research reports cited in this book, was made available to me through a source that I am not at liberty to disclose. Thanks to this source, to whom I am grateful, I was able to review a broad sample of reports that were written on Argentina during the period in question.

30–31   Information on the fevered atmosphere for emerging markets, especially in Latin America, comes from Danielle Robinson, "A More Mature Marketplace?" *Euroweek*, March 14, 1997; Robinson, "Wall Street's Latin Obsession:

Will It Last?" *Investment Dealers' Digest,* June 2, 1997; Robinson, "New World for Latin Sovereign Debt," *Euroweek,* August 29, 1997; and John R. Engen, "The Scramble for Latin America: Competition Among Investment Banks," *Institutional Investor,* September 1997.

35   Information on the money doled out by provincial legislators comes from a table of figures from an Argentine government report that was kindly furnished to me by Santiago O'Donnell. Further information comes from "The Legislative Gravy Train," *Latin America Weekly Report,* June 6, 2000; Pamela Druckerman, "Argentina, Land of Fiscal Loose Cannons," *Wall Street Journal,* March 2, 2001; and John Lyons, "Argentina Struggles to Rein in Provincial Spending," Bloomberg News, February 22, 2001.

36   Information on the distribution of gains among classes of workers after the decade's midpoint comes from the World Bank report, "Poor People in a Rich Country," pp. 3–7.

36–37   The story of Horacio Hinojosa comes from Anthony Faiola, "Argentina's Lost World; Rush into New Global Economy Leaves the Working Class Behind," *Washington Post,* December 8, 1999.

37   The Dresdner Kleinwort Benson report was titled "LatAm Bi-Weekly Bulletin," dated June 12, 1998.

37–38   The quotation from Daza comes from a J.P. Morgan report, "Global Equity Weekly," January 19, 1999.

Chapter 3

39–41   The figures on the numbers of IMF employees and economists come from the Fund's 2004 annual report, as well as from IMF spokesman Bill Murray; the size of the Fund's kitty comes from the IMF website.

42   The April 1997 internal IMF briefing paper, which is referred to extensively in this chapter, was titled "Briefing Paper for the Third Review Under the Stand-By Arrangement and Preliminary Discussions on an Extended Facility." It was, and is, a confidential document.

44–45   Information about Argentina's labor laws in the mid-1990s comes from "Carlos Menem, Labour Law, and the IMF," *The Economist,* April 18, 1998; Clifford Krauss, "Argentine Labor Code Largely Intact," *New York Times,* March 17, 1998; and the World Bank report, "Poor People in a Rich Country," pp. 25–26.

47–48   Teijeiro's paper is titled "La Política Fiscal Durante La Convertibilidad" (Fiscal Policy During Convertibility), Centro de Estudios Públicos, July 1996.

49–50   The IMF-related documents admitting the mistake on fiscal policy in the 1990s are Mark Allen, "Some Lessons from the Argentine Crisis: A Fund Staff View," from *The Crisis That Was Not Prevented: Argentina, the IMF, and Globalisation* (The Hague: Foundation on Debt and Development, 2003); the IMF staff's postmortem and the IEO report; and Michael Mussa, *Argentina and the Fund: From Triumph to Tragedy* (Washington, D.C.: Institute for International Economics, 2002).

Mussa's figures on the debt-to-GDP ratio in the mid-90s (which are also used in the chronology in this book, for the sake of consistency) differ slightly from figures in various IMF documents including the IEO report, even though Mussa himself derived his figures from other IMF documents. Regardless of which figures are precisely accurate, the trend that all of them show is the same—a significant rise in the debt-to-GDP ratio during a period of prosperity.

51   The memos by Loser acknowledging the qualms of other departments were, and are, confidential documents.

51   The award for "Issuer of the Year" was bestowed in "Deals of the Year," *LatinFinance*, January–February 1999.

53   The figures on provincial spending come from an IMF report, "Argentina: Recent Economic Developments," February 1999, pp. 35–37, on the IMF website.

54   Ter-Minassian's remarks about the dangers facing the economy were carried in, among others, Marcelo Bonelli, "Pronóstico con fondo rojo," *Clarin*, April 3, 1998. That article cited her as also saying that Argentina was afflicted with the same conditions that led to the crises in Asia. It quotes her as using the term "explosive cocktail," although other reports quote her as using "Molotov cocktail," one such item being "IMF Official Paints 'Disturbing' Picture for Argentine Economy,'" BBC Monitoring Service: Latin America, April 14, 1998.

54   The IMF letter, signed by Ter-Minassian and Tomás Reichmann and dated April 6, 1998, was addressed to Economy Minister Roque Fernández and Central Bank President Pedro Pou. It was, and is, a confidential document, but its contents were reported in the Argentine media at the time.

54–55   The April 7, 1998, memo that Ter-Minassian sent to IMF management was, and is, a confidential document.

55   Menem's comments, and their wide dissemination, were reported in "Display of Fury from Menem as IMF Warns of 'Pre-Crisis' Situation," *Latin American Weekly Report*, April 7, 1998.

55–56   Kiguel's comment was reported in Craig Torres, "Argentina, Its Economy Sizzling, Is Cool to IMF," *Wall Street Journal*, April 2, 1998.

56   Guidotti's comment was reported in Ken Warn, "IMF Breaks Up Argentina's Party," *Financial Times*, April 8, 1998.

56   The Credit Suisse First Boston report was titled "Argentina's Macro Concerns: Cry Wolf," April 14, 1998.

56–57   The Ter-Minassian memo dated July 29, 1998, was, and is, a confidential document.

57   The Paul Masson memo dated September 3, 1998, was, and is, a confidential document.

58   A transcript of Camdessus's October 1, 1998, press conference is on the IMF website.

59   The figure on the drop in Argentine exports to Brazil in 1999 comes from the IMF's *Direction of Trade Statistics* (Washington, D.C.: IMF, 2002).

60   The figure on the fall in the price of grain and other commodities that Argentina exported comes from the IMF staff postmortem on the crisis, p. 11; the figure on the drop in Argentine exports overall in 1999 comes from a table in the IEO report, p. 17.

Chapter 4

62   The data on the bond sales for which Salomon served as lead manager, and the fees it earned, come from Thomson Financial.

63   The e-mail in which Grubman used the term "pig" was reported in Ben White and Kathleen Day, "SEC Approves Wall Street Settlement; Conflicts of Interest Targeted," *Washington Post,* April 29, 2003.

63   The quotations from Rudloff come from a text of his speech, "Progress and Setbacks in the World Financial Infrastructure," delivered June 18, 2002.

64–65   The Salomon report stating that "the Argentine government may find it increasingly difficult to meet its financing needs unless domestic confidence can be restored quickly" was titled "Global Economic Outlook and Strategy," April 25, 2001.

66   The Morgan report stating that "the government's capacity to service its debt this year is not in question" was titled "Market Overview," March 1, 2001.

66   The ABN-AMRO report stating that neither default nor devaluation was "in the cards" was titled "Caught in the Crossfire," June 30, 2001.

66–67   The quotations from the Molano reports come from his publication "The Latin American Adviser."

71   The average weighting that Argentina and other countries had in the EMBI-Plus index during the period 1996–2001 was calculated by me using data kindly furnished by JPMorgan Chase.

72   The quotation from Tom Cooper comes from Elizabeth Stanton, "Argentina Bond Investors Eye Indexes," Bloomberg News, July 31, 2001.

73   The article quoting investors and analysts agreeing that the EMBI-Plus "poses some serious problems" is "Market Players Ponder Benchmark," *Emerging Markets Debt Report,* November 9, 1998.

74   Giacinto Innocenzi's story was reported in Keri Geiger, "Argentina's Broken Bonds," *LatinFinance,* October 2002. Felicia Migliorini was interviewed by my colleague Sarah Delaney, but her story was previously reported in Alina Trabattoni, "Italy Ruling on Argentine Assets May Help Investors," Bloomberg News, August 6, 2002.

76   The figures on *riesgo país* for Argentina come from data furnished by JPMorgan Chase.

76   The figures on the rise in real interest rates for Argentine companies in early 1999 come from the IMF staff postmortem, p. 18.

77–78   The figures on the decline in private capital flowing to major Latin American countries by mid-1999 come from Guillermo Calvo, Alejandro Izquierdo, and Ernesto Talvi, "Sudden Stops, the Real Exchange Rate, and Fiscal Sustainability: Argentina's Lessons," Inter-American Development Bank, March 2002.

78   There was one big catch in El-Erian's strategy—the EMBI-Plus. Like almost anyone who was managing money invested in emerging markets for pensions, endowments, foundations, and other institutions, El-Erian had to worry about how his performance compared with the EMBI-Plus: He could not afford to have PIMCO's emerging-markets portfolios miss out on the gains the index would post during rallies in Argentine bonds, the index's biggest component. But El-Erian engineered an ingenious way around that problem. As he sold Argentine bonds, he replaced them with Brazilian bonds, whose prices tended to track Argentina's fairly closely. That way, even though his position was very far underweight Argentina, his portfolios were able to reap at least some of the profits from upside moves in the country's bonds. Of course, he ended up heavily exposed to Brazil, which looked very costly when that country's markets plunged in 2002, but the strategy later paid off handsomely.

79–80   Data on the federal and overall public deficits for 1999 and 2000 come from "Argentina: 2002 Article IV Consultation—Staff Report; Staff Supplement," July 2003, pp. 42–43, available on the IMF website.

79   Information on the atmosphere during the final year of the Menem administration comes from Marcela Valente, "Menem Says 'Adios' Amid Corruption Scandals," Inter Press Service, December 7, 1999. Information on Menem's construction activities in his hometown come from Ian Phillips, "Menem Under Fire for Costly Transformation of His Andean Hometown," Associated Press, March 3, 1997; and Calvin Sims, "A Hometown Boy: Call Him Carlos the Bountiful," *New York Times,* July 18, 1996.

80   The figure on passports dispensed by the Italian embassy in the first half of 2000 was reported in Clifford Krauss, "With No Hope for Economy, Many Argentines Are Leaving," *New York Times,* November 24, 2000.

81   The figures on Argentine government bond issuance in 2000 come from calculations that I did using data on individual issues from the Bloomberg News database.

Chapter 5

88   The fall in Argentine government bond prices on the day of the flight taken by Summers and Marx was reported in John Lyons and Walter Siew, "Argentina Debt Plummets to 14-Month Low," Bloomberg News, October 25, 2000.

91 The results of the treasury bill sale on November 7, 2000, were reported in John Lyons and David Plumb, "Argentine Yields Soar at $1.1 Billion Treasury Auction," Bloomberg News, November 7, 2000.

91–92 The memo in which Ter-Minassian fretted about "a collapse of confidence" and other matters was, and is, a confidential IMF document.

92–93 Information on Köhler comes from Vinginie Montet, "IMF Makes Horst Köhler Its Chief at Pivotal Time," Agence France Presse, March 23, 2000; Alan Beattie, "Köhler Extends the Hand of Friendship to the World," *Financial Times*, September 22, 2000; James Smalhout, "Will Köhler Turn the Supertanker?" *Euromoney*, September 2000; and Klaus Engelen, "A Good Start; Horst Köhler, Managing Director of International Monetary Fund," *International Economy*, September 1, 2000.

94 A transcript of Köhler's speech, which was titled "The IMF in a Changing World," is on the IMF website.

95 The 11 percent rise in exports of manufactured goods in the first half of 2000 was reported in an IMF document titled "Argentina: Staff Report for the 2000 Article IV Consultation, First Review Under the Stand-By Arrangement, and Request for Modification of Performance Criteria," September 5, 2000, p. 5, available on the IMF website.

96 The August 1999 memo stating that exiting from convertibility "would be extremely difficult, if not chaotic" is cited in the IEO report, p. 34.

97 The memos by Peter Heller, Jesús Seade, and Miguel Savastano were, and are, confidential documents.

99–100 The October 2000 report by Arturo Porzecanski was titled "Argentina: A Stress Test of the 'New International Financial Architecture'?"

101 The 1997 projection by the Fund that public-sector debt would shrink to 34 percent of GDP by 2000 was contained in the confidential April 1997 briefing paper previously cited.

101 The assumptions underlying the IMF's debt projections in 2000 are contained in "Argentina: Second Review Under the Stand-By Arrangement and Request for Augmentation," January 4, 2001, p. 38, available on the IMF website.

102–103 The Plan Gamma memo was, and is, a confidential document.

105–106 The January 2, 2001, memo by Loser was, and is, a confidential document.

107 The statement that was circulated by Bernes was, and is, a confidential document.

108 The memo dated December 29, 2000, is cited in the IEO report, p. 73.

108 The statement issued after the January 12, 2001, board meeting is available on the IMF website.

109 The yield on treasury bills in the January 23, 2001, auction was reported in John Lyons and David Plumb, "Argentine T-Bill Yields Fall More Than Expected," Bloomberg News, January 23, 2001.

112–113   The activities of Binder's team were reported in Keri Geiger, "Outsmarting a Mean Market," *LatinFinance*, March 2003. I also interviewed Binder.

114   Daza's statement at the Americas Society on April 6 was reported in Vivianne Rodrigues, "Deutsche Bank's Daza on Argentina's Economy, Debt," Bloomberg News, April 6, 2001.

Chapter 6

116–117   Information about O'Neill comes from Joseph Kahn and Floyd Norris, "Industrialist with a Twist—Paul Henry O'Neill," *New York Times*, December 20, 2000; Leslie Wayne, "Designee Takes a Deft Touch and a Firm Will to Treasury," *New York Times*, January 16, 2001; Jacob M. Schlesinger and Michael M. Phillips, "Surprising Choices: Treasury's O'Neill Has Unusual Priorities, Miscues in Early Days," *Wall Street Journal*, March 19, 2001; Glenn Kessler, "First Impressions, Lasting Influence; O'Neill Has More Pull Than Meets the Eye," *Washington Post*, October 7, 2001; and Michael Lewis, "O'Neill's List," *New York Times Magazine*, January 13, 2002.

117   O'Neill's quotation about Wall Street traders was reported in Jacob M. Schlesinger and Michael M. Phillips, "Treasury Secretary O'Neill Indicates Proposal to Reduce Tax Withholdings," *Wall Street Journal*, January 26, 2001.

117–118   O'Neill's quotation about "the IMF rides in on its horse" was reported in David Ignatius, "O'Neill's Formula: Aid to Brazil but No Open Hand," *International Herald Tribune*, July 25, 2001.

118   Taylor's advocacy of the abolition of the IMF in 1998 came in a television program called "Uncommon Knowledge" on December 15, 1998. A transcript of the program can be found at http://www.uncommonknowledge.org/ 99winter/320.html.

118   O'Neill's comment that the IMF was "too often associated with failure" came in testimony on May 15, 2001, to the subcommittee on Foreign Operations of the House Appropriations Committee. His comment about money coming from "plumbers and carpenters" came in a speech on April 19, 2001, at the Economic Club of New York, which is available on the U.S. Treasury website, www.ustreas.gov.

118   Cavallo's comment "I am a legend" was reported in John Lyons, "Argentina's Domingo Cavallo Legend Gets Tarnished," Bloomberg News, July 13, 2001; other people who were present at the dinner in question have similar recollections of the stunning self-confidence he displayed.

118–119   Cavallo's comment predicting that Argentina's debt would soon be treated like Australia's or Canada's was reported in Germán Sopeña and Luis Cortina, "Con la nueva ley, el Gobierno espera generar un vigoroso crecimiento" (With the new law, the government expects to generate vigorous growth), *La Nación*, March 25, 2001.

119   Cavallo's comment predicting that 2001 "is going to be very similar to

1991" was reported in Richard Lapper and Thomas Catan, "Buying Time in Argentina," *Financial Times,* April 2, 2001.

119   The *Noticias* cover portraying Cavallo as Hannibal Lecter was the issue of March 24, 2001.

122   Calomiris's op-ed in the *Wall Street Journal,* "Argentina Can't Pay What It Owes," was published April 13, 2001.

122   Cavallo's vow that "Argentina will not be lured by the call of the sirens" came in his op-ed article titled "Debt Is Not the Problem for Argentina," *Financial Times,* April 26, 2001.

123   Information about the purchase by Argentine banks of billions of dollars in government bonds, and the ensuing fight between Cavallo and Pedro Pou, can be found in Michael Smith, "Argentina's Cavallo Blames 'Depression' on Central Bank," Bloomberg News, April 5, 2001; David Plumb, "Argentine Banks Agree to Buy \$3.5 bln Bonds from Govt," Bloomberg News, April 6, 2001; and Plumb, "Argentina Allows Banks to Use Bonds to Back Deposits," Bloomberg News, April 9, 2001.

124   Mussa's comments at the April 26, 2001, news conference, and Köhler's comments the next day, come from transcripts available on the IMF website.

124   The internal assessment by the Argentina task force stating that "the probability of a full-blown crisis in Argentina has increased" is cited in the IEO report, p. 80.

126   The passage reporting "lean times for investment bankers" comes from Graham Field, "Let the Hard Times Roll," *LatinFinance,* September 2001.

126   The passage reporting that investment banks "have been aggressively pursuing liability management transctions" comes from Danielle Robinson, "Bankers Celebrate as Cavallo Buys a Little Time," *Euromoney,* July 1, 2001.

128   Mulford's remarks to investors at the St. Regis Hotel were reported in Walden Siew and Vivianne Rodrigues, "CSFB's David Mulford: Argentina's Planned Bond Exchange: Comment," Bloomberg News, May 30, 2001.

128   Mulford's comments to reporters in Buenos Aires were reported in Thomas Catan and Peter Hudson, "Banker Says Argentine Bond Swap Will Set a Precedent," *Financial Times,* May 17, 2001.

128–129   The terms of the 2018 bond were reported in "Putting It at Face Value," *LatinFinance,* July 2001.

129   Molano's report likening the megaswap to "a modern Treaty of Versailles" was reported in Tom Vogel, "Don't Cheer for the Argentine Bond Swap," Bloomberg News, June 4, 2001.

129   Boorman's comment that the IMF viewed the swap as "an important complement to the authorities' program of economic stabilization and reform" was reported in Stephen Wisnefski, "Cavallo: May Tax Rev, Econ Growth Link Unclear," Dow Jones International News, May 30, 2001.

130   The admission that the megaswap "contributed to concerns about [Argentina's] solvency" comes from the IMF staff postmortem, p. 60.

130   Cavallo's declaration that "we have beaten those who were betting against Argentina" was reported in John Lyons and David Plumb, "Investors Swap $29.5 Billion in Argentine Bond Exchange," Bloomberg News, June 3, 2001.

130   Mulford's prediction that "future financing will be done at substantially lower rates" and his assertion that Argentina could try "various operations that would address that [high-interest] problem" were reported in John Lyons, "Argentina May Later Try to Buy Back Bonds: Mulford," Bloomberg News, June 6, 2001.

131   The rise in Argentine bond prices by June 12, and the reversal in following days, were reported in Diana Rochford, "Argentine, Brazil Bonds Fall on Real Tumble, Energy Rationing," Bloomberg News, June 14, 2001.

131   Mulford's explanation for why the megaswap failed was partially reported in "Architect: David Mulford," *LatinFinance,* July 2003.

131   The fee paid in the megaswap was reported in David Plumb, "CSFB, 9 Other Banks Earn $141 mln in Argentine Swap," Bloomberg News, June 15, 2001. The story reported that the government paid $137 million to the seven banks that led the exchange, with the remaining $4 million going to local units of banks that also participated.

131–132   Information about the markets' performance following Cavallo's announcement concerning the subsidies and duties that would affect exporters and importers comes from John Lyons and Diana Rochford, "Argentine Bonds Sink After Peso Devalued for Imports, Exports," Bloomberg News, June 18, 2001; and Elzio Barreto, "Argentine Bonds Rise 2nd Day After Govt Increases Global Sale," Bloomberg News, June 20, 2001.

132   Information about the markets' performance in late June and early July 2001, and the plethora of bad economic and political news during that period, come from Helen Murphy, "Argentine Bonds Fall on U.S. Fed Reserve Rate Cut, Weak Economy," Bloomberg News, June 28, 2001; Murphy and John Lyons, "Argentine Bonds Fall After IDB Official Calls for Spending Cuts," June 29, 2001; Lyons and David Plumb, "Latin Economies: Argentine June Tax Revenue Down 4.9%," Bloomberg News, July 2, 2001; Lyons, "Argentina's Cavallo Seeks to Resolve Province Funding," Bloomberg News, July 2, 2001; Lyons and Plumb, "Argentine Bonds Drop on Concern Politics Will Prevent Recovery," Bloomberg News, July 3, 2001; Lyons, "Argentina's de la Rúa Loses Grip on Power as Coalition Crumbles," Bloomberg News, July 4, 2001; Murphy, "Argentine Bonds Sink as Govt, Provinces Negotiate; Yields Soar," Bloomberg News, July 5, 2001; and Murphy, "Argentine Bonds Drop for 9th Day as Govt Seeks Province Accord," Bloomberg News, July 6, 2001.

133   Cavallo's statement that "we have to go immediately to a zero deficit"

was reported in Thomas Black, "Argentina's Cavallo Calls for Eliminating Deficit Spending," Bloomberg News, July 10, 2001.

133   The disastrous reception accorded the announcement of the zero deficit policy, and the accompanying collapse in Cavallo's remaining popularity, including the episode at his daughter's wedding, are recounted in Jenny Anderson, "Personality Politics," *Institutional Investor,* September 2001; "Austerity, or Bust," *The Economist,* July 21, 2001; Mark Mulligan, "Honeymoon over for Cavallo as Economy Falters," *Financial Times,* July 20, 2001; Clifford Krauss, "Argentine with a Headache: The Economy," *New York Times,* July 18, 2001; Bill Cormier, "Argentina's Cavallo Is Under Fire," Associated Press, July 16, 2001; and Chris Kraul, "Argentines Feel Betrayed by Economy's Shepherds," *Los Angeles Times,* July 16, 2001.

133   The *Veintitrés* cover showing Cavallo's face with clown paint and a sad frown was the issue of July 12, 2001.

134   Roubini's comments to the private IMF conference on July 26 came in a paper he wrote, "Bail-ins, Bailouts, Burden Sharing, and Private Sector Involvement in Crisis Resolution," which is available on his website, www.stern.nyu.edu/globalmacro.

Chapter 7

136   The figures on deposits and reserves were kindly furnished by Jens Nystedt of the IMF from files he had kept in his computer that were based on data from the Central Bank of Argentina. The Central Bank's website no longer seems to have similar data for that period.

136   The fact that the deposit withdrawals were concentrated among corporations and large investors comes from a confidential IMF document, "Argentina—Fourth Review Under the Stand-By Arrangement and Request for Rephasing of the Arrangement," August 31, 2001. This document states: "The bulk of the deposit withdrawals happened at the wholesale level—large corporate and institutional investors; withdrawals by small retail depositors have been quite limited ... [there is also] anecdotal evidence that many depositors chose to stay within the same banking group but to place their savings in offshore accounts."

142   Reinhart's memo on contagion was, and is, a confidential document.

143–144   The confidential staff report written for presentation to the executive board in August 2001 is the aforementioned "Argentina—Fourth Review Under the Stand-By Arrangement and Request for Rephasing of the Arrangement."

144   The words "implausible" and "extraordinarily favorable" come from the IMF staff postmortem on the crisis, p. 60.

146   Accounts of the Bush administration's explanation of its bailout policy can be found in Michael M. Phillips, "Bush Policy Is Familiar to Developing

Nations," *Wall Street Journal*, May 14, 2001; and Paul Blustein, "Stopping the Bailout Buck Here," *Washington Post*, June 5, 2001.

148   Taylor's disclosure that he favored dollarization came at a hearing of the International Monetary Policy and Trade Subcommittee of the House Financial Services Committee, February 6, 2002, available on the committee's website, http://financialservices.house.gov.

151   Rogoff's memo stating "there is no way to make $6 billion . . . worth more than $6 billion . . . but there are many creative ways to make it less" was, and is, a confidential document.

152–153   The press release issued August 21, "IMF Managing Director Prepared to Recommend Addition of US$8 Billion to Argentina's Stand-By Credit," is available on the IMF website.

153–154   The essay Eichengreen wrote on August 27 was titled "Argentina After the IMF" and is available on Eichengreen's web page at http://emlab.berkeley.edu/users/eichengr/reviews.html.

154   The press release issued September 7 following the board meeting, "IMF Augments Argentina Stand-By Credit to $21.57 Billion, and Completes Fourth Review," is available on the IMF website.

154–155   Wijnholds disclosed his abstention from the September 7 board vote in an article he wrote titled "The Argentine Drama: A View from the IMF Board," in *The Crisis That Was Not Prevented: Argentina, the IMF, and Globalisation* (The Hague: Foundation on Debt and Development, January 2003).

157   Mussa's accusation of "a failure of intellectual courage" is made in his book *Argentina and the Fund: From Triumph to Tragedy*, pp. 47–48.

Chapter 8

160–161   The reaction of investors to the government announcement of the September tax revenue decline and compensating spending reductions on October 2 was reported in Andrew J. Barden and Jeb Blount, "Argentina Stocks, Bonds Drop as Spending Cuts Heighten Concern," Bloomberg News, October 2, 2001.

161   Information about the patacón can be found in Larry Rohter, "Argentina's Stopgap Cash Gets Some Funny Looks," *New York Times*, August 26, 2001; Anthony Faiola, "Hard Times Tarnish a Sterling Symbol," *Washington Post*, August 30, 2001; and David Plumb, "Argentina's IOU's Buy Books, Burgers; Fetch Under $1," Bloomberg News, October 3, 2001.

161   The IMF's rescue was failing not only because of the poor reaction from the markets but also because of the lack of progress concerning the voluntary debt restructuring that Treasury Secretary O'Neill had envisioned. A number of investment banks drafted proposals—eleven of them, standing eighteen inches high when stacked atop each other—for how Argentina might use the Fund's $3 billion or other official resources as part of a deal to reduce the gov-

ernment's debt burden. The IMF rejected all these proposals, because some would have achieved little debt reduction; others had serious legal problems. (Specifically, they risked getting snarled in the courts because under their terms, the Argentine government would offer collateral to certain groups of bondholders as part of a debt exchange, which would invite lawsuits by other bondholders who did not get the same deal.) The IMF's objections were a source of frustration for Cavallo, because it seemed as if Fund officials were behaving petulantly toward an initiative they had not authored. But as far as IMF economists were concerned, the problems with most of the proposals boiled down to the difficulty inherent in O'Neill's plan—namely, that it was impossible to achieve a major debt restructuring on a voluntary basis with little money. The Argentines had tried to raise extra official funds from other donors, such as G-7 governments, to supplement the IMF's $3 billion and help make a voluntary restructuring more appealing, but those efforts had come to naught.

164   News reports in which the restructuring was described as both "orderly" and "voluntary" include Simon Gardner, "Argentina Seeks to Restructure Way Out of Crisis," Reuters, November 1, 2001; and Bill Cormier, "Bidding to Prevent Any Default, Argentine Leader Proposes Controversial Debt Swap," Associated Press, November 2, 2001.

169   Cavallo's declaration that Argentina was not defaulting was reported in "All Argentine Debt to Be Included in Swap: Cavallo," Reuters, November 1, 2001.

169   The quotation "It's like having a gun against your head" was reported in Kevin Gray, "Argentine Debt Plan Raises Alarms," Associated Press, November 2, 2001.

170   Information about the creation of the Argentine Bondholder Committee, its opposition to a "discriminatory" restructuring, and its consideration of litigation comes from Rebecca Bream, "External Creditors Challenge Argentina," *Financial Times*, November 20, 2001; Angela Pruitt, "Argentina Focuses on Orderly Restructuring," Dow Jones Newswires, November 21, 2001; "Argentine Intl Debt Swap to Offer Advantages to Foreign Lenders—Marx," AFX News, November 28, 2001; and Tim Loughran, "EMCA's Chair Says Group Not Planning Argentina Lawsuit," Dow Jones International News, November 27, 2001 (a story explaining that the Emerging Market Creditors Association, or EMCA, was not the same as the Argentine Bondholder Committee, and that some international investors were considering legal action).

171   Figures on reserves, as previously noted, were furnished by Jens Nystedt.

171   The fact that about $850 million of the reserves had been used to make interest and principal payments to the IMF and World Bank comes from my calculations based on data on those institutions' websites.

173   The Argentine government's acknowledgment that its deficit for 2001 was likely to be $7.8 billion was reported in David Plumb and Michael Smith,

"Argentina Budget Deficit to Widen More Than Forecast," Bloomberg News, November 19, 2001.

173   The objective for the IMF program of securing "a major improvement in market confidence, allowing the government to re-enter international bond markets in 2002" was contained in "Argentina—Letter of Intent, Memorandum of Economic Policies, Technical Memorandum of Understanding," August 30, 2001, available on the IMF website.

173   Loser's comment that "we already gave [Argentina] a large amount of aid" was reported in Marcela Valente, "Economy-Argentina: Downward Spiral Has No End in Sight," Inter-Press Service, November 19, 2001.

176–179   Krueger's speech, "A New Approach to Sovereign Debt Restructuring," is available on the IMF website.

176–177   O'Neill's recounting of what he had told Köhler and Krueger at breakfast came at a hearing of the U.S. Senate Committee on Banking, Housing, and Urban Affairs, September 20, 2001, a transcript of which can be found on the committee's website, http://banking.senate.gov.

181   The informal exchange rate for pesos at the end of the first week of December 2001 was reported in Thomas Catan and Richard Lapper, "Argentine Peso Devalues on the Streets," *Financial Times*, December 8, 2001.

181–182   The document "Steps to Reaching a Sustainable Program" was, and is, a confidential document.

184   Cavallo's statement "We completely agreed with the staff of the Fund on the numbers" was reported in Laura Bonilla, "Argentina Receives Instructions but No Money from IMF," Agence France Presse, December 9, 2001.

184–185   Information about the situation in mid-December 2001 can be found in Thomas Catan and Richard Lapper, "Argentina Appropriates Pension Funds to Pay Bills," *Financial Times*, December 7, 2001; Sophie Arie, "Nerves Fray in Depressed Argentina: Economic Crisis Has Led to Long, Angry Bank Queues and a Rise in Panic Attacks and Suicides," *The Observer*, December 9, 2001; John Lyons, "Argentina's Finance Secretary Daniel Marx Resigns," Bloomberg News, December 14, 2001; Catan and Lapper, "Argentina Braced for Mass Protests," *Financial Times*, December 13, 2001; and Catan and Lapper, "Argentina Narrowly Avoids Debt Default," *Financial Times*, December 15, 2001.

185   The quotation from the vendor at the news kiosk lamenting the decline in his sales was reported in "Día de adaptación en bancos y negocios" (Day of adaptation in banks and businesses), *La Nación*, December 4, 2001.

185–187   Information about the events of December 19, 2001, through January 6, 2002, can be found in Anthony Faiola, "State of Siege in Argentina," *Washington Post*, December 20, 2001; Clifford Krauss, "Reeling from Riots, Argentina Declares State of Siege," *New York Times*, December 20, 2001; Faiola, "Besieged President Resigns in Argentina," *Washington Post*, December 21, 2001; Hector Tobar, "Rioting Forces President Out in Argentina," *Los Angeles Times*, December 21, 2001; Faiola and Steven Pearlstein, "Argentina to Suspend Debt

Payment," *Washington Post,* December 23, 2001; Krauss, "Argentine Leader Declares Default on Billions in Debt," *New York Times,* December 24, 2001; Marc Lifsher, "Crisis Management: Argentina Will Halt Some Debt Payments in the Wake of Unrest," *Wall Street Journal,* December 24, 2001; Larry Rohter, "Fiscal Shift by Government Adds to Doubts of Argentines," *New York Times,* December 28, 2001; Rohter, "Unity Eludes Argentina's Governing Party," *New York Times,* December 30, 2001; Rohter, "Within Hours, Two Quit as Argentine Leader," *New York Times,* December 31, 2001; Matt Moffett and Michelle Wallin, "New Argentine Leader Resigns as Support Falls," *Wall Street Journal,* December 31, 2001; Faiola, "Crisis-Wracked Argentina Seeks Fifth President in Two Weeks," *Washington Post,* January 1, 2002; Rohter, "Argentina Drifts, Leaderless, as Economic Collapse Looms," *New York Times,* January 1, 2002; Moffett and Wallin, "Argentina Picks Peronist Duhalde as Fifth President in Two Weeks," *Wall Street Journal,* January 2, 2002; Rohter, "Argentina Unlinks Peso from Dollar, Bracing for Devaluation and Even Harder Times," *New York Times,* January 7, 2002; and Wallin and Moffett, "Argentina Says It Is Devaluing Its Peso by 29%," *Wall Street Journal,* January 7, 2002.

Chapter 9

190–193   Information about the situation in the first half of 2002 comes from Thomas Catan, "Hope—and Everything Else—Is Running Out in Buenos Aires," *Financial Times,* February 2, 2002; Paul Blustein, "Argentina Lets Peso Float," *Washington Post,* February 12, 2002; Blustein, "In Argentina, Going Without; International Suppliers Cut Shipments After Default," *Washington Post,* February 19, 2002; Anthony Faiola, "Argentines Lose Confidence in Banks; Depositors Angered by Curbs Placed on Withdrawals During Economic Crisis," *Washington Post,* March 8, 2002; Kevin Gray, "Argentina Orders Banking 'Holiday,'" Associated Press, April 19, 2002; Heather Walsh and Helen Murphy, "Argentine Businessmen Await Economic Plan to End Cash Shortage," *Bloomberg News,* April 25, 2002; Larry Rohter, "Freeze on Deposits Is No Holiday, Argentines Find," *New York Times,* April 25, 2002; Hector Tobar, "Economic Rut in Argentina Grows Deeper," *Los Angeles Times,* April 27, 2002; Tony Smith, "Plummeting Real Estate Market Gives X-Ray View of Argentina's Problems," Associated Press, May 7, 2002; and John Barham, "No Leaders, No Money, No Hope," *LatinFinance,* May 2002.

193   The article describing "empty businesses, movie theaters without audiences," was Cristian Alarcón, "Postcard from the Still City," *Página/12,* April 26, 2002.

195–196   My colleague Jon Jeter reported the Machado family's postcrisis travails in "Scrap by Scrap, Argentines Scratch Out a Meager Living," *Washington Post,* June 7, 2003, and the quotations in this section are from that article. As noted previously, Machado was reinterviewed for this book, especially concerning his lifestyle during the boom.

196–197   The point about how well market-oriented countries such as Chile performed relative to Venezuela and Cuba is made in Pedro-Pablo Kuczynski and John Williamson, *After the Washington Consensus: Restarting Growth and Reform in Latin America* (Washington, D.C.: Institute for International Economics, 2003).

197–198   The most influential explanations advanced by academics at universities, think tanks, and other institutions concerning the Argentine crisis include Martin Feldstein, "Argentina's Fall: Lessons from the Latest Financial Crisis," *Foreign Affairs,* March/April 2002; Steve H. Hanke and Kurt Schuler, "What Went Wrong in Argentina?" *Central Banking Journal* 12, 3 (2002); Mussa, *Argentina, and the Fund*; Birdsall, "What Went Wrong in Argentina?"; Mark Weisbrot and Dean Baker, "What Happened to Argentina?" Center for Economic and Policy Research, January 2002; Ricardo Hausman and Andrés Velasco, "Hard Money's Soft Underbelly: Understanding the Argentine Crisis," *Brookings Trade Forum 2002* (Washington, D.C.: Brookings Institution, 2003); Joseph Stiglitz, "Argentina, Shortchanged; Why the Nation That Followed the Rules Fell to Pieces," *Washington Post,* May 12, 2002; Andrew Powell, "Argentina's Avoidable Crisis: Bad Luck, Bad Economics, Bad Politics, Bad Advice," also in *Brookings Trade Forum 2002*; Calvo, Izquierdo, and Talvi, "Sudden Stops, the Exchange Rate, and Fiscal Sustainability: Argentina's Lessons"; and Guillermo Perry and Luis Servén, "The Anatomy and Physiology of a Multiple Crisis: Why Was Argentina Special and What Can We Learn from It?" Latin America and Caribbean Regional Office, World Bank.

An insightful summary of the debate is provided in William R. Cline, "Restoring Economic Growth in Argentina," World Bank Policy Research Working Paper, October 2003, in which the author rebuts the arguments of those who contend that Argentina's fiscal policy was too tight rather than too loose. The paper is available at http://econ.worldbank.org/files/30460_wps3158.pdf.

199   The assertion that the IMF's projections of Argentine growth in the mid-to-late 1990s were based on "overly favorable" views about the nation's reforms comes from the IMF staff's postmortem, p. 69.

202   The assertion that the second rescue loan "only postponed the inevitable" and caused the costs of collapse to be "all the greater" comes from the IMF staff's postmortem, p. 31.

204–207   Information about the state of the 2003–2004 economy comes from data on the World Bank website and from the monthly editions of "Argentine Panorama," published by Buenos Aires economist Federico Thomsen. Information about the disputes between Argentina and its bondholders can be found in Alan Beattie, "Creditors Lose Faith in Argentina's Intentions over Debt," *Financial Times,* November 3, 2003; David Glovin, "Argentina Sued for

$172 Mln by NML over Bond Default," Bloomberg News, November 7, 2003; Matt Moffett, "Going South: After Huge Default, Argentina Squeezes Small Bondholders," January 14, 2004; Mike Esterl, "US Judge Backs New Bondholder Suits Against Argentina," Dow Jones International News, March 8, 2004; Joshua Goodman, "Crying Poor Won't Work Anymore," *Business Week*, May 10, 2004; Daniel Helft, "Argentina's Creditors Shun Debt Talks, Reject Offer," Bloomberg News, June 8, 2004; and Angela Pruitt, "Class Action Suits Against Debtor Argentina Piling Up," June 10, 2004. Information about the periodic game of chicken between Argentina and the IMF can be found in Paul Blustein and Anthony Faiola, "Argentina Defaults on Debt Payment," *Washington Post*, November 15, 2002; Blustein, "IMF Approves $3 Billion Loan for Argentina; Fund's Action Signals End of Rift With Nation, but Voting Abstentions Reveal Dissent," *Washington Post*, January 25, 2003; Beattie and Adam Thomson, "Argentina Misses IMF Deadline on $3bn Loan," *Financial Times*, September 10, 2003; Beattie, "Argentine-IMF Rancour Starts to Turn Personal," *Financial Times*, January 30, 2004; Michael Casey and Michael M. Phillips, "IMF, Argentina Go to the Brink in Debt Talks," *Wall Street Journal*, March 9, 2004; and Casey, "Argentina Averts Default on IMF Loan," *Wall Street Journal*, March 10, 2004. Information about the mind-set of the Argentine body politic can be found in Kevin G. Hall, "As Protesters' Ranks Swell, Argentina's Middle Class Turns on Poor," Knight Ridder newspapers, September 19, 2004; Casey, "Kirchner's Next Challenge—Ire at Argentine Activists Highlights Need for Sustained Job Creation," *Wall Street Journal*, August 31, 2004; Eliana Raszewski, "Argentina's Kirchner Rebuffs Investor Demands to Quell Violence," Bloomberg News, August 27, 2004; and Daniel Helft, "Argentina's Kirchner Snubs Fiorina, IMF, for 'Political Appeal,'" Bloomberg News, October 1, 2004.

Chapter 10

209–211   Information about the bubbly conditions in emerging-market bonds in early 2004 can be found in Kevin Morrison, Päivi Munter, and Adrienne Roberta, "Asset Bubbles Resting on a Bed of Investors' Ambition," *Financial Times*, January 15, 2004; and Munter, "Emerging Market Debt Soars," *Financial Times*, February 2, 2004. The *Financial Times* editorial asking "Is this another bubble?" was titled "A Dash for Yield."

210   The 347-point decline in the spread on emerging-market bonds in 2003 was reported in the IMF's *Global Financial Stability Report*, April 2004, p. 27.

211   Dallara's quotation at the news conference of the Institute of International Finance was reported in Alan Beattie, "Rush of Investors into Emerging Markets 'Too Far Too Fast,'" *Financial Times*, January 16, 2004.

211   *The World Economic Outlook* of autumn 2003 containing the chapter about emerging-market debt levels is available on the IMF website.

212   Information about the bubbly conditions that were taking hold anew in emerging-market bonds at the end of 2004 can be found in Päivi Munter, "Emerging Market Debt Hits Record Levels," *Financial Times,* October 13, 2004.

215   The 2003 IMF paper questioning the benefits of financial integration for emerging-market nations is Eswar S. Prasad, Kenneth Rogoff, Wei Shang-Jin, and Ayhan Kose, "Effects of Financial Globalization on Developing Countries: Some Empirical Evidence," and is available on the IMF website.

216   Information on the settlement between the Securities and Exchange Commission and Wall Street can be found in Stephen Labaton, "Ten Wall St. Firms Reach Settlement in Analyst Inquiry," *New York Times,* April 29, 2003; and in the SEC's press release, "Ten of Nation's Top Investment Firms Settle Enforcement Actions Involving Conflicts of Interest Between Research and Investment Banking," on the SEC website, www.sec.gov.

217–218   Truman's proposal for a fee on cross-border investment was made in his speech "Perspectives on External Financial Crises," December 10, 2001, available on the website of the Institute for International Economics, www.iie.com.

218   The paper that Rogoff coauthored with Bulow is "Cleaning Up Third-World Debt Without Getting Taken to the Cleaners," *Journal of Economic Perspectives* 4 (Winter 1990): 31–42.

219   Information on the controversy over the Bush administration's position on capital controls can be found in Edward Alden, "US Backs Curbs on Capital Controls," *Financial Times,* April 2, 2003. For an excellent critique of the administration's stance, see Jagdish Bhagwati and Daniel Tarullo, "A Ban on Capital Controls Is a Bad Trade-off," *Financial Times,* March 17, 2003; and Tarullo's statement before the House subcommittee on Domestic and International Monetary Policy, Trade, and Technology, April 1, 2003, available on the website of the House Financial Services Committee, http://financialservices.house.gov.

220–221   The paper by Haldane and Kruger, "The Resolution of International Financial Crises: Private Finance and Public Funds," Bank of Canada Working Paper 2001-20, is a joint study with the Bank of England, available on the Bank of Canada website at http://www.bankofcanada.ca/en/res/r02-2-ea.htm.

222–223   Roubini and Setser make their case for being simultaneously tougher and more generous in their book *Bailouts or Bail-Ins? Responding to Financial Crises in Emerging Economies* (Washington, D.C.: Institute for International Economics, 2004).

224   I am indebted to Nancy Birdsall for helping me refine my proposal about how an independent body of outside experts would act to help stiffen the IMF's backbone.

225   Information about Uruguay's restructuring comes from John Barham,

"Cooking Up a New Solution," *LatinFinance*, June 2003; and from Roubini and Setser, *Bailouts or Bail-ins?*

227-228   Information about Kenneth Dart comes from Laurie P. Cohen and Thomas T. Vogel Jr., "Tug of War: Brazil Debt Deal Pits Nation and U.S. Banks Against Dart Family," *Wall Street Journal*, November 30, 1993; Al Kamen, "Belize, the Billionaire, and Sarasota," *Washington Post*, September 11, 1995; Elizabeth Lesly, "The Darts: Fear, Loathing, and Foam Cups," *Business Week*, July 10, 1995; and John Kenyon, "Who Is Kenneth Dart?" *Moscow Times*, June 1, 1999.

227-229   Dart's lawsuit is *EM Ltd. v. The Republic of Argentina*, filed in the United States District Court for the Southern District of New York. Information about the suit can be found in Jonathan Karp and Aaron Lucchetti, "Kenneth Dart Gets a Cup of Cash," *Wall Street Journal*, September 16, 2003; and Lucchetti and Karp, "Billionaire's Award May Snag Progress on Argentine Debt," September 22, 2003. The quotation from his lawyer, David Rifkin of Debevoise & Plimpton, comes from John Dizard, "Argentina Up Against the Ropes over Bonds," *Financial Times*, September 13, 2004.

229   The IMF study showing high returns for investors who file lawsuits to block sovereign debt restructurings is Manmohan Singh, "Recovery Rates from Distressed Debt—Empirical Evidence from Chapter 11 Filings, International Litigation, and Recent Sovereign Debt Restructurings," August 2003, available on the IMF website.

230   Taylor's April 2002 speech was reported in Blustein, "IMF Crisis Plan Torpedoed," *Washington Post*, April 3, 2002.

232-233   The paper by Rubin, Orszag, and Sinai is available on the Brookings Institution website at http://www.brookings.edu/views/papers/orszag/20040105.htm.

233   Snow's comments dismissing the possibility that foreigners might decide to dump U.S. assets came at a hearing of the House Financial Services Committee on March 25, 2004, a transcript of which is on the committee's website, http://financialservices.gov.

233-234   The op-ed article in which Snow argued that the trade deficit "reflects foremost the strengths of the U.S. economy" was titled "A United Effort Will Restore the Global Economy," *Financial Times*, April 23, 2004.

Index

PublicAffairs is a publishing house founded in 1997. It is a tribute to the standards, values, and flair of three persons who have served as mentors to countless reporters, writers, editors, and book people of all kinds, including me.

I. F. STONE, proprietor of *I. F. Stone's Weekly*, combined a commitment to the First Amendment with entrepreneurial zeal and reporting skill and became one of the great independent journalists in American history. At the age of eighty, Izzy published *The Trial of Socrates*, which was a national bestseller. He wrote the book after he taught himself ancient Greek.

BENJAMIN C. BRADLEE was for nearly thirty years the charismatic editorial leader of *The Washington Post*. It was Ben who gave the *Post* the range and courage to pursue such historic issues as Watergate. He supported his reporters with a tenacity that made them fearless and it is no accident that so many became authors of influential, best-selling books.

ROBERT L. BERNSTEIN, the chief executive of Random House for more than a quarter century, guided one of the nation's premier publishing houses. Bob was personally responsible for many books of political dissent and argument that challenged tyranny around the globe. He is also the founder and longtime chair of Human Rights Watch, one of the most respected human rights organizations in the world.

For fifty years, the banner of Public Affairs Press was carried by its owner, Morris B. Schnapper, who published Gandhi, Nasser, Toynbee, Truman, and about 1,500 other authors. In 1983, Schnapper was described by *The Washington Post* as "a redoubtable gadfly." His legacy will endure in the books to come.

Peter Osnos, *Publisher*